CATHOLICISM, LIBERALISM, AND COMMUNITARIANISM

Catholicism, Liberalism, and Communitarianism

The Catholic Intellectual Tradition and the Moral Foundations of Democracy

Edited by
Kenneth L. Grasso,
Gerard V. Bradley,
and
Robert P. Hunt

with a foreword by
Richard John Neuhaus

ROWMAN & LITTLEFIELD PUBLISHERS, INC.

ROWMAN & LITTLEFIELD PUBLISHERS, INC.

Published in the United States of America
by Rowman & Littlefield Publishers, Inc.
4720 Boston Way, Lanham, Maryland 20706

3 Henrietta Street
London WC2E 8LU, England

Copyright © 1995 by Rowman & Littlefield Publishers, Inc.

An earlier version of chapter 5, "Subsidiarity: The 'Other' Ground of Limited Government," appeared in *Providence: Studies in Western Civilization* 1, no. 2 and is
reprinted by permission.
Chapter 6, "Catholic Social Thought, the City, and Liberal America," originally appeared in *Catholicism and Liberalism,* ed. Bruce R. Douglass and David Hollenbach
(New York: Cambridge University Press, 1994), and is reprinted with permission.
An earlier version of chapter 12, "The Importance of Being Catholic," appeared in *Lis-
tening* 25, no. 1 and in *First Things* (March 1990), and is reprinted by permission of
both journals.

British Cataloging in Publication Information Available

Library of Congress Cataloging-in-Publication Data

Catholicism, liberalism, and communitarianism / edited by Kenneth L. Grasso, Gerard
V. Bradley, and Robert P. Hunt ; with a foreword by Richard John Neuhaus.
    p. cm.
    Includes bibliographical references and index.
    1. Catholic Church—United States—History—1965– 2. Sociology, Christian
(Catholic) 3. Democracy—Religious aspects—Catholic Church. 4. Liberalism. 5. Community. I. Grasso, Kenneth L., 1958– II. Bradley, Gerard V.,
1954– . III. Hunt, Robert P., 1955– .
    BX1406.2.C365 1995 261.8′08′822—dc20 95-6446 CIP

ISBN 0-8476-7994-2 (cloth: alk. paper)
ISBN 0-8476-7995-0 (pbk: alk. paper)

Printed in the United States of America

♾ ™ The paper used in this publication meets the minimum requirements of American National Standard for Information Sciences—Permanence of Paper for Printed Library Materials, ANSI Z39.48–1984.

Contents

Acknowledgments

We would be remiss if we did not express our heartfelt gratitude to the individuals and institutions whose assistance helped make this volume possible. Thanks are in order to our contributors both for their essays and, in several cases, for their sage advice with respect to the volume as a whole. We particularly wish to thank the Reverend Francis Canavan, S.J., who was the teacher of two of the editors. Father Canavan offered encouragement and wise counsel at every stage of our work.

Special thanks to Jonathan Sisk, Rowman & Littlefield's editor-in-chief, for unfailing faith in our volume, constant trust in our judgment, and willingness to invest the time and effort necessary to understand an admittedly unorthodox project. It was a pleasure working with Jon, Julie Kirsch, and everyone at Rowman & Littlefield. We also wish to thank Rebecca A. Liounis for her tireless work in the preparation of the final manuscript.

We also need to express our gratitude to our institutions — Southwest Texas State University, Notre Dame University Law School, and Kean College of New Jersey — for their ongoing encouragement and support of our scholarship. Most of all, we wish to thank our wives and our children for their patience and encouragement.

Foreword

This book makes a very ambitious proposal. The proposal is that Catholic social thought can contribute significantly to revivifying the American experiment in liberal democracy. That there is a need, an urgent need, for such a revival is today widely recognized by thinkers across the political and philosophical spectrum. Some of the essays here are polemical and others apologetic, but the book taken all in all is a proposal. As such, it must make its case sometimes in conversation with and sometimes against other proposals that are advanced in the public square of democratic discourse.

The fact that it is a Catholic proposal does not give it privileged status. Indeed, in the opinion of many, that fact may make it distinctly suspect. Catholicism and democracy, after all, have had a rather rocky history. For many readers, the arguments pressed in these essays will have to win acceptance despite, not because of, their Catholic provenance. Part of the ambitiousness of this project is to demonstrate that Catholic also means catholic; that Catholic social thought is truly comprehensive of the truths and concerns important to those who are not Catholic, and that its being comprehensively catholic is fully faithful to its being authentically Catholic.

Readers would be suspicious, and rightly so, of Catholics presenting an otherwise convincing public philosophy that does not square with the teaching of the Catholic Church. Just as rightly, they would have slight interest in an argument that does no more than demonstrate that democracy is compatible with Catholic teaching. That argument was of great concern to an earlier generation of Catholics, but it is chiefly of interest to Catholics. On the far side of the older argument over the compatibility of Catholicism and democracy, this book seeks to convince us that the principles and practices of the free society are made necessary by Catholic teaching. Beyond that, we are asked to examine the claim that Catholic teaching proposes the most compelling understanding of a society that is both free and just.

There could not have been a book like this fifty years ago. And maybe not even fifteen years ago. Fifty years ago, a self-consciously immigrant Catholicism was still in a largely defensive posture, uncertain about its place in the American experiment, and even more uncertain about the fit between Catholic teaching and the constituting principles of the American public order. Fifteen years ago, also in an essentially defensive mode, Catholic thinkers were eager to demonstrate that they could be good liberals just like everybody else — it being assumed that everybody else defined what it meant to be a good liberal. Of course, both fifty and fifteen years ago, there were exceptions, but as a rule Catholics had neither the confidence nor the inclination to propose Catholic social thought as a critical and constructive resource for putting the American experiment on more solid philosophical and moral foundations.

The new moment of which this book is one evidence is made possible, in large part, by the much-discussed "crisis of liberalism." As more and more secular intellectuals became aware that they could not offer a philosophical defense of the liberalism that they cherished, an opening was created for substantively different arguments. Aside from those who, like Richard Rorty, are content to say that the liberal society is their "ironic" preference, thoughtful citizens recognize that this kind of experiment must be philosophically and morally legitimated if it is to be sustained. The crisis of liberalism coincided with the dramatic development of Catholic teaching on the free and just social order. The magna carta of that development was the Second Vatican Council, and it has been vigorously advanced and elaborated by the pontificate of John Paul II. One edges only a little distance out on the limb by saying that this book could not have been written before *Centesimus Annus*.

But then one quickly edges back again, lest the impression be given that these essays subscribe to the pernicious notion that there are two Catholic Churches, the preconciliar and the postconciliar (or the pre-John Paul II and John Paul II churches). The Catholic intellectual tradition and, more specifically, Catholic social teaching long predate our historical moment, as, for that matter, does reflection on "the moral foundations of democracy." The singular nature of this moment may be that it provides the opportunity for a less inhibited engagement of Catholic teaching and democratic theory — less inhibited from the Catholic side because of the historical ascendancy of democracy in the framework of the Anglo-American experience, rather than the French revolutionary framework with its powerful animus against religion in general and Catholicism in particular. And the engagement is less inhibited on the side of the friends of democracy because it has become evident also to many non-Catholics that, at the edge of the Third Millennium, the Catholic Church is, intellectually and institutionally, the world's most influential champion of human freedom.

That the Catholic Church is such a champion may not be self-evidently true to some readers. These essays may not convince them of that claim, but they are surely a persuasive invitation to entertain the possibility of its being true. In his encyclical *Redemptoris Missio,* John Paul II writes, "The Church imposes nothing; she only proposes." A critically important question is whether that is a statement of principle or only an acknowledgment of limitations upon the Church's power under contemporary circumstances. John Paul clearly intends to say that, even if the Church could impose, she should not and would not. The free society is composed of free persons who are called to respond freely to the truth proposed by the Church. No other kind of response is desired by the Church or pleasing to the Church's Lord. In Catholic teaching, human freedom is not grudgingly acknowledged but theologically imperative. Freedom is ordered to truth but freedom can never be coerced to truth.

This book should be viewed, then, as a proposal. It proposes a more secure moral foundation for liberalism, community, and democracy, and it proposes better ways of understanding liberalism, community, and democracy. Put differently, this is not just a case of Catholicism coming to the moral rescue of liberal democracy in crisis. It is catholic thought in the service of better understanding of how the crisis came about, and it is Catholic thought proposing a different, more morally compelling, and more enduring idea of the democratic experiment. To be sure, a few of the essayists perhaps are not entirely untouched by a suspicion that the democratic experiment was and remains a misbegotten idea. In that sense, these pages reflect a reciprocal testing—a testing of democratic theory and practice by Catholic thought, and a testing of Catholic thought by democratic theory and practice. For a few participants in this discussion, the suspicion may be that one or the other must prevail; for most, the clear hope is that both will emerge stronger by virtue of their mutual and vigorous engagement.

Richard John Neuhaus

1

Introduction: Catholic Social Thought and the Quest for an American Public Philosophy

Kenneth L. Grasso

Civilization, Thomas Aquinas observed, is formed by men and women locked together in argument. Whatever may be the case with regard to societies in general, this is certainly an apt description of the United States. At the heart of American political culture—from the debates of the Philadelphia Convention and the struggle over the ratification of the Constitution through the Lincoln–Douglas debates down to today—has been an ongoing argument about the moral foundations and dimensions of our continuing experiment in self-government. This perennial American debate manifests itself in a variety of ways in our contemporary public life. One thinks immediately here of today's *Kulturkampf* over the role of religion and religiously grounded values in American public life. One also thinks immediately in this context of today's debate over the relationship of the individual to the community, over the rights of the individual and the common good, which finds academic expression in what has come to be known as the liberalism–communitarian debate.

In the spirit of the Second Vatican Council's call for serious dialogue between the Church and modern culture, this volume seeks to bring the Catholic tradition in social thought into conversation with the ideas and intellectual systems that inform the contemporary American public argument, as well as with men and women of good will who, regardless of their religious convictions, are

1

concerned about the future of the American democratic experiment. It seeks to demonstrate that Catholic social thought can make an important contribution to our ongoing national debate about the moral foundations of our public life. The nature and significance of this contribution can perhaps best be seen against the backdrop of the debate between the proponents of liberalism and the advocates of communitarianism, a debate which has emerged as one of the central issues in contemporary political theory and social philosophy.

Liberalism, Communitarianism and the Moral Foundations of the American Democratic Experiment

In recent decades America has witnessed the ascendancy of a new variety of liberal individualism. At its heart is found the idea that, as John Rawls puts it, the self is prior to the ends it chooses. Thus, human beings are conceived of as, in Michael Sandel's words, "free and independent selves unclaimed by ties antecedent to choice."[1] The self is thereby "installed as sovereign, cast as the author of the only obligations that constrain."[2] Human beings, in this view, are essentially sovereign wills.

From the starting point of human beings as unencumbered selves, as sovereign individuals, the proponents of this new liberalism develop a whole theory of politics. At the center of this theory are found three premises. The first is a radical individualism: social relations are thus something artificial, external, and contractual rather than being rooted in man's nature as a social being. All social institutions and relations must be understood as nothing more than the purely conventional product of the wills and interests of naturally autonomous individuals: there is thus no particular structure of social relations demanded by human nature as such. The second is the rejection of any conception of substantive human good transcending the desires, preferences, and choices of particular individuals. This rejection culminates in a commitment to what George F. Will has aptly termed the "moral equality of appetites."[3] The third premise is the elevation, be it explicit or implicit, of individual choice to the status of the highest good. The anthropology of the sovereign self issues in what Francis Canavan has described as "an unrelenting subordination of all allegedly objective goods to the subjective good of individual choice."[4]

According to the proponents of this new liberalism, a properly organized polity merely seeks to provide a framework of public order within which individuals are free to pursue their disparate visions of the good life. Far from embodying a particular substantive conception of the good life, the law must instead afford all lifestyles and belief systems equal treatment. The state exists simply to make public arrangements designed to secure individuals the greatest possible amount of freedom to lead their lives in the way they choose consistent with the exercise of that same freedom by others.

This new liberalism thus issues in the construction of what has been called "the naked public square," the establishment of a body politic that excludes "all particularist religious and moral belief" from its public life and civil conversation.[5] While individuals or groups must be left free to profess whatever beliefs and values they choose, the liberal conception of the human good dictates that no individual or group be allowed to impose their particular subjective preferences as to the nature of the good life upon others. Substantive conceptions of the good life must under no circumstance be allowed to impinge upon the making of law or public policy. The public square, accordingly, must be hermetically sealed to such beliefs; substantive conceptions of the good life — including and especially those whose origins are religious in nature — must be checked at its door.

Championed by such prominent intellectuals as John Rawls, Ronald Dworkin, Laurence Tribe, Robert Nozick, and Bruce Ackerman, in the past few decades, this new variety of liberalism has come to have a far-reaching and revolutionary effect on American public life. Increasingly, our public agenda has been set by a variety of movements seeking to refashion our laws and public policies so as to bring them into conformity with the political morality it champions. Even more importantly, the new liberalism has come to supply the prism, so to speak, through which we interpret key provisions of the Constitution; and, as such, a host of Supreme Court decisions involving the First Amendment and the right to privacy bear its imprint. Perhaps most importantly of all, this liberalism has come to supply the conceptual framework within which we think about politics. Indeed, our public argument increasingly takes place within the idiom it establishes. Today, this new liberalism seems on the verge of establishing itself as the public philosophy of contemporary America.[6]

In recent years, however, growing doubts have emerged about liberal individualism's ability to sustain a democratic body politic. On the political level, a host of critics have argued that this liberalism erodes the very virtues whose presence is a precondition of a democratic society's proper functioning. In a manner reminiscent of Tocqueville, they have argued that the individualism fostered by liberalism threatens our free institutions by sapping the ethos of self-restraint, public spiritedness, and responsibility on which they depend for their vitality and stability.[7] Still other critics have questioned whether a society committed to the maintenance of a naked public square can sustain the belief in the sacredness of the human person that is the inspiration and organizing principle of a free society.[8] On what grounds, these critics ask, can a society whose public life lacks a transcendent point of reference affirm the sacredness of the human person and the inviolable order of human rights that flows from it?

Other influential critics have argued that the philosophy informing liberal theory is flawed. Some have stressed the inadequacy of liberalism's philosophical anthropology. Human beings, they argue, are not essentially separate and independent individuals whose selfhood is independent of the ends they may have chosen for themselves at any given moment. Rather, because the communities of which we are a part and the roles we play are partly constitutive of our identity, our selfhood is inseparable from our membership in an array of communities and the roles that we, by virtue of this membership, play.[9]

Similarly, eminent scholars have raised grave doubts about the compatibility of liberalism's epistemology and metaphysics with the moral principles that inform democratic government. Rather than providing a secure basis for the affirmations of the moral absolutes that constitute the moral and intellectual foundation of democratic government, these scholars have argued, liberalism's metaphysics and epistemology inevitably issue in a thoroughgoing moral subjectivism, in what might more technically be termed value noncognitivism. This value noncognitivism, in turn, precludes in principle an affirmation of the moral absolutes that are the charter and justification of a free society.[10]

In recent years a new intellectual movement has emerged with the objective of providing us with an alternative model of democracy capable of supplanting liberalism as the foundation of American public life. What is generally known as "communitarianism" is a heterogeneous movement. What unites the diverse thinkers and schools of thought that compose this movement is not a shared anthropology and model of society but a common conviction as to the inadequacy of liberalism, and a common desire to forge a new public philosophy taking its bearings from man's nature as a social being and emphasizing the importance of public spiritedness, participation, and the public good. Indeed, if at times some communitarians seem to long for a return to the classical political world with its ideal of what Jean Bethke Elshtain has aptly termed "armed civic virtue,"[11] many seem to see the communitarian project as consisting largely in the fine-tuning of modern liberalism with which they have no fundamental quarrel.

Recent essays by two prominent communitarians are illustrative of this latter approach. William Sullivan and Michael Sandel seek to draw on the work of seminal figures in the liberal tradition—in Sullivan's case, John Dewey and T. H. Green, and in Sandel's case, John Locke—in devising an alternative public philosophy to that provided by contemporary liberal theory.[12] Sullivan and Sandel are hardly alone in believing that the liberal intellectual tradition contains within itself the resources necessary to address the crisis of contemporary liberalism.

Although in the past few years it has begun to emerge as a real force in American intellectual life, it may be questioned whether communitarianism represents a satisfactory alternative to liberal individualism. Although its heterogeneous character makes generalizations difficult, at least three points need to be made in this context. To begin with, while communitarianism has articulated an incisive critique of the shortcomings of liberalism, it is doubtful whether it has succeeded in supplying us with a coherent, intellectually sophisticated, and compelling alternative to the dominant liberal model of man and society. Even if the differences among communitarians themselves are left aside, the fact remains that an incisive critique of liberalism combined with rhetorical appeals to fraternity, participation, and community does not in itself constitute such an alternative. Communitarians have tended to be vague regarding both the exact nature of the theory of politics they espouse, and the philosophical foundations of that theory. "When it comes to providing a constructive and affirmative philosophical foundation for the communitarian viewpoint," as Thomas A. Spragens, Jr., has noted, "we find rather thin fare."[13]

Second, it is unclear—especially in the case of those communitarians who look back nostalgically toward the classical political world—just how the communitarian emphasis on community and its insistence that the common good must take precedence over pursuit of private self-interest is to be reconciled with the emphasis on the value and rights of the individual to which the American democratic experiment has from its inception been committed. How, in other words, can a theory of politics centering upon the good of the community rather than the rights of the individual serve as the moral foundation of a free society?

Third, the claim of many communitarians that the liberal tradition possesses the intellectual resources required to address the crisis besetting contemporary liberal theory would appear to be highly problematic. As numerous scholars have pointed out, the difficulties besetting contemporary liberal theory are no accident, but rather are deeply rooted in the anthropological, metaphysical, and epistemological premises that lie at the heart of the liberal tradition. The corrosive skepticism and, in the final analysis, utter nihilism that issue from those premises entails the denial of the existence of order of human and political ends, which imposes itself on the conscience as obligatory independent of, and prior to, any antecedent voluntary consent to seek these ends. Without such an order of ends, however, politics is necessarily reduced to a matter of sheer power, sheer will. Thus, the only political question becomes whose will is to be absolutized: that of the group or that of the "sovereign" individual?

In the former case, what results is some sort of tribalism or collectivism; in the latter case what emerges is what we see in contemporary liberal theory: an individualism that is paradoxically both illimitable and unjustifiable. By "why not"—a publicly unanswerable question—the corrosive skepticism issuing from liberalism's metaphysics produces a political culture in which the subjective will of the individual inevitably trumps all other claims, in which the desires or wants of the individual are automatically transformed into rights. This same corrosive skepticism, however, precludes in principle the affirmation that this dignity and these rights have any foundation in reality itself. As a result, politics is reduced to a matter of mere expediency and self-interest, and a situation is created in which our commitment to human freedom and dignity hangs precariously suspended over a moral abyss. The crisis besetting contemporary liberal theory is thus no accident. It is the direct and inevitable result of the very premises that are the foundation of the liberal tradition itself. Under the circumstances, it is difficult to see how the attempt to salvage contemporary liberalism by drawing upon the internal resources of the liberal intellectual tradition can succeed.

Our difficulties in forging a public philosophy capable of undergirding the American democratic experiment are closely related to the limited range of intellectual traditions on which contemporary America has attempted to draw in articulating such a philosophy. Our efforts to formulate such a philosophy have drawn almost exclusively upon two such traditions: the classical tradition— one thinks here of the contemporary revival of classical republicanism or civic humanism—and the liberal individualist tradition. As far as the former is concerned, one cannot but suspect that any attempt to revive the ancient polis with its ideal of armed civic virtue is destined to fail. Such a return, as one suspects even its proponents ultimately recognize, is neither possible nor desirable. It is not possible because of the far-reaching and seemingly irrecoverable transformation in human self-understanding that brought an end to classical civilization in the first place. It is not desirable because many aspects of this changed self-understanding represent real progress, a real gain for humanity. In any case, it is rather doubtful that classical political thought has the resources necessary to generate the intellectual affirmations—for example, the existence of an order of human rights antecedent to the state, the dignity and value of each and every human being considered as a unique and irreplaceable self, the distinction between state and society and the limited scope of the former, and so on—that constitute the very political substance of the free society.

This, in effect, leaves liberalism as the only game in town. This is why even many of liberalism's communitarian critics find themselves in the rather embarrassing position of being compelled to turn to the liberal tradition itself in search of the intellectual resources necessary to address the crisis of contemporary liberalism. As we have seen, such efforts appear doomed to fail for the simple reason that the problematic features of contemporary liberalism would appear to the inevitable consequence of the internal dynamic of liberalism itself, of the inner logic of the very premises that define the liberal tradition itself. To address the crisis that besets us today, therefore, something more is required than what Unger aptly terms a mere "partial" critique of liberalism. What is required is an alternative starting point for our thinking about politics.

Today's debate regarding the political morality that should govern American public life thus seems to have arrived at an impasse. Although the deficiencies of liberal individualism have become glaringly obvious, we lack a viable alternative. To paraphrase Matthew Arnold, we remain trapped between an old public philosophy that is dying and a new one that refuses to be born.

America's "Catholic" Moment and the Catholic Human Rights Revolution

In 1987, Richard John Neuhaus, at the time one of America's most prominent Protestant theologians, published a widely read and highly influential study of the role of the Church in the contemporary world. One of the principal theses of this study is that "this can and should be the moment in which the Roman Catholic Church in the United States assumes its rightful role in the culture-forming task of constructing a religiously informed public philosophy for the American experiment in ordered liberty."[14] If many readers found it surprising to hear such a thesis defended by a prominent Lutheran theologian, the thesis itself was by no means new.

In the last century, prominent Catholics such as Bishop John Ireland and Orestes Brownson had eloquently argued that only the Catholic intellectual tradition had the depth and richness necessary to provide American democracy with the public philosophy it required to endure and prosper.[15] In more measured tones and a more nuanced form, this view was echoed in this century by the influential Jesuit public theologian John Courtney Murray. In the face of what he saw as a far-reaching apostasy among both the people at large and our intellectual elite from the moral and political tradition in which the American democratic experiment was rooted, Murray maintained that it was incumbent on the Catholic community, in which "this tradition has found, and still finds, its intellectual home," to take the lead in championing "the ethical and political principles" that had originally "inspired the American republic."[16] "Political and social democracy in their modern realizations owe much to the inspiration of Christian truth," he insisted, "but relatively little to the action of the men and women of the Church." Confronted with this apostasy and the crisis it represented, "we the people of the Church," he said, "must have the intelligence and courage to come to their rescue, by restoring their inspiration."[17]

At first glance, the Catholic intellectual tradition might seem an unlikely source of a theory of democratic politics capable of sustaining the American democratic experiment. In the last century, as is well known, the Church enjoyed a close alliance with the *ancien regime,* and exhibited, to say the least, a profound suspicion of democratic government and its characteristic institutions and practices (e.g., religious freedom). Less well known perhaps is the far-reaching renewal of Catholic social teaching that began with the pontificate of Leo XIII and culminates in the social and political teaching of Vatican II.

While both the history of this development and the nature of the theory of politics that emerges from it are too complex to summarize here, some indication of its character and the surprise with which it has been greeted in certain circles can be conveyed by way of an anecdote that George Weigel is fond of relating: "In a conversation in the early 1980s," he recalls,

> Sir Michael Howard, the regius professor of modern history at Oxford, suggested that there had been two great revolutions in the twentieth century. The first took place when Lenin's Bolsheviks expropriated the Russian people's revolution in November 1917. The second was going on even as we spoke: the transformation of the Roman Catholic Church from a bastion of the ancien regime into perhaps the world's foremost institutional defender of human rights. It was a fascinating reading of the history of our century. One also sensed, in Sir Michael's story, just the slightest hint of an element of surprise: Fancy that—the Vatican as a defender of the rights of man![18]

In the aftermath of what Weigel has termed the Catholic human rights revolution, the Church's social teaching and activity in the temporal sphere have been rooted in the affirmation of, in Paul Sigmund's words, "the moral superiority of democratic government and guarantees of human rights."[19]

Neither Classical Nor Liberal— The Distinctiveness of Catholic Social Thought

Some might very well be tempted to dismiss this revolution as old hat, as nothing more than a belated endorsement by the Church of a set of political institutions and practices long ago embraced as normative by all men and women of good will. To grasp the true significance of the Catholic human rights revolution to contemporary America's quest for a public philosophy, it is necessary to first recognize the distinctiveness of Catholic social thought.

Catholic social thought differs fundamentally from both classicism and liberalism. It cannot be assimilated to any other tradition in political theory because it constitutes an intellectual tradition *sui generis.* On the one hand, while drawing upon the heritage of the classical tradition, Catholic social thought breaks decisively with both classical political practice and classical political theory. For purposes of brevity here, we might say that this break is essentially twofold. To begin with, it rejects the understanding of the structure of political society that informed the political orders of the classical world. "It is an historical commonplace," as Murray has written,

> to say that the essential political effect of Christianity is to destroy the classical view of society as a single homogenous structure, within which the political power stood forth as the representative of society both in its religious and political aspects. Augustus was both *Summus Imperator* and *Pontifex Maximus;* the *ius divinum* was simply part of the *ius civile.* . . . "Two there are, August Emperor, by which this world is ruled on title of original and sovereign right—the consecrated authority of the priesthood and the royal power." In this celebrated sentence of Gelasius I . . . the emphasis laid on the word "two" bespoke the revolutionary character of the Christian dispensation.

In the distinction between church and state introduced by Christianity, and Christianity's insistence on the freedom of the church both to define itself and to discharge its divinely appointed mission, lay, in Murray's words, "the virtualities of a great revolution," a revolution marking "the beginning of a new civilizational era."[20] The distinction of church and state and "the pregnant idea" of the freedom of the church both involved the assertion of "the existence of a whole wide area of human concerns which were remote from the competence of government." Implicit in this assertion was the idea "that the state is distinct from society and limited in its offices toward society"[21]; implicit in it, in short, was the idea of limited government.

Second, there is what has been described as Christianity's exaltation of the individual. In classical antiquity, as Elshtain (drawing upon the work of Peter Brown) has argued, human beings were understood as "instruments to be put to a civic purpose" and "the human body was wholly conscripted into society." For Christianity, on the other hand, a human being was not "the creature of any government, any polis, any empire."[22] On the contrary, for Christianity in Jacques Maritain's words, each individual not only possesses an "absolute dignity,"[23] but "a single human soul is of more worth than the whole universe of bodies and material goods."[24] The social and political consequences of the dignity conferred upon each and every individual in the Christian vision of the human person were far-reaching and revolutionary. It meant that individual human beings must be treated as ends in themselves, never as mere means; that human beings must always be treated with a respect commensurate with their dignity as persons; that, as Glenn Tinder notes, all human beings "deserve attention" and that "no one, then, belongs at the bottom, enslaved irremediably poor, consigned to silence."[25] It means, as Maritain puts it, that "society exists for each person, and is subordinated thereto,"[26] and thus, that the state exists to serve the person, rather than vice versa.

On the other hand, if the Christian understanding of man and society is at odds with the classical understanding, it is equally true that—as the long and bitter quarrel between the two attests—it is incompatible with the vision of man and politics that informs liberalism. It is no accident, of course, that liberalism develops on the soil of what had once been Christendom, in a cultural environment that, if undergoing a process of rapid de-Christianization, was still shaped in decisive respects by the Christian understanding of man and the universe. "The individualism on which it [i.e., liberalism] rests," as Kenneth Minogue has observed, "clearly descends from a Christian conception of the soul and its destiny on earth."[27]

To suggest that the roots of liberalism's individualism are found in Christianity is not to imply that the substance of its individualism is Christian in character. Liberalism, as Reinhold Niebuhr pointed out, "transplanted" the Christian exaltation of the individual "to the soil of classic rationalism to produce a new concept of individual autonomy which is known in neither classicism or Christianity."[28]

What modern liberalism did was to lay claim to one of the consequences of the revolution in human self-understanding brought about by Christianity—the recognition of the irreplaceable worth and unique value of each and every human being—while rejecting its source. Repudiating Christianity's metaphysics of the person, liberalism sought instead to transplant the Christian exaltation of the individual—its assertion of the dignity and value of each and every human being as a unique irreplaceable self—to the new soil of its own fundamentally different vision of man and the universe. Implicit in this vision, even if its adherents failed to recognize it, were a denial both of man's creaturehood, and the existence of an order of human ends bending upon human beings independently of, and prior to, any free consent on our part to strive for these ends. In this new soil, however, the Christian vision of the value and dignity of the individual human person either withered and died, or mutated into something quite different: the sovereign individual of contemporary liberal theory. The latter conception of man—involving as it does the idea that the individual is the sole arbiter of right and wrong, true and false—is quite simply irreconcilable with the Christian conception of the nature and destiny of man. Indeed, from the Christian perspective, this idea, by conferring upon the individual the prerogatives of God alone, involves nothing less than idolatry.

Catholicism possesses its own distinctive intellectual tradition. Two millennia old, it contains a rich body of reflection on the fundamental problems epistemology, metaphysics, anthropology, and political theory. From the perspective of the Catholic tradition, human beings are neither the polis animals of classical antiquity nor the autonomous selves of contemporary liberal theory.

It is for this very reason that the Catholic tradition is uniquely equipped to enrich our contemporary public argument regarding the moral foundations and future direction of America's ongoing experiment in ordered liberty. The impasse at which we have arrived in our search for a public philosophy for contemporary America is a direct result of the deficiencies and limitations of the intellectual traditions to which our political theorizing has been captive. To escape this impasse, a new starting point—a different intellectual tradition possessing a different anthropology, metaphysics, and epistemology—is required.

Precisely because it is rooted in an anthropology and intellectual tradition that differ fundamentally from that of both the classical tradition and the liberal tradition, the Catholic human rights revolution has the ability to generate a theory of politics that will provide us with the real alternative to liberal individualism we so badly need. Precisely because it is rooted in an anthropology and intellectual tradition deeper and richer in decisive respects than that of classicism or liberalism, the Catholic human rights revolution offers us the possibility of a theory of democratic government that can combine an insistence upon the importance of the individual human person as the focal point of political life with an insistence upon man's social nature and the primacy of the common good; a recognition of the limited character of the goals of political life with a recognition of the importance of civic virtue, participation, and public spiritedness. Precisely because it is rooted in an anthropology and intellectual tradition capable—in sharp contrast to either that of classicism or liberalism—of firmly grounding the moral affirmations that lie at the heart of democracy, the Catholic human rights revolution has the potential of supplying our democratic experiment with the solid intellectual and moral foundation it needs. The Catholic human rights revolution thus opens to us the prospect of a model of democratic government that can combine all the truth contained in both liberalism and communitarianism while avoiding the errors of either.

What the Catholic human rights revolution offers us, in short, is the foundation upon which the new and better public philosophy we so urgently need can be constructed.

Catholicism and the American Civil Conversation: The Agenda of This Volume

The essays that compose this volume examine a host of different aspects of Catholic social thought. Some explore the teaching of the official statements— papal encyclicals and pronouncements, and conciliar documents—in which the Church has articulated its social doctrine. Others examine the key concepts that inform Catholic social teaching (i.e., the common good, the dignity of the human person, natural law, subsidiarity, etc.). Still others analyze some of the intellectual movements (i.e., neo-Thomism, personalism) and thinkers that have played key roles in the Catholic human rights revolution.

In doing so, these essays have a fourfold objective. The first is to acquaint readers with the Catholic tradition in social thought, and the theory of man and society that form it. Whereas several decades ago, several representatives of the tradition were widely known and respected figures on the American intellectual scene—one thinks immediately in this context of Murray, Maritain, and Yves Simon—today few if any Americans (including, tragically, American Catholics) have any real knowledge of this tradition, much less of the recent developments within it.

The second objective is to contribute to the further development of the political theory of the Catholic human rights revolution. Although it is rooted in ideas that lie at the very foundation of the Catholic intellectual tradition, the revolution itself is a relatively recent development and its political theory is by no means a finished project. It is hoped that by exploring the central theoretical issues raised by the revolution, and by bringing Catholic social thought into contact with rival traditions, this volume can both clarify the theory of politics that informs this revolution and contribute substantively to the completion of the important intellectual project it represents.

The volume's third objective is to demonstrate that Catholic social thought is neither narrow nor sectarian. One of the reasons that Catholic tradition in social thought is capable of making an important contribution to the public argument of our religiously pluralist society is because one need not be Catholic to appreciate the insights of the Catholic tradition's two millennia of reflection on the right ordering of human social life. Thus, these essays are avowedly ecumenical in character. Contributors include three respected non-Catholic scholars—Jean Bethke Elshtain, Stanley Hauerwas, and Matthew Berke—who share the conviction of the volume's Catholic contributors that Catholic social thought can play an important role in contemporary America's quest for a public philosophy. The essays themselves, moreover, are not written with an exclusively, or even primarily, Catholic audience in mind. On the contrary, they seek to illustrate how Catholic social thought can enrich the reflections on the problems of political order of all men and women of goodwill.

The volume's final, and perhaps most important, objective is to show the new light that Catholic social thought can cast on the issues that lie at the heart of the contemporary American public argument, and thus to help both revivify this argument and reorient our ongoing search for a public philosophy. Toward this end, these essays do more than merely articulate the model of man and society that informs Catholic social thought. They contrast this model of man and society with those that dominate the contemporary American intellectual scene; bring Catholic social thought to bear on the issues confronting us today, and into conversation with the intellectual traditions that inform our ongoing discussion of the moral foundations of democratic government, so as to make it a full-fledged participant in the American public argument; and demonstrate its ability to assist us in our quest for an American public philosophy. In doing so, it is hoped that they will help foster a serious dialogue between Catholic social thought and the various ideas and intellectual traditions that inform the contemporary American civil conversation. In addition to being called for by the Second Vatican Council, there is reason to believe, as we have seen, that such dialogue is important to the future of America's democratic experiment.

Notes

1. Michael J. Sandel, "Freedom of Conscience or Freedom of Choice?" in *Articles of Faith, Articles of Peace,* ed. James Davison Hunter and Os Guinness (Washington, D.C.: The Brookings Institution, 1990), 76.

2. Ibid., 75.

3. George F. Will, *Statecraft As Soulcraft* (New York: Simon & Schuster, 1983), 158.

4. Francis Canavan, S.J., "The Pluralist Game," *Law and Contemporary Problems* 44 (Spring 1987): 34.

5. See Richard John Neuhaus, *The Naked Public Square* (Grand Rapids, Mich.: Eerdmans, 1984), 89.

6. The literature on this point is too voluminous to be cited here. Good introductions to this new liberalism's impact on, respectively, our culture as a whole, and our legal culture in particular, are found in William A. Donahue, *The New Freedom* (New Brunswick, N.J.: Transaction Publishers, 1990); and Mary Ann Glendon, *Rights Talk* (New York: The Free Press, 1991).

7. Here again the literature is voluminous. A good example of such a critique from the political right is found in Will's *Statecraft As Soulcraft*. For a good example of such a critique from the political left, see Robert N. Bellah et al., *Habits of the Heart* (Berkeley: University of California Press, 1985).

8. See Neuhaus, *Naked Public Square*.

9. See, for example, Sandel, *Liberalism and the Limits of Justice* (New York: Cambridge University Press, 1982).

10. On this point, see Thomas A. Spragens, Jr., *The Irony of Liberal Reason* (Chicago: University of Chicago Press, 1988). Spragens's volume is perhaps the single best study of the difficulties created for liberal political theory by its metaphysics.

11. Elshtain, "In Common Together: Unity, Diversity, and Civic Virtue" in *"The*

Constitution of the People": Reflections on Citizens and Civil Society, ed. Robert E. Calvert (Lawrence: University Press of Kansas, 1991), 72.

12. Sandel, "Freedom of Conscience or Freedom of Choice" in *Articles of Faith, Articles of Peace,* 74–92; and William M. Sullivan, "Bringing the Good Back In," in *Liberalism and the Good,* ed. R. Bruce Douglass, Gerald M. Mara, and Henry S. Richardson (New York: Routledge, 1990), 148–66.

13. Thomas A. Spragens, Jr., *Reason and Democracy* (Durham, N.C.: Duke University Press, 1990), 7–8.

14. Neuhaus, *The Catholic Moment: The Paradox of the Church in the Postmodern World* (San Francisco: Harper & Row, 1987), 283.

15. For a brief discussion of John Ireland's view on this matter, see George Weigel, *Catholicism and the Renewal of American Democracy* (New York: Paulist, 1988). For an overview of Brownson's thought see Gregory S. Butler, *In Search of the American Spirit: The Political Thought of Orestes Brownson* (Carbondale: Southern Illinois University Press, 1992).

16. Murray, *We Hold These Truths: Catholic Reflections on the American Proposition* (Kansas City: Sheed & Ward, 1960), 41–43.

17. Murray, "The School and Christian Freedom," *Proceedings of the National Catholic Educational Association* 48 (August 1951): 64.

18. George Weigel "Catholicism and Democracy," *The Washington Quarterly* 12 (Autumn 1985): 5.

19. Paul Sigmund, "The Catholic Tradition and Modern Democracy" in *Religion and Politics in the American Milieu,* ed. Leslie Green (Notre Dame, Ind.: *The Review of Politics* and Office of Policy Studies, n.d.), 20.

20. Murray, *We Hold These Truths,* 202.

21. Ibid., 35.

22. Elshtain, "In Common Together: Unity, Diversity, and Civic Virtue," 70–71.

23. Maritain, *Christianity and Democracy and the Rights of Man and Natural Law* (San Francisco: Ignatius Press, 1988), 89.

24. Ibid., 98.

25. Glenn Tinder, *The Political Meaning of Christianity* (San Francisco: Harper San Francisco, 1991), 32–33.

26. Maritain, 98.

27. Kenneth Minogue "Theorizing Liberalism and Liberalizing Theory," in *Traditions of Liberalism,* ed. Knud Haakonssen (Canberra: The Centre for Independent Studies, 1988).

28. Niebuhr, *The Nature and Destiny of Man* (New York: Scribner's, 1941), vol. 1, 61.

2

The Image of Man
in Catholic Thought

Francis Canavan, S.J.

Some readers will regard the above title as a misnomer, since this essay is
based entirely on the social encyclicals of modern popes from Leo XIII on.
Popes, however, are not by office originators of Catholic thought, but custodi-
ans and teachers of the Catholic trdition. They draw upon the work of Catholic
thinkers through the ages, give it approval as authentic expression of the
Church's doctrine, and apply it to contemporary social problems. They can
also draw, at least indirectly, upon the thought of thinkers outside the Church,
but only insofar as they find it capable of being incorporated into the Catholic
tradition. We may therefore safely take the image of man presented in the papal social encyclicals as being the image in Catholic thought. Those who prefer the idea of man favored by theologians with "creative ideas" may do so if
they please, but they will not find it here.

Nor will they find the search for inconsistencies in papal thought so beloved
by certain scholars. In the successive papal documents there are certainly nu-
ances, shifts of emphasis, and developments of certain points of doctrine, some
of which will be pointed out here. But the premise of this piece is that the encyclicals are a body of Catholic thought marked by a fundamental consistency
of ideas and principles.

In this image of man, one notices a certain progress from the Thomism of
Leo XIII to the personalist Thomism of John Paul II, which contains a richer
and fuller idea of the human person, but not a different one. This essay will

therefore view the encyclicals as presenting a harmonious picture of what it is to be a human person. The major thrust of these encyclicals, to be sure, is toward a theory of society, but that will be touched on only incidentally here. A certain image of man is at the heart of the social theory, and that alone is the subject of this piece of writing.

Popes Leo XIII and Pius XI did not dwell at length on man's personhood. In *Rerum Novarum* (1981), Leo referred, however, to "the essential nature of human beings," in an argument for the right of private property, which we need not explain here. But the premise of his argument is this: "Since man by his reason understands innumerable things, linking and combining the future with the present, and since he is master of his own actions, therefore, under the eternal law, and under the power of God most wisely ruling all things, he rules himself by the foresight of his own counsel."[1] Man is by nature rational, therefore free and master of his own actions, but under God's eternal law.

Leo, and Pius XI in *Quadragesimo Anno* (1931), confronted the liberal state and a capitalist economic order founded on individualistic premises. Their purpose was not to abolish capitalism, but to bring about its reform, to alleviate class warfare, and to establish a more just community on Christian principles. As Pius XI said, "Leo XIII's whole endeavor was to adjust this economic regime to the standards of true order, whence it follows that the system itself is not to be condemned" and "is not vicious of its very nature."[2] It was the rise of the totalitarian state in the first half of the twentieth century that led the papacy, while still advocating social reform, to put a greater stress on the individual human being as a person.

This idea was not entirely new, of course. "No one may with impunity outrage the dignity of man, which God Himself treats with great reverence, nor impede his course to the level of perfection which accords with eternal life in heaven," Leo XIII had said.[3] But in October 1939, just after the outbreak of the Second World War, Pius XII in his first encyclical, *Summi Pontificatus,* felt obliged to denounce Nazi racism, as his predecessor, Pius XI, had done two years earlier in the encyclical *Mit Brennender Sorge.* In contrast to racism, he called attention to the human race's "one common origin in God," its "unity of nature," its "unity of the immediate end and mission in the world," its "unity of dwelling place, the earth," and "its unity of the supernatural end, God Himself," on which is founded the "law of human solidarity and charity."[4] There is only one human race, and all men are equally members of it.

Toward the end of the war, in his Christmas message of 1944, Pius XII pointed out a lesson he thought people had learned:

> Taught by bitter experience, they are more aggressive in opposing the concentration of dictatorial power that cannot be censured or touched, and call for a system of government more in keeping with the dignity and liberty of the citizens. These

multitudes, uneasy, stirred by the war to their innermost depths, are today firmly convinced—at first, perhaps, in a vague and confused way, but already unyieldingly—that had there been the possibility of censuring and correcting the actions of public authority, the world would not have been dragged into the vortex of a disastrous war, and that to avoid for the future the repetition of such a catastrophe, we must vest efficient guarantees in the people itself.

It was not only the threat of totalitarian dictatorship, however, but the power of the modern state in general that led the pope to advocate democracy as a requirement of natural law: "If, then, we consider the extent and nature of the sacrifices demanded of all the citizens, especially in our day when the activity of the state is so vast and decisive, the democratic form of government appears to many as a postulate of nature imposed by reason itself."[5] This is not an argument that moves from the original right of every individual in "the state of nature" to govern himself to the conclusion that he has by nature the right to vote in elections, still less to the proposition that the social contract generates a "general will" that is its own supreme law. Rather, it asserts that the power and activity of the state in the modern world is so extensive that reason requires democracy to control it.

Democracy itself, Pius XII said, must be subject to natural law and divine revelation:

> A sound democracy, based on the immutable principles of the natural law and revealed truth, will resolutely turn its back on such corruption as gives to the state an unchecked and unlimited power, and moreover makes of the democratic regime, notwithstanding an outward show to the contrary, purely and simply a form of absolutism. State absolutism . . . consist[s] in fact in the false principle that the authority of the state is unlimited and that in face of it—even when it gives free rein to its despotic aims, going beyond the confines between good and evil—to appeal to a higher law obliging in conscience is not admitted.[6]

Given their continuing criticism of economic and political liberalism, it is clear that Pius XII and subsequent popes did not subscribe to the kind of individualism presupposed by classical liberal theories. Yet they espoused a certain individualism, one that is implied by the Christian belief that every man is destined for eternal life or damnation on his individual merits or demerits. Paul VI expressed this Christian individualism, in terms drawn from the Catholic philosopher Jacques Maritain, in his encyclical *Populorum Progressio*.

"In the design of God," he wrote, "every man is called upon to develop and fulfill himself, for every life is a vocation." This statement implies a teleological view of nature, of human nature in particular. "At birth, everyone is granted, in germ, a set of aptitudes and qualities for him to bring to fruition." His education and his personal efforts "will allow each man to direct himself toward the destiny intended for him by his Creator." Every man is therefore a responsible subject of action:

> Endowed with intelligence and freedom, he is responsible for his fulfillment as he is for his salvation. He is aided, or sometimes impeded, by those who educate him and those with whom he lives, but each one remains, whatever be these influences affecting him, the principal agent of his own success or failure. By the unaided effort of his own intelligence and his will, each man can grow in humanity, can enhance his personal worth, can become more a person.

But, the pope continues, this self-fulfillment is an obligation, not a mere private choice:

> Just as the whole of creation is ordained to its Creator, so spiritual beings should of their own accord orientate their lives to God, the first truth and the supreme good. Thus it is that human fulfillment constitutes as it were, a summary of our duties. But there is much more: this harmonious enrichment of nature by personal and responsible effort is ordered to a future perfection. By reason of his union with Christ, the source of life, man attains to new fulfillment of himself, to a transcendent humanism which gives him his greatest possible perfection: this is the highest goal of personal development.[7]

This is not the individualism that sees man as a sovereign will free to make of itself and the world what it pleases. Rather, it envisions a person who is obliged to frame his life through free choices in accordance with a law built into our common human nature by the Creator, who is the first truth and supreme good, and by Christ's call to a higher, supernatural life. Christian humanism is something more than mere individualism.

The main theme of the encyclical *Veritatis Splendor,* issued by John Paul II in 1993, is "the unbreakable bond between freedom and truth."[8] He had already said in 1981 that the "new humanism" makes it necessary, "on the part of all to recover an awareness of the primacy of moral values, which are the values of the human person as such."[9] The human person shares in divinely created human nature, which is what confers dignity and worth on his individuality. Without awareness of this truth about the source of this dignity as man, modern man degenerates into a secular humanism in which discrete individuals pursue their own satisfactions under a social contract to which they consent out of enlightened self-interest, or into the mass egalitarianism of socialism.

The Catholic "concept of the person," in the words of John Paul II, is that of "the autonomous subject of moral decision, . . . the very subject whose decisions build the social order."[10] Man as the free subject of action is a favorite theme of Pope John Paul. As he said in his encyclical *Mulieris Dignitatem,* "All of God's action in human history respects the free will of the human 'I'."[11] His designation of man as a "subject" is meant to call attention to human subjectivity, to the fact that the person is the subject who acts, and this by his own choice, rather than being an object acted upon. Since the subject is intelligent, his free choice of action is to be governed by his recognition of a moral law higher than his own mere will. In John Paul's philosophy, the self is not prior to the ends affirmed by it, as it is for John Rawls. Choice does not constitute the good, but the true and objective good governs, without physically determining, choice.

Nor is the autonomy intended here that of the Kantian individual, who spins the moral law out of his own reason, but rather that of the person who, by reason of his nature and eternal supernatural destiny, transcends the state, and therefore participates in building the social order in accordance with God's plan, not that of the government, as the ultimate authority. (The operative term in that last phrase is "ultimate," for no pope denies that the authority of government to govern for the good of society comes from God.[12])

Hence, John XXIII could say: "The cardinal point of this teaching [of the Catholic Church on social life] is that individual men are necessarily the foundation, cause, and end of all social institutions." Institutions are for men, not men for institutions. Furthermore, the men for whom all institutions exist are individuals, not a collective mass. Yet John XXIII adds in the next sentence, "We are referring to human beings insofar as they are social by nature, and raised to an order of existence that transcends and subdues nature."[13]

Man is an animal, but one that thinks and chooses, therefore neither an angel nor a beast. Instead, he is "an incarnate spirit, that is a soul which expresses itself in a body and a body informed by an immortal spirit."[14] That he is an animal is the source of the sociality inherent in the common nature of the human species. John Paul II remarks that "the transcendent reality of the human being . . . is seen to be shared from the beginning by a couple, a man and a woman (cf. Genesis 1:27), and is therefore fundamentally social."[15] According to the text in Genesis, "God created man in His own image, in the image of God He created him, male and female He created them." Neither sex exhausts human nature; it requires and is constituted by two sexes, who are twin principles of generation and therefore destined by nature to found families and to live in society.

Animality is not the whole of human nature, of course. Because "every human being is a person, that is, his nature is endowed with intelligence and free will . . . he has rights and obligations flowing directly and simultaneously from his very nature. And as these rights and obligations are universal and inviolable so they cannot in any way be surrendered."[16] This statement of John XXIII's casts doubt on the notion, advanced by some, that the recent popes have switched from traditional natural law to a modern natural-rights theory. It would be more accurate to say that, in the face of the expansive power of the modern state, they have incorporated human rights into their doctrine of natural law, and have made both the protection of the rights and the fulfillment of the obligations of the person the natural and God-given purposes of society. Both the rights and the obligations depend upon the teleology inherent in man's nature and supernatural destiny; the obligations are not derived from the rights but from the goods that are the goals of human nature. Papal thought, therefore, differs from a rights-based liberalism, and can furnish criteria for judging that asserted "rights" are valid ones, a distinction that liberalism finds it more and more difficult to make.

John Paul II's concept of man as the subject of action is the basis of his criticism of both capitalism and socialism. In his encyclical *Laborem Exercens,* he attributes to nineteenth-century liberal economists the doctrine that work is a commodity that the worker sells to the employer, who then owns it and has a right to all the profit. "Since then," he says, "explicit expressions of this sort have almost disappeared. . . . Nevertheless, the danger of treating work as a special kind of 'merchandise,' or as an impersonal 'force' needed for production . . . always exists, especially when the whole way of looking at the question of economics is marked by the premises of materialistic economics."

The radical flaw in that way of thinking is this:

> Man is treated as an instrument of production, whereas he—he alone, independently of the work he does—ought to be treated as the effective subject of work and its true maker and creator. Precisely this reversal of order, whatever the program or name under which it occurs, should rightly be called "capitalism"—in the sense more fully explained below . . . [i.e.], the liberal sociopolitical system, which, in accordance with its "economistic" premises, strengthened and safeguarded economic initiative by the possessors of capital alone, but did not pay sufficient attention to the rights of the workers, on the grounds that human work is solely an instrument of production, and that capital is the basis, efficient factor and purpose of production.[17]

Pius XI had said much the same thing fifty years earlier in *Quadragesimo Anno* about a capitalism motivated only by the desire for profit: "And so bodily labor, which was decreed by Providence for the good of man's body and soul even after original sin, has everywhere been changed into an instrument of strange perversion: for dead matter leaves the factory ennobled and transformed, where men are corrupted and degraded."[18]

John Paul II made a similar criticism of socialism in his later encyclical *Centesimus Annus* (where he praised a more positive conception of capitalism):

> The fundamental error of socialism is anthropological in nature. Socialism considers the individual person simply as an element, a molecule within the social or-

ganism, so that the good of the individual is completely subordinated to the functioning of the socio-economic mechanism. Socialism likewise maintains that the good of the individual can be realized without reference to his free choice, to the unique and exclusive responsibility which he exercises in the face of good or evil. Man is thus reduced to a series of social relationships, and the concept of the person as the autonomous subject of moral decisions disappears, the very subject whose decisions build the social order.[19]

We see here the basic reason for John Paul's frequent condemnation of "consumerism." He regards it as the consequence of reducing man to a factor in the process of production, and compensating him with a cornucopia of material goods, while depriving him of the role in work through which he realizes himself as a human being. "Work," he insists, "is a good thing for man—a good thing for his humanity— because through work man not only transforms nature, adapting it to his own needs, but he also achieves fulfillment as a human being and indeed, in a sense, becomes 'more a human being.'"[20]

As was said above, Paul VI's *Populorum Progressio* is based upon a teleological understanding of the nature of man and of the world. It is a view that runs through all the social encyclicals. As Pius XI said, if the natural moral law "be faithfully observed, the result will be that particular economic aims, whether of society as a body or of individuals, will be intimately linked with the universal teleological order, and as a consequence we shall be led by progressive stages to the final end of all, God Himself, our highest and lasting good."[21]

Human nature is a teleological principle of development toward higher human ends. "Man is only truly man," says Paul VI, "insofar as, master of his own acts and judge of their worth, he is author of his own advancement, in keeping with the nature which was given to him by his Creator and whose possibilities and exigencies he himself freely assumes."[22] But, Paul says, development is not only individual but social:

> Each man is a member of society. He is part of the whole of mankind. It is not just certain individuals, but all men who are called to this fullness of development. Civilizations are born, develop and die. But humanity is advancing along the path of history like the waves of a rising tide encroaching gradually on the shore.[23]

John Paul II also sees human history as a record of the progress of the race: "The story of the human race described by Sacred Scripture is, even after the fall into sin, a story of constant achievements, which, although always called into question and threatened by sin, are nonetheless repeated, increased and extended in response to the divine vocation given from the beginning to man and to woman . . . and inscribed in the image which they received."[24] Yet he does not conceive of history as the working out of an inexorable law of progress, but as dependent on the right use of men's free wills: "History is not simply a fixed progression towards what is better, but rather an event of freedom, and even a struggle between freedoms that are in mutual conflict."[25]

As was said earlier, inscribed in the image of God that man and woman received was the vocation to marry and to found that first and most basic human society, the family. "Behold, therefore, the family," said Leo XIII, "or rather the society of the household, a very small society indeed, but a true one, and older than any polity! For that reason it must have certain rights and duties of its own entirely independent of the State."[26] John Paul II repeats this thought: "The family . . . in God's plan is the basic cell of society and a subject of rights and duties before that State or any other community."[27]

There are large implications in the proposition that the family is a natural and divinely willed institution. Although the individual person is the foundation, cause, and end of all social institutions, it does not follow that institutions exist to protect and foster him as a discrete and insular individual. On the contrary, the individual realizes and develops himself through communion with other persons in institutions, beginning with the family. Says John Paul:

> In that it is, and ought always to become a communion and community of persons, the family finds in love the source and constant impetus for welcoming, respecting and promoting each one of its members in his or her lofty dignity as a person, that is, as a living image of God. . . . The moral criterion for the authenticity of family and conjugal relationships consists in fostering the dignity and vocation of the individual person, who achieve their fullness by sincere self-giving.[28]

All of this is implied in saying that man is social by nature. He cannot fully be himself except in and through community.

John Paul continues: "In creating the human race 'male and female,' God gives man and woman an equal personal dignity, endowing them with the inalienable rights and responsibilities proper to the human person."[29] But they are designed by nature to form families and to raise society's next generation, from which certain consequences for their roles in social life flow:

> There is no doubt that the equal dignity and responsibility of men and women fully justifies women's access to public functions. On the other hand the true advancement of women requires that clear recognition be given to the value of their maternal and family role, by comparison with all other public roles and all other professions. Furthermore, these roles and professions would be harmoniously combined, if we wish the evolution of society and culture to be truly and fully human.

Therefore, he concludes, the Church must insist "that the work of women in the home be recognized and respected by all in its irreplaceable value," and "society must be structured in such a way that wives and mothers are not in practice compelled to work outside the home, and that their families can live and prosper in a dignified way even when they themselves devote their full time to their own family."[30] If institutions exist for the sake of their members, then children deserve families that can raise them in the best way.

The equality of men and women is therefore not an identity of function that makes them interchangeable parts in the social machine. (According to Leo XIII, something similar should be said of the different roles that workers perform in society.[31] All are necessary, but their functions are not the same.)

While the family is the basic institution of society, it is not the only one that grows out of man's social nature. Nor is the state the only other such institution, as John Paul II explains:

> According to *Rerum Novarum* and the whole social doctrine of the Church, the social nature of man is not completely fulfilled in the State, but is realized in various intermediary groups, beginning with the family and including economic, social, political, and cultural groups which stem from human nature itself and have their own autonomy, always with a view to the common good.[32]

Leo XIII and Pius XI had laid heavy stress on these intermediary groups as the agents of social reform to cure the abuses of capitalism without recurring to socialist statism. In such questions as "the number of hours of work in each kind of occupation and the health safeguards to be provided, particularly in factories," said Leo XIII, "it will be better, in order to avoid unwarranted governmental intervention, especially since circumstances of business, season, and place are varied, that decision be reserved to the organizations of which We are about to speak."[33] The chief of these (on which we need not go into detail here) are associations of workers, or of workers and employers.[34]

Pius XI would have preferred not to have to rely on the state for social reform, but felt it necessary to do so in the circumstances of the liberal society:

> When we speak of the reform of the social order it is principally the state we have in mind. Not indeed that all salvation is to be hoped for from its intervention, but because on account of the evil of "individualism" as We called it, things have come to such a pass that the highly developed social life which once flourished in a variety of prosperous institutions organically linked with each other, has been damaged and all but ruined, leaving thus virtually only individuals and the state.[35]

The reform of the social order, therefore, must seek to restore institutions that mediate between the individual and the state, in accordance with what has come to be called the "principle of subsidiarity":

Just as it is wrong to withdraw from the individual and commit to the community at large what private enterprise and industry can accomplish, so, too, it is an injustice, a grave evil and a disturbance of right order for a larger and higher organization to arrogate to itself functions which can be performed efficiently by smaller and lower bodies. This is a fundamental principle of social philosophy, unshaken and unchangeable, and it retains its full truth today. Of its very nature the true aim of all social activity should be to help individual members of the social body, but never to destroy or absorb them.[36]

The energies of society, that is to say, well up from below as persons freely organize themselves to pursue a wide variety of common goals. The principle of subsidiarity is rooted in the image of man as intelligent, free, and social by nature, as God made him and meant him to be.

But subsidiarity does not suppose that enlightened self-interest, the free market, and competition, useful though they undoubtedly are, are enough to produce a just and humane society through the automatic working of economic laws modeled on the laws of the physical world. That is what Paul VI meant when he condemned "unchecked liberalism" as a system "which considers profit as the key motive for economic progress, competition as the supreme law of economics, and private ownership of the means of production as an absolute right that has no limits and carries no corresponding social obligation."[37] As Pius XI had said, "free competition, though within certain limits just and productive of good results, cannot be the ruling principle of the economic world."[38] Men must choose to cooperate in creating a social order that corresponds to the universal order that flows, as we saw above, from "God, the first truth and supreme good,"[39] in order to produce a society that adequately serves the basic needs of all its members.

John Paul II said nothing different when he defended the legitimate pursuit of self-interest in *Centesimus Annus:*

One can transcend one's immediate interest and still remain bound to it. The social order will be all the more stable, the more it takes this fact into account and does not place in opposition personal interest and the interests of society as a whole, but rather seeks ways to bring them into fruitful harmony.[40]

For the common good of the community is not opposed to private goods. Rather, it is composed of them, and would not exist if private citizens did not pursue their personal and familial interests in ways that do not harm but contribute to the overall welfare of the community. This they do, for example, by running legitimate and useful businesses, performing well the jobs by which they serve the needs of others as well as earning their livelihood, and raising their children to be good human beings. Nevertheless, the common good is more than a sum total of private goods. Human nature is social as well as individual, and therefore community is natural to man, and serves a good that is not reducible to a sum total of private goods. It is a good that persons can only enjoy by taking part and sharing in it, as they take part in a real conversation, that is, one that is not just a series of monologues.

The popes refer often to the common good as the goal of civil society, but without offering a full definition of it. John XXIII perhaps comes closest when he says of the common good:

This embraces the sum total of those conditions of social living, whereby men are enabled more fully and more readily to achieve their own perfection. Hence, we regard it as necessary that the various intermediary bodies and the numerous social undertakings wherein an expanded social structure primarily finds expression, be ruled by their own laws, and as the common good itself progresses, pursue this objective in a spirit of sincere concord among themselves. Nor is it less necessary that the above mentioned groups present the form and substance of a true community. This they will do, only if individual members are considered and treated as persons, and are encouraged to participate in the affairs of the group.[41]

The common good itself is produced by free persons. Here again, one must be struck by the centrality that this whole series of papal documents attributes to the freedom of the human person. It is, however, a distinctive idea of freedom and stands in sharp contrast to a conception of liberty widely entertained among secularists today. A young professor at the University of Southern California gave poignant expression to the latter more than a quarter of a century ago in a little paperback book intended for college courses:

It may be that the Enlightenment resulted in the alienation of modern man from a dead and indifferent nature; that we must now, according to modern science, regard man "as little more than a chance deposit on the surface of the world, carelessly thrown up between two ice ages by the same forces that rust iron and ripen corn, a sentient organism endowed by some happy or unhappy accident with intelligence indeed, but with an intelligence that is conditioned by the very forces that it seeks to understand and control" (C. Becker). It is not necessarily true, of course, that a godless universe and a silent nature deprive human life of meaning. It is only true that, in a meaningless universe men must bear the responsibility for giving value to a world which they did not make and which will outlast them. A consciousness of this task is the lasting legacy of the Enlightenment.[42]

If there is no God, then man is perforce the only god there is. In this view, man does not make the world, but he has to be the creator of whatever meaning and purpose his life in this meaningless world has.

In the Catholic view, man is neither God nor a god, but a creature. He is, however, as John Paul II has said, "the only creature on earth which God made for its own sake."[43] Made in the image and likeness of God, he is the intelligent and free creature. Because he is free, he shapes his life and destiny by his own self-determining choices. But because he is intelligent, he is obliged to shape them by obedience to the truth: "If you continue in my word, you are truly my disciples, and you will know the truth, and the truth will make you free."[44]

Notes

All references to papal documents are to the editions published by the Daughters of St. Paul (50 St. Paul's Avenue, Boston, Mass. 02130) unless otherwise noted. References are to the numbered paragraphs or sections into which those documents are divided, but to page numbers where they are not so divided. Where, as in more recent documents, the numbered sections cover more than one page, references are to section and page numbers.

1. *Rerum Novarum,* no. 11.
2. *Quadragesimo Anno,* 49.
3. *Rerum Novarum,* no. 57.
4. *Mit Brennender Sorge,* 17–19.
5. *Papal Thought on the State,* ed. Gerard F. Yates, S.J. (New York: Appleton-Century-Crofts, 1958), 116–17.
6. Ibid., 121.
7. *Populorum Progressio,* nos. 15–16; cf. nos. 20 and 42, where it is called a "new humanism" and a "complete humanism."
8. *Veritatis Splendor,* no. 87, 109.
9. *Familiaris Consortio,* no. 8, 19.
10. *Centesimus Annus,* no. 13, 21.
11. *Mulieris Dignitatem,* 18–19.
12. See, e.g., *Pacem in Terris,* no. 47.
13. *Mater et Magistra,* no. 219.
14. *Familiaris Consortio,* no. 11, 22.
15. *Sollicitudo Rei Socialis,* no. 29, 52.
16. *Pacem in Terris,* no. 9.
17. *Laborem Exercens,* nos. 7–8, 18, 20.
18. *Quadragesimo Anno,* 66.
19. *Centisimus Annus,* no. 13, 20–21.
20. *Laborem Exercens,* no. 9, 23.
21. *Quadragesimo Anno,* 22.
22. *Populorum Progressio,* no. 34.
23. Ibid., no. 17.
24. *Sollicitudo Rei Socialis,* no. 10, 53.
25. *Familiaris Consortio,* no. 46, 71.

26. *Rerum Novarum,* no. 19.
27. *Familiaris Consortio,* no. 46, 71.
28. Ibid., no. 22, 38.
29. Ibid., no. 22, 39.
30. Ibid., no. 23, 40.
31. *Rerum Novarum,* no. 26.
32. *Centesimus Annus,* no. 13, 21.
33. *Rerum Novarum,* no. 64.
34. Ibid., no. 68.
35. *Quadragesimo Anno,* 40.
36. Ibid.
37. *Populorum Progressio,* no. 26.
38. *Quadragesimo Anno,* 44.
39. *Populorum Progressio,* no. 16.
40. *Centesimus Annus,* no. 25, 36.
41. *Mater et Magistra,* no. 65.
42. Robert Anchor, *The Enlightenment Tradition* (New York: Harper & Row, 1967), 144.
43. *Centesimus Annus,* no. 53, 75.
44. John 8: 31–32.

3

Beyond Liberalism: Human Dignity, the Free Society, and the Second Vatican Council

Kenneth L. Grasso

The past half century has witnessed a far-reaching development in Catholic social teaching that George Weigel has dubbed "the Catholic human rights revolution."[1] For Catholics, this revolution constitutes a historic development in their Church's understanding both of its mission in the temporal sphere and of the implications of the deposit of faith entrusted to it for the ordering of social and political life. Yet one need not view it through the prism of the Catholic faith to see in this revolution an intellectual event of considerable note. At a minimum, it marks a far-reaching development in an ancient, venerable, and influential intellectual tradition's teaching about the right ordering of human life in society.

The goal of this essay is to analyze the theory of politics that informs this revolution, to address some of the questions to which it has given rise, and to explore its significance to the contemporary debate regarding the moral foundations of democratic government. Before doing so, it is necessary to examine the exact nature of the development in the Church's social teaching of which Weigel speaks.

Vatican II and the Catholic Human Rights Revolution

The Catholic human rights revolution was a result of a long, gradual evolution that began during the pontificate of Leo XIII, and whose roots extend to the very foundations of the Catholic intellectual tradition. An examination of the history and intellectual roots of this revolution is far too ambitious a task for this essay.[2] Inasmuch as this revolution crystallized in the teaching of the Second Vatican Council, its broad contours can be seen by examining the council's Constitution on the Church in the Modern World (*Gaudium et Spes*) and Declaration on Religious Liberty (*Dignitatis Humanae*).[3]

The Preferential Option for Constitutional Democracy

The Council emphatically reaffirms the traditional truth that the Church "is not committed to any one culture or to any political, economic or social system" (GS 42, 942). She is neither to be "identified with any political community nor bound by ties to any political system" (GS 74, 984). Likewise, it affirms that "the concrete forms of structure and organization of public authority in any political community may vary according to the character of various peoples and their historical development" so long as political power is "exercised within the limits of the moral order and directed toward the common good" (GS 74, 981). At the same time, in scrutinizing "the signs of the times," the conciliar fathers note that "a sense of the dignity of the human person has been impressing itself more and more deeply on the consciousness of contemporary man" (DH 1, 162); and that "modern man is in a process of fuller personality development and of a growing discovery of his own rights" (GS 41, 940). As a result, the people of our time have come to "prize freedom very highly and strive eagerly for it" (GS 17, 917). "The demand is increasingly made," they observe, "that men should act on their own judgment, enjoying and making use of a responsible freedom, not driven by coercion but motivated by a sense of duty" (DH 1, 162).

In the political sphere, this newfound appreciation of human dignity and the desire for freedom it has fostered have prompted "the demand that constitutional limits . . . be set to the powers of government" so as to protect "the rightful freedom of the person and of associations" from encroachment. This demand for freedom manifests itself "chiefly [as] regards [to] the quest for the values proper to the human spirit" (DH 1, 162–63).

Confronted with this new "keener awareness of human dignity" and the political aspirations engendered by it, the council, having searched "into the sacred tradition and doctrine of the Church," pronounces them to be "greatly in accord with truth and justice" (DH 1, 163). More specifically, the council makes a series of affirmations that, taken together, constitute what John Courtney Murray describes as "a political commitment, however discreet, to constitutional government,"[4] a preferential option, as it were, for constitutional democracy.

First, the council affirms that the protection and promotion of human rights is at the very heart of the political task. "In virtue of the Gospel entrusted to it," the council announces, "the Church proclaims the rights of man" (GS 41, 941). Indeed, the very common good that government exists to promote "consists chiefly in the protection of the rights, and in the performance of the duties, of the human person." Thus, "the protection and promotion of the inviolable rights of man ranks among the essential duties of the government" (DH 6, 173–74).

Second, the council strongly affirms the importance of the principle of limited government as a defining feature of a rightly ordered polity. Limited government, the council insists, is an exigency of both the "inviolable" rights of the person (DH 6, 174) and the "principle of the freedom of the Church," which "among the things which concern the good of the Church and indeed the welfare of society . . . certainly is preeminent" (DH 12, 185). The "sacred rights of the person" (DH 6, 176) and the "sacred" principle of the freedom of the Church (DH 13, 185) combine to mandate both that government be restricted to "the order of terrestrial and temporal affairs" (DH 3, 170) and even here be limited in its scope. They combine, in other words, in the emphatic affirmation that the ends of government are coextensive neither with the ends of human life, nor even with those of human society.

Third, the council vigorously affirms that the right ordering of political life requires that the principle of subsidiarity be respected. Human nature, it maintains, gives rise to a host of "social ties" some of which "correspond more immediately to . . . [man's] innermost nature" such as "the family," and "others [that] flow rather from free choice" (GS 25, 926). These groups, it stresses, not only possess inviolable rights but also make an indispensable contribution to human well-being. Accordingly, government must

> take care not to put obstacles in the way of family or cultural groups, or of orga-
> nizations and intermediate institutions, nor to hinder their lawful and constructive
> activity; rather they should eagerly seek to promote such activity. Citizens, on the
> other hand, either individually or in association, should take care not to vest too
> much power in the hands of public authority nor to make untimely and exagger-
> ated demands for favors and subsidies, lessening in this way the responsible role
> of individuals, families and social groups. (GS 75, 982)

The state, in short, must seek neither to absorb these groups nor to usurp their functions, but must respect their autonomy and provide them with the assistance they need to flourish. Governmental intervention "in social, cultural and economic matters," therefore, must have the goal of bringing about "more favorable conditions to enable citizens and groups to pursue freely and effectively the achievement of man's well-being in its totality" (GS 75, 983).

Fourth, the council affirms that freedom must take its place alongside the traditional triad of truth, justice, and love, as a foundational component of a genuinely human social order. For the council, freedom becomes, in Murray's apt phrase, "the political method par excellence." While political authority must "guide the energies of all towards the common good," it must do so "not mechanically or despotically, but by acting above all else as a moral force based on freedom and a sense of responsibility" (GS 74, 981). In the terse formulation of the *Declaration:* "the freedom of man [must] be respected as far as possible, and curtailed only when and insofar as necessary" (DH 7, 178).

Fifth, the council affirms that there should exist "a system of positive law . . . providing for a suitable division of the function and organs of public authority and an effective and independent protection of citizens' rights," a system of positive law in which "the rights of all individuals, families, and organizations" are "acknowledged" (GS 75, 982). The council, in other words, calls upon societies to establish written constitutions specifying the organization, operations, and scope of government; defining the rights of individuals, families, and groups; and providing mechanisms for the protection of these rights. Such a juridical order is necessary to "guarantee . . . the rights of the person" (GS 73, 980). The council thus embraces the idea of constitutional government, of the juridical state: the scope and exercise of political power must be defined and limited by positive law.

Finally, the council affirms that this juridical order should include

> structures providing all citizens without any distinction with ever improving and effective opportunities to play an active part in the establishment of the juridical foundations of the political community, in the administration of public affairs, in determining the aims and the terms of reference in public bodies, and in the election of political leaders. (GS 75, 982)

In affirming that such "politico-juridical structures" are "fully consonant with human nature" (GS 75, 982), the Council embraces not merely the idea of the juridical state but also constitutional democracy.

Embracing constitutional democracy, the council in no way contradicts its simultaneous insistence that the Church is not committed to any particular political system. Nor does the council's preference for constitutional democracy involve the rejection per se of other forms of government. Circumstances, it makes clear, may not only make another form of government legitimate, but may require it. What the council affirms is that, in principle, constitutional democracy is preferable to other forms of government; and that it ought to be instituted whenever and wherever the preconditions for its actualization and proper operation are present.

The council is well aware, however, that this posture marks a development in the Church's political teaching. Its political teaching, the council readily admits, is intended "to develop the doctrine of the recent Popes on the inviolable rights of the human person and on the constitutional order of society" (DH 1, 165). In the teaching of the council, as Paul Sigmund has observed, the Church's traditional "indifference as to the various forms of government has . . . yielded to the recognition of the moral superiority of democratic government and guarantees of human rights," to the recognition that constitutional democracy is the form of government "most in keeping with the nature of man, and with Christian values."[5] The Church's understanding of human nature, and, consequently, of the demands of the common good, the council maintains, has deepened in the course of history. The result has been the recognition that although a variety of governmental forms is capable of advancing the common good, constitutional democracy provides the political medium—the matter, as it were—through which the demands of the common good can receive their best and most complete realization. Constitutional democracy, in short, is capable of incarnating the substance of the common good more fully, more perfectly, than its rivals.[6]

Interpreting the Council

Not surprisingly, the development in the Church's social doctrine that finds expression in the teaching of the council has given rise to many questions. There is, for example, the question of the internal coherence of the theory of politics that informs this revolution. Some have wondered how the Council's embrace of freedom and human rights is to be reconciled with the traditional emphasis of Catholic social thought on duty, virtue, and the common good.[7]

Similarly, there is the whole question of the relationship of the Catholic human rights revolution to liberalism. The last century, as is well known, witnessed the rise of a succession of revolutionary movements that, appealing to the ideas of democracy, the rights of man, and religious freedom, sought to effect the transformation of European social and political life. As is also well known, the Church exhibited toward these movements the same unrelenting hostility they exhibited toward it and vigorously condemned the ideology underlying these movements. Liberalism, as it called this ideology, was, the Church insisted, quite simply incompatible with Catholicism. The obvious question is whether by embracing constitutional democracy, the rights of man, and religious freedom, the Church has thereby embraced liberalism; whether, in other words, the Catholic human rights revolution constitutes a belated capitulation to this old adversary.[8]

To address these questions, it will be necessary to return to the documents of the council both to ascertain the nature of the theory of politics that informs them, and to compare it with that that lies at the heart of the liberal tradition.

Human Dignity, the Rights of the Person,
and the Constitutional Order of Society:
The Conciliar Vision

Not surprisingly, given the Catholic tradition, the starting point of the council's theory of politics is the idea of a common, intelligible, and divinely created human nature from which obligatory norms of conduct flow. An understanding of the teleological structure of this common human nature results in the understanding that man is "a social being" (GS 12, 913) who "by his very nature stands completely in need of life in society" (GS 25, 926). "Life in society is not something accessory to man" (GS 25, 913) because it is "through his dealings with others through mutual service, and through fraternal dialogue, [that] man develops all his talents and becomes able to rise to his destiny." "Man's development" thus necessitates a wide array of "social ties."

Among the communities to which man's "innermost nature" gives rise is "the political community" (GS 25, 926). Because "individuals, families and the various groups which make up the civil community are aware of their inability to achieve a truly human life by their unaided efforts," the council states, "they see the need for an even wider community." Lest this community "be ruined while everyone follows his own opinion, an authority is needed to guide the energies of all towards the common good." Precisely for this reason, "it is clear that the political community and public authority are based on human nature" (GS 74, 980–81).

Both the political community and the public authority "exist for the common good" in which is found their "full justification and meaning and the source of . . . [their] specific and basic right to exist" (GS 74, 981). The common good consists in "those conditions of social life under which men may enjoy the possibility of achieving their own perfection in a certain fullness of measure and also with some relative ease" (DH 6, 173), wherein they may live "a genuinely human life" (GS 26, 927).

It is precisely because of the teleological structure of human nature that we distinguish between actions that are consistent with a truly human life, which enable man to achieve his "true and full humanity" (GS 53, 958), and actions that are inconsistent with a truly human life, which are destructive of man's humanity. The human mind, in short, can discern a moral order, a moral law, inherent in the very structure of human nature. "The entire universe," the council states, "is ordered, directed and governed" by a "divine law," which is "eternal, objective and universal." "Man," it continues, "has been made by God to participate in this law, with the result that . . . he can come to perceive ever increasingly the unchanging truth" (DH 3, 169). Man thus "discovers the existence of a law which he has not laid upon himself," a law embodying "objective standards of moral conduct" (GS 16, 916). This law constitutes the "highest norm of human life" (DH 3, 169), and men have "the moral obligation" to "order their whole lives in accord with . . . [its] demands" (DH 2, 168).

Likewise, precisely because the common good that constitutes the justification and goal of political life has a moral dimension—precisely because advancing the common good involves the fostering of human perfection—politics becomes a moral enterprise with a moral objective. The proper objective of law extends, in this view, beyond the management of conflict. Law, properly understood, has the duty of pointing men towards "a truly human life" (GS 74, 980), of fostering the life of virtue. The Council's theory of politics, like the broader tradition of which it is part, is unabashedly perfectionist in nature.

The Dignity of the Human Person

Up to this point, the theory of politics elaborated by the council neither breaks new ground nor entails the affirmations that constitute the Catholic human rights revolution. The most important of the different aspects of the council's teaching that converge to lay the groundwork for these affirmations is the council's understanding of the demands of human dignity.[9] The idea of the dignity of the human person, it is true, had long been a foundational element in the Church's anthropology. What spurs the far-reaching development in the Church's social teaching that crystallizes in the conciliar documents, however, is a new emphasis upon man's personhood, and a new and deeper understanding of the dignity this implies and of its implications for the organization of social and political life.[10]

Even if contemporary man's growing awareness of his own dignity has at times been distorted by false understanding, the council is emphatic in viewing this awareness as a great advance in human self-understanding. Man, it avows, "is not deceived when he regards himself as superior to bodily things and as more than just a speck of nature or a nameless unit in the city of man." By virtue of his "sublime dignity," man "stands above all things." Hence, human beings may not be regarded as mere objects, or as mere cogs in the social machine.

What is the source of this sublime dignity? To begin with, human beings are more than individual exemplars of a common human nature. Human reason attests to the fact that human beings are "persons—that is, beings endowed with reason and free will and therefore privileged to bear personal responsibility" (DH 2, 167–68). By virtue of his intelligence, man can not only "search out the secrets of the material universe" but "can with genuine certainty, reach to realities known only to the mind." Man can thus discover "what is true and good" (GS 15, 915–16) and recognize "with certainty" the existence of "God, the first principle and last end of things."[11] Through his freedom, moreover, "man can turn himself towards what is good." He is capable of "freely choosing" the good and, "by his diligence and skill securing for himself the means suited to this end" (GS 17, 917). By their freedom, this is to say, men can "order their whole lives in accord with the demands of truth" (DH 2, 168), and, by their "personal assent . . . adhere to it" (DH 3, 169).

By virtue of man's personhood a very real ontological gulf separates human beings from the world of mere objects. Indeed, the human intellect can recognize the ontological foundation of this gulf and of the dignity that flows from it. Reason tells us that, unlike mere objects, man possesses a "rational" nature and a "spiritual and immortal soul" (GS 14, 915).

If we rely on human reason alone, however, "man remains a question to himself, one that is dimly perceived and left unanswered" (GS 21, 921). Only divine revelation—by simultaneously throwing "a new light on all things" (GS 11, 912), and opening up "new horizons closed to human reason" (GS 24, 925)—can enable us to recognize "the nature and greatness of . . . man" (GS 22, 924), and to perceive "his dignity . . . and vocation . . . in their true light" (GS 12, 913). What then does revelation teach us about man's "high calling" (GS 13, 914)? "Sacred scripture," to begin with, "teaches us that man was created 'to the image of God' as able to know and love his creator and as set by him over all earthly creatures that he might rule them, and make use of them, while glorifying God" (GS 12, 913). This image manifests itself through the very capabilities that are constitutive of man's personhood: the human intellect represents a "sharing in the light of the divine mind" and "that which is truly freedom is an exceptional sign of the image of God in man" (GS 17, 917).

Man's full dignity, however, only emerges in and through God's definitive revelation of himself in Jesus Christ: "In reality," the Council declares, "it is only in the mystery of the Word made flesh that the mystery of man becomes clear." On the one hand, "human nature, by the very fact that it was assumed, not absorbed, in Him, has been raised in us also to dignity beyond compare." On the other hand, Christ, who is simultaneously "the 'image of the invisible God'" and "the perfect man," by revealing to man "the mystery of the Father and of His love" both "fully reveals man to himself and brings to light his most high calling" (GS 22, 922).

Indeed, the "full meaning" of man can only be grasped in the light of "man's eternal destiny" (GS 51, 955), as revealed to us by Christ. In Christ, we learn "man is the only creature on earth that God has wanted for its own sake" (GS 24, 925); and that "all men are in fact called to one and the same destiny" (GS 22, 924), a destiny that is "blessed" and "lies beyond the limits" of this world (GS 18, 918). Man is "called as a son to intimacy with God and to share in His happiness" (GS 21, 921). Indeed, "God has called man . . . to cleave with all his being to Him in sharing forever a life that is divine and free from all decay" (GS 19, 918). Man, therefore, is called to a "destiny, which is divine" (GS 22, 924). Men are called upon to do nothing less than to "become sharers in the divine nature."[12] Man's dignity, the Council concludes, "is grounded and brought to perfection in God" (GS 21, 920).

To be a person thus implies a task and involves a grave responsibility. The human person, as we have seen, exists in a universe that is intelligible and that contains inscribed in its very structure an order of moral oughtness. As persons, "all men should be at once impelled by nature and also bound by a moral obligation to seek the truth, especially religious truth. They are also bound to adhere to the truth, once it is known, and to order their whole lives in accord with the demands of truth" (DH 3, 169). As persons, men and women are both impelled by their very nature and morally obligated to seek the true and the good. As persons, they are called on to organize their lives, indeed to shape their very selves, in response to the imperatives that flow from their nature.

Man, however, is not called upon merely to confront and actualize himself in terms of an impersonal order of truth and goodness. Human beings are called upon to confront and actualize themselves in terms of other persons. "The Lord Jesus, when praying to the Father 'that they may all be one . . . even as we are one' " implies "that there is a certain parallel between the union existing among the divine persons and the union of the sons of God in truth and love. It follows, then, that . . . man can fully discover this true self only in a sincere giving of himself" (GS, 24, 925). Inasmuch as God is love, man, made in God's image and called upon to manifest this image in his actions, can fulfill himself only by freely sharing himself with others, only by love. Likewise, for human relations to serve the cause of the development and fulfillment of human beings, these relations must be "enlivened by love" (GS 26, 927), they too must be a communion of persons in love.

The communion of persons through which man discovers and fulfills himself is not restricted to the level of human social relations. Man is called to enter into communion with the persons of the Trinity, to respond to God's love by giving himself to God in love:

> The dignity of man rests above all on the fact that man is called to communion with God. The invitation to converse with God is addressed to man as soon as he comes into being. For if man exists it is because God has created him through love and through love continues to hold him in existence. He cannot live fully according to

truth unless he fully acknowledges that love and entrusts himself to God his creator. (GS 19, 918)

Only in responding to God's call, "by a sincere giving of himself" can "man fully discover his true self" (GS 24, 925).

Human Dignity and the Political Order

The understanding of the person just sketched constitutes the foundation of the political theory of Vatican II, and supplies the dynamic that propels the Catholic human rights revolution. Man's dignity as a person, the council declares, is the fundamental moral fact from which social life must take its bearings. As a person, man "stands above all things" and is the subject of "rights and duties [that] are universal and inviolable." Precisely because "the order of things must be subordinate to the order of persons," it follows that "the social order and its development must constantly yield to the good of the person" (GS 26, 927). Accordingly, the social and political order must be organized in a manner consonant with the dignity of the human person.

What then is the relationship of this dignity to the affirmations that constitute the Catholic human rights revolution? Man is both impelled by his dynamic orientation towards the perfection of his nature and morally obligated to seek truth and goodness. "Truth," however, must "be sought after in a manner proper to the dignity of the human person." Likewise, "as the truth is discovered, it is by personal assent that men are to adhere to it" (DH 2, 169). Truth and goodness, in short, are to be sought in a manner consistent with the nature and dignity of the person: "Man's dignity . . . requires him" to seek truth and goodness through a "conscious and free choice, as moved and drawn in a personal way from within, and not by blind impulses in himself or by mere external constraint" (GS 17, 917). Indeed, "God willed," the council concludes, "that man should 'be left in the hand of his own counsel' so that he might of his own accord seek his creator and freely attain his fully and blessed perfection by cleaving to him" (GS 17, 917). Men, therefore, "cannot discharge" the obligations inherent in their personhood "in a manner in keeping with their own nature unless they enjoy immunity from external coercion as well as psychological freedom" (DH 2, 168).

As a person, man is called upon to respond freely to the call of truth and goodness, moved by an inner sense of responsibility. "External coercion" is obviously inconsistent with the pursuit of truth or goodness "in a manner in keeping" with the nature of the human person. Moreover, such coercion is useless: truth requires free, personal assent. What is true of man's confrontation with the order of truth and justice is even more true of his relationships with other persons. The gift of oneself in love to others must be made personally and freely. It is of the nature of such a gift that it cannot be compelled: a coerced gift is no gift; it is in the nature of love that it cannot be created through external coercion.

From this understanding of the nature and dignity of the human person flow two conclusions central to the council's theory of politics. The first is that the very responsibilities inherent in man's personhood mandate a zone of personal freedom within which human beings can confront these responsibilities in a manner consistent with their nature as persons. Man's moral responsibilities, in other words, are creative of rights vis-à-vis government, and demand that constitutional limits be placed on the scope of government. The authentic rights of the human person thus have their foundation "not in the subjective disposition of the person, but in his very nature." Precisely because its roots are in man's very ontological status as a person, these rights "continue to exist even in those who do not live up to their obligation of seeking the truth and adhering to it" (DH 2, 168).[13]

Government, of course, has the duty to protect society from abuses of these rights. It may intervene and restrict the exercise of these rights when necessary to protect "that basic component of the common welfare" that the council designates as the "public order." The public order has a threefold content, encompassing the "effective safeguard of the rights of all citizens" and the provision "for peaceful settlement of conflicts of rights"; "an adequate care of genuine public peace, which comes about when men live together in good order and in true justice"; and "a proper guardianship of public morality" (DH 7, 177).

The second conclusion is that because, as John XXIII has aptly put it, "there is nothing human about a society that is welded together by force,"[14] freedom is elevated to the status of the political method par excellence. It is true that this principle leaves the question of exactly when freedom should be curtailed to the determination of prudence. It does, however, establish a bias toward the method of freedom. Freedom is to be the rule; coercion, the exception. Obviously, the principle of subsidiarity figures centrally in this context.[15]

Admittedly, the conciliar documents are not systematic treatises in political theory. Nevertheless, as Murray has pointed out, the nature of the argument whose broad outlines they sketch is clear enough. It begins, he writes,

with the traditional truth that every man has the innate dignity of a moral subject. He is endowed with intelligence, with a capacity for self-awareness. He is therefore called to a consciousness of the sense of his own existence—its meaning and purpose as determined by a transcendent order of truth and moral values, which is not created by himself but is to be discovered by him in the total reality of existence itself. Man is also endowed with freedom, a capacity for love and choice. As a subject sui juris, he is called to realize the sense of his own existence through a lifelong process of self-determination, motivated by his own personal judgments.

As a moral subject, man is "responsible" both "for the conformity of his judgments of conscience with the imperatives of the transcendent order of truth" and "for the conformity of his external actions with the inner imperatives of conscience." As a moral subject, therefore,

> man exhibits three characteristics. The first is personal autonomy. That is to say, in his necessary search for the sense of human existence, he is subject only to the laws that rule the order of truth—truth is so accepted only on pertinent evidence, the assent is to be pursued in free communion with others. The second characteristic is the irreplaceability of personal judgment and choice in the moral life. Moral worth attaches only to a human act done deliberately and freely. The human subject cannot be endowed with moral worth from the outside, by the action of others that would attempt to substitute itself for the inner dynamisms of intelligence and freedom. The third characteristic is inviolability. Man's native condition as a moral subject, who confronts the demands of a transcendent order of truth and goodness, requires that he be surrounded by a zone or sphere of freedom within which he may take upon himself his ineluctable burden—that of responsibility for his own existence.

This requirement of a zone of freedom is even "more stringent in what concerns man's relation with God" on account of its immediacy, its "person to person" character, and each person's "responsibility for the nature" of their individual "response" to God's call.

For all these reasons

> it clearly appears that coercion brought to bear upon the human subject, especially in what concerns his relation to God, is not only a useless irrelevance but also a damaging intrusion. It does injury to man's personal autonomy. It stupidly seeks to replace what is irreplaceable. It does violence to the very texture of the human condition, which is a condition of personal responsibility. The conclusion is that an exigence for immunity from coercion is resident in the person as such. It is an exigence of his dignity as a moral subject.

This "exigence for immunity from coercion" extends to all those "areas of human life in which the values of the human spirit are directly at stake" and is validly "asserted against . . . other individuals, others organized in social groups, and especially that impersonal other that is the state." It is thus "the source of the fundamental rights of the person—those political–civil rights concerning the search for truth, artistic creation, scientific discovery, and the development of man's political views, moral convictions, and religious beliefs."

Inasmuch as "this exigence is a thing of the objective order . . . rooted in the given reality of man as man," it follows that it is "permanent and ineradicable and altogether stringent. It is identically the basic requirement that man should act in accordance with his nature." The state thus bears "the burden of proving that it has the right" to restrict the exercise of these rights, which it can only do by showing that "its fundamental responsibility" has become "controlling" — that is, in the case of a violation of public order in the previously defined sense.[16]

Perfectionism, Limited Government, and the Conciliar Theory of Politics

To properly understand the Catholic human rights revolution, it is essential that the affirmations that constitute this revolution not be detached from the broader theory of politics of which they are a part. To be properly understood, the new aspects of the council's political teaching must be situated in the context of its traditional aspects.

The council's insistence upon the right of individuals to immunity from coercion in the sense just adumbrated does not mean that the council believes that the goal of politics is reducible to the protection of individuals from external coercion. Rather, the council's assertion of the rights in question must be seen in the context of its entirely traditional affirmation that government exists to serve the common good. The common good, in turn, encompasses the creation of "conditions of social life under which men enjoy the possibility of achieving their own perfection in a certain fullness of measure and also with relative ease" (DH 6, 173). Government has the responsibility of helping to create conditions in which human beings "have ready access to all that is necessary for living a genuinely human life" (GS 26, 927) of creating social conditions that facilitate "the integral development of the human person" (GS 59, 963). Obviously, this constitutes a broader and more positive conception of the goals of politics than the merely "negative" function of protecting individuals from coercion.

In the council's view, respect for the exigence for immunity from coercion inherent in man's dignity as a person is a demand of the very common good that government exists to serve. Far from being incompatible with its insistence as to the primacy of the common good, the protection of the rights that flow from this exigence is demanded by the common good itself. The common good demands that human beings "have ready access to all that is necessary for living a genuinely human life." Insofar as this exigence from coercion is a demand of human dignity itself, the zone of freedom it demands is necessary to a truly human life.

The protection of these rights is thus an integral element of the common good itself. A government that violates this immunity has not only violated the dignity of the person; it has thereby failed in its responsibility to secure the common good because it has failed in its fundamental responsibility to provide the conditions "necessary to a truly human life." Precisely because this common good is the good of a community whose members are persons, to violate this immunity is to betray the common good itself. These rights do not "trump" the demands of the common good but rather are themselves a function of the common good.[17]

The doctrine of rights invoked by the council thus does not imply a rejection of the idea that the common good constitutes the raison d'être of political life. Nor are these rights to be understood in opposition to—as a limitation upon—the common good. These rights specify the content of the common good and the permissible means of its advancement, so as to enable government to more effectively secure it and assure that the benefits that comprise it are distributed to all.

Even with regard to the rights in question, moreover, the role of government is not limited to the purely negative objective of their protection. The council speaks also of their "promotion" (DH 6, 174). Likewise, the council speaks of governments' role in facilitating "the performance of the duties" of the human person in which these rights have their origins. The example of religious freedom is instructive in this regard. With regard to this right, the council insists that it is not enough for government merely to abstain from coercing individuals in religious matters. Rather, a more positive governmental role is necessary. Government must "promote" this right and facilitate the performance on the part of individuals of the duties in which it originates. Thus, it must "help [to] create conditions favorable to the fostering of religious life" (DH 6, 175) by taking "account of the religious life of the people" and showing "it favor" (DH 3, 170).

The council's teaching about human rights, furthermore, must be seen against the backdrop of its perfectionist understanding of politics. This understanding pervades the conciliar documents and finds expression in the council's affirmation that the common good that government exists to serve consists in the establishment of social conditions conducive to human "perfection," social conditions that foster "the integral development of the human person"; its identification of the "guardianship of public morality" as a "basic component" of the government function; and its insistence on the duty of the laity to "impress the divine law on the earthly city" (GS 43, 944). It finds expression in the council's insistence that government has "a sacred duty to acknowledge the true nature of marriage and the family, to protect and foster them"; that civil authorities proscribe "abortion, euthanasia, willful suicide, and prostitution" (GS 27, 928); and that government "help create conditions favorable to the fostering of religious life." Governments thus have a moral mission.

Yet, if the common good confers a moral function upon the state, it is important to recognize the limited character of government's responsibilities in this regard. To begin with, it is important to recognize the exact character of the common good that government is charged with advancing. This common good is defined not in terms of securing the "perfection" of men per se, but in the creation of conditions "under which men enjoy the possibility of achieving their own perfection . . . with some relative ease" (DH 6, 173). The common good consists in the creation of "circumstances" that "allow man to be conscious of his dignity and rise to his destiny" (GS 31, 931). It is not the responsibility of the state to make men paragons of virtue, to lead them to God, to transmit to them the divine life in which we are invited by God to share, or to transform them into saints. Government has the much more modest task of creating conditions within which men can "with relative ease" achieve their own destiny; conditions that permit men "ready access" to all the things necessary to a "truly human life," conditions that allow them to recognize their own dignity and respond to its imperatives.

Second, it is important to recognize the limited nature of government's responsibility for the common good. The care of the common good does not devolve upon government alone: it is shared by "the people as a whole," "social groups," "government," and "the Church and other religious communities." In "the manner proper to each," each group must seek to advance the common good (DH 6, 173). Indeed, beyond its special responsibility for the securing of public order, government's responsibility for the common good is largely of a subsidiary character: it is government's duty "to bring about more favorable conditions to enable citizens and groups to pursue freely and effectively the achievement of man's well-being in its totality" (GS 75, 983). Government's responsibility is not so much to secure the common good, as to assist other institutions (i.e., family, locality, professional and occupational groups, etc.) in securing it.

Third, it is important to appreciate that in performing its responsibilities government must act in a manner consistent with both the exigencies of human dignity and the nature of the common good itself. Inasmuch as the common good itself "consists chiefly in the protection of the rights, and, in the performance of the duties, of the human person" (DH 6, 173), both the nature of the common good itself and the moral reality of human dignity demand that in performing its responsibilities government must respect the limitations placed on its scope and powers by the rights of the person. Similarly, human dignity demands that government must seek to minimize its use of coercion, acting in accordance with the maxim that "the freedom of man [must] be respected as far as possible, and curtailed only when and in so far as necessary" (DH 7, 178).

The council's teaching about the importance of freedom as a defining attribute of a body politic fully in accord with human nature does not issue in the rejection of a politics of the common good in favor of a thoroughgoing individualism, or in the rejection of a perfectionist theory of politics. On the contrary, on both scores the conciliar teaching is emphatically traditional. What is new in the conciliar teaching is its emphatic embrace of the idea of a limited government: human dignity, it argues, demands that sharp limits be placed on the use of coercion in the pursuit of the common good. What the council does is to wed a perfectionist theory of politics to a theory of limited government. The result is a theory of politics in which the state is simultaneously sharply limited in its scope and powers, yet dedicated to the moral development of its citizens. There is no inconsistency between these two commitments because it is the very moral order that government exists to serve that demands that the scope and powers of the state be limited.

Liberal Individualism and the Political
Teaching of the Second Vatican Council

Before proceeding to the question of the relationship of the Council's theory of politics to the liberal tradition, it is necessary first to clarify what is meant by liberalism. Sometimes the term *liberal* is used to designate a particular practical political orientation rather than a particular theory of politics. The liberal tradition, in this broad usage of the term, would consist of those thinkers and movements supportive of the cause of constitutionalism, limited government, the rule of law, and so on, over and against the cause of absolutism. So understood, liberalism becomes virtually synonymous with constitutionalism or Whiggism.

Sometimes, however, the term *liberalism* is used in a narrower fashion to designate a particular tradition in political theory, a particular model of man and society, which first emerged in the seventeenth century. Originally championed by a small group of intellectuals, this tradition gradually eclipsed its rivals and eventually came to dominate the public life and social and political discourse of the Western world. Understood in this manner, there can be no disputing Harold Laski's description of liberalism as "in the last four centuries, the outstanding doctrine of western civilization,"[18] or Roberto Mangabeira Unger's more recent characterization of it as the modern West's "dominant system of ideas."[19]

Now if liberalism is employed in the first sense, it is not inappropriate to describe the council's political teaching as liberal. This should not be surprising. Historically, the Catholic Church has hardly been hostile to the cause of constitutionalism. Indeed, it has done much to inspire and encourage certain currents within liberalism so understood. The real issue concerns the relationship of the council's teaching to liberalism in the second sense, to this peculiarly modern model of man and society. It was against liberalism understood in this fashion that the Church directed its repeated and emphatic condemnations in the last century; and the relationship of the council's social teaching to liberalism so understood constitutes one of the most important questions prompted by the Catholic human rights revolution. Before addressing the question of whether the Catholic human rights revolution indeed represents a belated capitulation to this old adversary, it is necessary to clarify the model of man and society that defines the liberal intellectual tradition.

The Liberal Model of Man and Society: Its Logic and History

What are the core premises that lie at the heart of the liberal model of man and society, which define it as a distinct intellectual tradition? To begin with, liberalism's most striking feature is its individualism, its insistence, as Douglass and Mara have noted, that "politics is justifiable only by appeal to the well being, rights or claims of individuals." Yet to fully grasp the nature of liberalism and of the individualism it champions, it is equally important to recognize that this individualism must be understood in the context of what Douglass and Mara term the "rejection of teleology . . . [of] the claim that there is a discoverable excellence or optimal condition . . . which characterizes human beings."[20] Liberalism, it might be said, is that theory of man and society that combines a methodological individualism with an emphatic rejection of teleology, with an emphatic rejection of any notion of natural or God-given goals. Planted in the soil of its antiteleological metaphysics of the person, liberalism's individualism issues in a view of human beings as essentially sovereign wills, subject to no order of obligations not of their own creation, subject to no order of human ends that obligate independent of, and prior to, an act of free consent to strive for these ends.

This conception of human beings as unencumbered selves has profound implications for liberalism's understanding of the human good. It issues in the rejection of any substantive conception of the good life. Substantive conceptions of the good life are nothing more than "value judgments"—mere expressions of the subjective desires, the personal preferences, of the individual—with no objective foundation in reality. If, as a result, liberalism at first glance appears to exhibit an agnosticism on the question of the good, closer examination reveals that absent a substantive conception of the human good, liberalism—

either implicitly or explicitly—elevates individual choice to the status of the human good, of the highest good for man. Thus, liberalism issues in what Francis Canavan aptly characterizes as "a steady choice of individual freedom over any other human or social good that conflicts with it, an unrelenting subordination of all allegedly objective goods to the subjective good of individual choice."[21]

It is this conception of the human good that shapes the political morality and conception of the goal of politics around which liberalism seeks to organize social life. "For all forms of liberalism . . . the ideal situation," as Canavan notes, "is one in which the individual freely . . . sets norms for himself. If regulation is necessary . . . its ultimate justification is that it contributes to the individual's freedom to shape his life as he will."[22] Precisely because choice is *the* human good, individuals must respect the freedom of others to live in the way they choose, and thus must refrain from imposing their own subjective preferences on others. For this reason, liberalism insists that the purpose of political institutions is to create a framework of order within which individuals can pursue their self-chosen conceptions of the good. In a community organized in accordance with this conception of the human good, the freedom of individuals to live their lives in the way they choose may be restricted only by the right of others to that same freedom.

The political morality that emerges from liberalism's understanding of the human good demands that substantive conceptions of the good be prevented from impinging on the making of law and public policy because allowing them to do so is tantamount to giving to some individuals license to "impose" their subjective preferences upon others. Creating a society consistent with the demands of liberal political morality thus requires the construction of a public square hermetically sealed off from substantive conceptions of the good life. Obviously, in a society organized in accordance with liberal political morality, liberalism and its conception of the human good enjoy a privileged position. It alone orders both the community's common life and its discussion of what this common life should be; it alone directs the making of law and public policy; and it alone supplies both the idiom and conceptual framework informing the public argument.

The privileging of the liberal conception of the good, in turn, demands what might be called the privatization of nonliberal belief systems. On the one hand, these belief systems must refrain from intruding themselves and their conceptions of the good into the community's public life. They must, in short, embrace liberalism's political morality and accept the privileged position this confers upon the liberal conception of the good that this entails. On the other hand, privatization necessitates a subtle change in the way nonliberal belief systems understand themselves. They must understand themselves as liberalism understands them: not as embodying universally valid and obligatory truths, but as mere subjective preferences. They must recognize that these convictions are true only for those who believe them to be true and morally binding only on those who choose to be bound by them.[23]

The obvious objection to this description of liberalism is that it is misleading because it attributes to liberalism positions held only by some proponents of the liberal model and only by some currents within liberalism. It might be argued that whereas the positions attributed to liberalism are indeed characteristic of the Continental Liberalism so uncompromisingly condemned by the Church in the last century, and the highly influential current in contemporary Anglo-American liberalism represented by figures such as Rawls, Dworkin, and Tribe, they may not fairly be attributed to figures like Grotius, Locke, Jefferson, and Madison, or to the forms of liberalism they inspired. Indeed, it might even by suggested that the latter forms of liberalism are more authentic expressions of liberalism than the former, that the sovereign self and privatization of the good are aberrations restricted to certain historical currents within liberalism rather than defining characteristics of the liberal tradition as such.[24]

Here it is necessary to distinguish between the inner logic of the core premises constitutive of a tradition itself, and the various historical manifestations of the tradition, the various efforts by individual thinkers to construct theories of politics based upon its premises. In understanding an intellectual tradition, it is necessary to appreciate that its proponents may not grasp the conclusions that their premises logically entail. There is, after all, necessarily a time lag between the formulation of new ideas and the appreciation of their full implications.

Taken together, the work of John H. Hallowell and Thomas A. Spragens, Jr., provides a superb overview of the difficulties experienced by liberal thinkers in coming to grips with the implications of the core premises—political, anthropological, metaphysical, epistemological—informing their thought.[25] The potentially revolutionary implications of liberalism's individualism were checked initially by the countervailing belief, inherited by early liberals such as Locke and Grotius from the medieval tradition, in the existence of a moral law discoverable by reason that transcended the subjective wills and desires of individuals. The commitment of liberalism to the existence of such a moral order was inherently precarious both because it was ultimately at odds with liberalism's commitment to individual autonomy, and because it was unsustainable in light of the philosophical premises that informed liberalism. As time went on, it gradually became apparent that the very rejection of teleology entailed by liberalism's nominalism and rationalism was incompatible with the affirmation of the type of objective and universally obligatory moral order whose existence early liberals had taken as axiomatic. The result of the efforts of liberal theoreticians to understand the implications of their own premises was thus the demise of integral liberalism and its replacement by varieties of liberalism in which the inner logic of liberalism's own core premises were given free rein.

The history of liberalism is thus the story of the triumph of the will: the triumph of the subjective will of the individual over the objective moral good, of the individualism that lies at the heart of liberalism over the inherited ideas that had initially acted to restrain it. What needs to be stressed in this context is that this triumph is no mere accident. While all adherents of liberalism may not recognize it, the anthropology of the sovereign self and the conception of the human good and political morality that issues from it are the inevitable consequences of the liberal model's own inner logic, of liberalism's own internal dynamic. For this reason, neither nineteenth-century Continental Liberalism nor today's liberalism of the autonomous self may be dismissed as aberrations. Rather, they reveal the implications of the core principles that define liberalism as a tradition, the fundamental commitments of liberalism as such.

The Liberal Model and the Catholic Human Rights Revolution

Even a cursory comparison of the theory of politics put forward by the council with that which informs the liberal tradition indicates that a gulf separates the two. The liberal understanding of man, social and political life, and the human good is simply incompatible with the Catholic understanding; and the privatization of religion demanded by liberalism is incompatible with both the Catholic understanding of the principles constitutive of a rightly organized body politic and with the Church's understanding both of itself and of the nature and epistemological status of the truth entrusted to it.

The council seems to be aware that some may mistakenly interpret its teaching as a disavowal of its former condemnation of liberalism. On the fundamental points at issue between the two, therefore, the council is at pains to reiterate, albeit in a more measured tone and in a somewhat different idiom, its unalterable and unequivocal rejection of the liberal position. As we have seen, the council reiterates that both reason and revelation disclose to us the existence of an objective moral order. There is, it insists, an order of human and political ends that exists independently of, and obliges prior to, any free consent on our part to pursue these ends. The liberal understanding of the human good as sheer choice is thus mistaken. Likewise, it insists both that man is a social and political creature; and that a rightly ordered body politic must take its bearings from, and seek to foster, this objective moral order and the substantive conception of the human good it embodies.

The council is equally emphatic in its rejection of the privatization of religion that follows from the liberal understanding of man and the human good. It accepts neither the closure of public life to substantive conceptions of the good life deriving from religion nor the privileging of the liberal conception of good consequent upon the liberal conception of a rightly organized body politic. The council insists upon not only the right of the Church to define itself, but on the right of the Church and other religious societies to bring their understanding of the good to bear on law and public policy. "It comes within the meaning of religious freedom," the council declares, "that religious societies should not be prohibited from freely undertaking to show the special value of their doctrine in what concerns the organization of society and the inspiration of the whole of human activity" (DH 4, 171–72). Based upon both this right to religious freedom and the freedom "in human society and in the face of government" peculiar to "herself in her character as a spiritual authority established by Christ the Lord" (DH 13, 186), the council asserts the right of the Church "at all times and in all places . . . to proclaim its teaching about society . . . and to pass moral judgments even in matters relating to politics, whenever the fundamental rights of man or the salvation of souls requires it" (GS 76, 285).

Likewise, the council emphatically rejects the reformation of its self-understanding implicit in the liberal privatization of religion. On the contrary, the council emphatically reasserts the Church's ancient understanding of itself, and in the process makes an array of truth claims flatly incompatible with liberalism. "God Himself," the council declares, "has made known to mankind the way in which men are to serve Him." Indeed, He has revealed that the "one true religion subsists in the Catholic and apostolic Church." The Church is established "by the will of Christ" as "the teacher of the truth" whose "duty" it is to "give utterance to, and authoritatively to teach, that Truth which is Christ Himself and also to declare and confirm by her authority those principles of the moral order which have their origin in human nature itself" (DH 14, 187).

The council is also emphatic in rejecting the liberal conception of freedom, contrasting the "true freedom" it champions with the "false" freedom championed by liberal individualism. If the council "proclaims the freedom of the sons of God" (GS 41, 941), it is careful to contrast the freedom it celebrates from the type of freedom to which the doctrine of the sovereign self gives rise. "That which is truly freedom," the Council avows, "is an exceptional sign of the image of God in man." Thus, "the people of our time," it concludes, "are right" to "prize freedom very highly and strive eagerly for it" (GS 17, 917).

Tragically, however, people today "often cherish" freedom "improperly, as if it gave them leave to do anything they like, even when it is evil" (GS 17, 917). Indeed, some have embraced "a false notion of freedom" (GS 65, 971), in which freedom becomes "the pretext for refusing to submit to authority and for making light of the duty of obedience" (DH 8, 178). Some assert a "false autonomy" arguing that "our personal rights are fully maintained only when we are exempt from every restriction of divine law" (GS 41, 941).

In the face of the misunderstandings fostered by liberalism, the council insists that "true freedom" involves "respect [for] the moral order" and obedience "to lawful authority," the making of decisions "in the light of truth," the striving "after what is true and right," and "a sense of responsibility" (DH 8, 178). God, it insists, does not destroy human freedom but grounds and perfects it. The obligations issuing from the objective moral order do not obstruct human dignity, but are its essential condition. The "true freedom" it champions thus differs fundamentally in its foundations, spirit, and substance from that espoused by liberalism.[26] If the former is a blessing, the Council suggests, the latter can—and today does—constitute a threat to the cause of human dignity.

The Achievement of the Council

In the Catholic understanding, the Church's doctrine develops. While the truth entrusted to the Church does not change, this is to say, the Church's understanding of this truth does indeed grow over the course of time. In the formulation of Dei Verbum: "The Tradition that comes from the apostles makes progress in the Church, with the help of the Holy Spirit. There is a growth of insight into the realities and words that are being passed on."[27] The political teaching of the council represents the culmination of just such a process of development. "The maturing influence of centuries of past experience" (GS 43, 945) during which "the quiet ferment of the Gospel" has been at work, the council declares, has both clarified the Church's "relationship to the world" and made "the requirements" of human dignity regarding the right ordering of social and political life "more adequately known" (DH 9, 179).

As such, the political theory of the Catholic human rights revolution is simultaneously new and traditional. If the political affirmations comprising this revolution are new, the truths that are the inspiration and foundation of these affirmations are, as Maritain and Murray so brilliantly demonstrated, ancient. On the one hand, their roots are found in the distinctions between Church and state, and state and society, and the dedivinization of politics, which are implicit in Christian dualism and the idea of the freedom of the Church. On the other hand, their roots are found in the affirmation of the unique worth and value of each and every human being implicit in Christian revelation, and in the personalist anthropology that emerges from it.

Thus, to interpret the Catholic human rights revolution as representing little more than a belated embrace of liberalism or of the political institutions and procedures generated by the liberal model of man and society is to miss both the originality of the council's theory of politics and the ambitious character of the intellectual project that it involves. The Catholic human rights revolution does much more than to put a Catholic veneer on ideas originating in intellectual systems incompatible with Catholicism, or on the institutions that such ideas have inspired. Indeed, the key to understanding this revolution is the recognition that it takes place in the context of an ongoing and uncompromising rejection of the liberal model of man and society with which constitutional democracy has been so closely linked for so long. What the council has done is to formulate a theory of democratic government rooted in the Church's distinctive vision of man and society.

Far from being rooted in the liberal conception of man and the human good, the democratic society envisioned by the Council is predicated upon, and informed by, the Church's ancient and distinctive understanding of the nature and destiny of man, and of the human good. Thus, the council affirms a right to religious freedom not because religious truth is unattainable or unimportant but because this truth itself demands the recognition of such a right. It affirms the need to place limitations on the scope and power of government—and thus upon the state's responsibility for, and power over, the moral and religious lives of its citizenry—not because it denies that there exists an objective moral order, but because this moral order itself demands such limitations. It defends a regime dedicated to political freedom and human rights not because it rejects the idea of a substantive human good but because this good itself demands such a regime. Thus, as the council emphasizes, the religious freedom it defends "has to do with immunity from coercion in civil society." It "leaves untouched traditional Catholic doctrine on the moral duty of men and societies toward the one true religion and the one Church of Christ" (DH 1, 165).

Likewise, the Catholic human rights revolution does more than offer an alternative justification for the institutions, procedures, and practices championed by liberalism. The fact is that constitutional democracy is not a univocal concept. There are a number of different theories of democracy rooted in divergent understandings of politics and animated by disparate conceptions of the nature and destiny of man. Although superficially similar in their institutions, procedures, and practices, the democratic regimes engendered by these competing theories will differ markedly in their spirit and substance.

The whole question of religious freedom and the role of religion in public life illustrates this point. *Dignitatis Humanae* is at one with liberalism in affirming the existence of a right to religious freedom. Yet its understanding of the foundation, nature, and scope of this right is fundamentally at odds with the liberal understanding. The right to religious freedom affirmed by the council differs so profoundly in spirit and substance from the right to religious freedom championed by theoreticians of liberalism (e.g., Locke, etc.) that one might even go so far as to say that it is not the same right at all. The right to religious freedom therefore cannot simply be equated with the liberal understanding of that right. And, although on the surface a society rooted in the teaching of *Dignitatis* might seem virtually indistinguishable from one taking its bearings from liberal theory—the constitutional law of both, for example, would establish religious freedom as a basic civil right—the former society would differ radically in spirit and society from the latter.[28]

The point is that the Catholic human rights revolution does not simply embrace the institutions and practices generated by liberalism, while rejecting the premises from which they were projected. What it proposes is an alternative to the liberal model of democracy—a model of democratic politics that, if loosely similar in its institutional framework and practices to that which issues from liberalism, nevertheless differs dramatically from it in spirit and substance precisely because its conception of man and the human good differs fundamentally from that of liberalism.[29]

Catholicism, Liberalism and the Free Society: Four Conclusions

Of the conclusions regarding the nature of the Catholic tradition and the intellectual foundations of the free society toward which the foregoing analysis points, four deserve mention here. The first concerns the distinctiveness of the Catholic tradition itself. The Catholic human rights revolution makes it clear that a gulf separates Catholic social thought from both the classical and the liberal traditions. On the one hand, the Catholic understanding of man and politics constitutes far more than an interesting variant of the Aristotelian tradition, or a Platonism debased for consumption by the masses. Catholic social thought shares with the classical tradition a conviction that political life is natural to man, that its objective is the advancement of the common good, and that at the center of this common good is the promotion of human excellence and hence of moral virtue. In other essential respects, however, it breaks fundamentally with both classical political philosophy and classical political practice. For Catholicism, the polity is not the polis of classical antiquity, and a human being is far more than the rational polis animal whose contours are so brilliantly sketched in the work of Aristotle. On the other hand, although both the Catholic and liberal traditions afford a value to the individual human being foreign to classical antiquity, they differ—and differ fundamentally—about the nature of man, about exactly what an individual human being is. The sovereign self of liberal theory is not the person exalted by Christian revelation: it is what is left of the Christian exaltation of the person when that idea is transplanted to the soil of a fundamentally anthropocentric metaphysical vision, and hence projected against the backdrop of a non-Christian, and, ultimately, godless and meaningless universe.

Indeed, one of the major sources of confusion about the Catholic human rights revolution has been the tyranny of various theoretical frameworks that obscure the distinctiveness of the Catholic tradition. As long, for example, as we view political theory through the prism of theoretical categories that reduce the history of political theory to a conflict between the "classical" and "modern" traditions, we are virtually forced to assimilate Catholic social thought to either the classical or liberal traditions. By collapsing it into a tradition that differs from it fundamentally, we badly distort Catholic social thought. Such categories render us effectively incapable of understanding either the Catholic tradition or the development within that tradition that comes to term in the work of the council.

The second conclusion concerns the falsity of the widely asserted claim that liberalism constitutes the necessary and essential intellectual foundation for a free society. Now there can be no denying that liberalism has dominated modern theorizing about human rights, no denying that the liberal understanding of man has provided the foundation from which the most influential rights theories of the past several centuries have been projected. Likewise, our very propensity to refer to our system of government as a liberal democracy attests to the role liberalism has played historically in inspiring and supplying an intellectual foundation for the institutions and practices of modern constitutional democracy.

Nevertheless, it simply does not follow that liberalism provides the only possible intellectual foundation for the institution, practices, and principles that are constitutive of the free society. Nor does it follow that a principled commitment to these institutions, practices, and principles entails the acceptance of the liberal model of man and society. Simply stated, the Catholic human rights revolution demonstrates that the institutions and practices of constitutional democracy and human rights can be projected from foundations other than the premises of liberalism, and thus that a principled commitment to democracy and human rights does not entail the acceptance of the liberal model of man and society.

The third conclusion concerns the falsity of the widely asserted claim about the incompatibility of the affirmation of a substantive conception of the human good with a principled commitment to a free society. It is widely held that the inner logic of such an affirmation tends inexorably toward political authoritarianism, and thus that such an affirmation necessarily constitutes some kind of incipient fascism. For the proponents of a substantive conception of the good life, it is widely believed, the free society can only be accepted for reasons of expediency, that is, on the grounds that no better regime is practical under prevailing conditions. Yet, although widely asserted, the truth of this claim is by no means self-evident. From the premise that we can know the human good it does not automatically follow that it is the right—much less the duty—of government to compel all to embrace it. If some substantive conceptions of the good life may foster an authoritarian politics, others may foster a commitment to government that is sharply limited in its scope and responsible to those it governs. As a matter of fact, the political theory of the Catholic human rights revolution provides conclusive proof of the unsustainability of this claim. What this revolution demonstrates is that regardless of whether some substantive conceptions of the human good are indeed inconsistent with a principled commitment to a free society, at least one such conception—namely, that which informs the council's teaching—is perfectly consistent with such a commitment.

The fourth conclusion concerns the relevance of the political theory informing the Catholic human rights revolution to the future of the American democratic experiment. In recent years, it has become apparent to an increasing number of observers that, far from providing its essential intellectual foundation, liberalism has today come to constitute perhaps the most important threat facing constitutional democracy.[30] Unfortunately, despite the rapidly growing recognition both of the inadequacies of liberalism as a theory of man and politics and of its inability to sustain a democratic society, no systematic break with the liberal model has taken place.

For purposes of the present discussion, perhaps the most important factor explaining this state of affairs is found in the fact that, notwithstanding whatever reservations they may harbor about liberalism, for the overwhelming majority of our contemporaries liberalism has become, in effect, the only game in town. So deeply embedded in our intellectual climate are the assumptions of liberalism that our intelligentsia is unfamiliar with any living intellectual tradition that simultaneously differs fundamentally from liberalism, is at least its equal in depth and intellectual power, and is fully compatible with a principled commitment to the free society.

What Catholic social thought can offer us is just such a tradition. Its relevance to contemporary America consists in the possibility it opens to us of a democratic regime that differs decisively from that which issues from liberalism. Thus, although it may be surprising to some in light of the conflict that has characterized the Church's relationship to modernity, Catholic social thought may today offer us our best hope of bringing the modern world's quest for the social and political emancipation of humanity to a successful conclusion. Ironically, given the suspicion and even hostility with which the Church responded to the rise of modern democracy and the frequently asserted incompatibility of Catholicism with a free society, the Catholic intellectual tradition may today offer us our best hope—perhaps our only hope—of saving liberty from liberalism.

For those who remain satisfied with liberalism and with what it has wrought, of course, the Catholic human rights revolution will perhaps be of little more than academic interest. But, for the growing number of thinkers of a variety of religious commitments who recognize the deficiencies of the liberal model, and who seek—however tentatively—an alternative to it, this revolution must be numbered among the most important and welcome intellectual developments of our era.

Notes

I wish to thank the Reverend Francis Canavan, S.J., of Fordham University, Dr. Robert P. Hunt of Kean College, three colleagues of mine at Southwest Texas State University—Drs. Randall W. Bland, Arnold Leder, and George Weinberger—and my wife, Rebecca Liounis, for taking the time to read and comment upon an earlier draft of this essay. The essay has benefited immensely from their helpful suggestions. I also wish to express my gratitude to one of my former students, Jeffrey C. Herndon, for his able assistance with some of the research for the essay. Needless to say, I alone am responsible for the views it expresses.

1. See George Weigel, "Catholicism and Democracy," *The Washington Quarterly* 12 (Autumn 1985): 5–25; and *Catholicism and the Renewal of American Democracy* (New York: Paulist Press, 1989).

2. For an incisive analysis of the development of modern papal thought on human rights and the role of the state, see John Courtney Murray, S.J., *The Problem of Religious Freedom* (Westminister, Md.: The Newman Press, 1965). For a good account of the intellectual roots of this revolution by a thinker whose seminal work did much to spur it, see Jacques Maritain, *Christianity and Democracy and the Rights of Man and Natural Law* (San Francisco: Ignatius Press, 1986).

3. Our examination of these documents will necessarily be restricted to those aspects of their teaching that relate most directly to the theory of democratic government. For a good overview of the social teaching of the council as a whole, see Rodger Charles, S.J., *The Social Teaching of Vatican II* (San Francisco: Ignatius Press, 1982). References to *Dignitatis Humanae* are from the translation by John Courtney Murray, S.J., in *Religious Liberty: An End and a Beginning,* ed. John Courtney Murray (New York: Macmillan, 1946), which was reprinted from *The Documents of Vatican II,* ed. Walter M. Abbot, S.J. (New York: Guild Press, 1966). References to *Gaudium et Spes* are from the translation in *Vatican II: The Conciliar and Post-Conciliar Documents,* ed. Austin Flannery, O.P. (Collegeville, Minn.: The Liturgical Press, 1975). The documents will be cited parenthetically as DH and GS, respectively; and the section number will be given followed by the page number in the volume containing the translation.

4. Murray, "The Issue of Church and State at Vatican Council II," Theological Studies (December 1966): 599.

5. Paul Sigmund, "The Catholic Tradition and Modern Democracy" in *Religion and Politics in the American Milieu,* ed. Leslie Green (Notre Dame, Ind.: *The Review of Politics* and the Office of Policy Studies, n.d.), 20, 13.

6. See Maritain, *Christianity and Democracy.*

7. See, for example, Ernest Fortin, "The Trouble with Catholic Social Thought," *Boston College Magazine* (Summer 1988): 37–42. The development in Catholic social doctrine under discussion here, Fortin argues, has produced "a number of tensions" (37) in contemporary Catholic social teaching. These tensions stem, he argues, from the fact that the Church's traditional social teaching, which "presented itself as first and foremost a doctrine of duties" (38) and spoke in the idiom of "virtue, character formation, and the common good" (42) has been juxtaposed with ideas that derive from the "natural or human rights doctrine" developed by Hobbes and his successors, in which "rights," rather than duties, are "paramount" (39). As a result of this juxtaposition, Fortin suggests, the Church's social teaching combines traditional Christian ideas with "ideas that once were and still may be fundamentally antithetical to it," and, as a result, "suffers from a latent bifocalism that puts it at odds with itself and thereby weakens it to a considerable extent" (37).

8. Cf. Michael Novak, *Free Persons and the Common Good* (Lanham, Md.: Madison Books, 1989), and *Freedom with Justice: Catholic Social Thought and Liberal Institutions* (San Francisco: Harper & Row, 1984), and David Hollenbach, S.J., "Liberalism, Communitarianism, and the Bishops' Pastoral Letter," in *Church Polity and American Politics: Issues in Contemporary American Catholicism,* ed. Mary C. Segers (New York: Garland Publishing, Inc., 1990), 99–118, and "Religion and Political Life," Theological Studies 52 (March 1991): 86–106. Novak argues that Catholic social thought "has slowly but steadily come to embrace the institutions of liberal society" (FWJ, 38). At an even deeper level, he maintains, the council's teaching betokens an impending "marriage between the liberal tradition and the Catholic tradition" (FPCG, 2). Ironically, in view of their disagreements regarding the Church's teaching on economic life, David Hollenbach seems to be in basic agreement with Novak here. Hollenbach would seem to accept Novak's contention that Vatican II affirms "the desirability and indeed the moral demand" for "liberal institutions" (RPL, 91), for the institutions generated by the liberal model of man and society. Likewise, he suggests that there are strong affinities between the council's political teaching and liberalism, albeit "a liberalism of a strongly revisionist kind" (LC, 107). The conciliar account of the hallmarks of a rightly organized society, for instance, "bears a remarkable resemblance to what Rawls calls a just basic structure of social, political, and economic institutions" (LC, 109).

9. A comprehensive presentation of the theory of politics that underlies these affirmations would thus have to include a discussion of three aspects of its teaching not examined here, which, if not as central to the council's theory of politics as the line of argument developed here, are nevertheless significant. Specifically, such a presentation would have to include an examination of the council's insistence on the centrality of the freedom of the Church to the right ordering of social and political life; its insistence

on the rightful autonomy of temporal matters; and its insistence simultaneously upon both the transcendental dimension of the human person and the temporal character of the state's competence.

10. It is commonplace that the idea of the person as a theological and philosophical concept emerged as a byproduct of the Christological controversies of the Patristic era. If not incompatible with the classical conception of man as a rational animal, the idea of man as a person nevertheless goes decisively beyond it, and thereby constitutes an historic advance in man's self-understanding. The rediscovery and development of this concept as a foundational element in Catholic anthropology has been one of the driving forces behind the *ressourcement* in Catholic thought that culminates in the work of the council and constitutes the thread connecting the work of many of the thinkers who have propelled this *ressourcement* (i.e., Maritain, De Lubac, Guardini, Marcel, von Hildebrand, Rahner, Lonergan, Wojtyla, etc.). For an important recent effort to explore the philosophy of the person from the standpoint of Thomas's metaphysics of being, see W. Norris Clarke, S.J., *Person and Being* (Milwaukee: Marquette University Press, 1993).

11. *Dei Verbum* in *Vatican II: The Conciliar and Post-Conciliar Documents*, section 5, p. 752. The council is here quoting from the First Vatican Council's *Dogmatic Constitution on the Catholic Faith.*

12. Ibid., 2, 751.

13. Several obvious questions suggest themselves here. If these rights have their foundation in man's obligation to seek the true and the good, why does the man who ignores or rejects this obligation not thereby forfeit his rights? If our dignity as person is grounded in our ability to pursue the true and good, does not such a man forfeit his dignity and thus the rights which are consequent upon it? To address these questions, it is necessary to fully articulate a distinction implicit in the council's teaching, namely, the distinction here between man's ontological dignity and his moral dignity. These rights have their foundation in man's ontological dignity as persons. Whereas a man may forfeit his moral dignity by taking "little trouble to find out what is true and good" or allowing his "conscience" to become "by degrees almost blinded through the habit of committing" (GS 16, 917), his ontological dignity remains: "The person in error never loses his dignity as a person" (GS 28, 929), and thus retains the rights that have their source in it.

14. John XXIII, *Pacem in Terris* in *The Encyclicals and Other Messages of John XXIII* (Washington, D.C.: TPS Press, 1964), section 34, p. 335.

15. On the connection between subsidiarity and the free society, see Johannes Messner, "Freedom as a Principle of Social Order," *The Modern Schoolman 27* (January 1951): 97–110. Cf., Thomas C. Kohler, "In Praise of Little Platoons," in *Building the Free Society: Democracy, Capitalism, and Catholic Social Teaching,* ed. George Weigel and Robert Royal (Grand Rapids, Mich.: Eerdmans, 1993), 31–50.

16. Murray, "The Declaration of Religious Freedom: A Moment in its Legislative History," in *Religious Liberty: An End and a Beginning,* 38–41.

17. For the classic account of the implications of man's personhood for our understanding of the common good, see Maritain, *The Person and Common Good* (New York: Charles Scribner's Son, 1947).

18. Harold J. Laski, *The Rise of European Liberalism* (London: George Allen & Unwin, 1936), 9.

19. Roberto Mangabeira Unger, *Knowledge and Politics* (New York: Free Press, 1975), 5.

20. R. Bruce Douglass and Gerald M. Mara, "The Search for a Defensible Good: The Emerging Dilemma of Liberalism" in *Liberalism and the Good,* ed. R. Bruce Douglass, Gerald M. Mara, and Henry S. Richardson (New York: Routledge, 1990), 257–58.

21. Francis Canavan, S.J., "The Pluralist Game," *Law and Contemporary* Problems 44 (Spring 1981): 23.

22. Ibid.

23. For an insightful discussion of liberalism and the privatization of religion, see Gerard V. Bradley, "Dogmatomachy—A Privatization Theory of the Religion Clause Cases," *St. Louis Law Journal* 30 (1986): 275–330.

24. This, for example, would appear to be the position of Michael Novak. Liberalism, Novak suggests, "has many strands and many diverse positions" (FPCG, 222). He contrasts the main current of Anglo-American liberal thought that finds expression in the work of thinkers such as Locke, Smith, Bentham, John Stuart Mill, Madison, and Jefferson, with other varieties of liberalism whose very "claim . . . to the title of 'liberal' is not beyond dispute" (FPCG, 158). The "liberalism" championed by Rawls, Dworkin, Ackerman, etc., would appear to be an example of the latter type of "liberalism," as, by implication, would nineteenth-century Continental Liberalism. The latter two varieties of liberalism, Novak seems to argue, differ fundamentally from the variety of liberalism championed by Locke et al.

25. See Hallowell, *The Decline of Liberalism as an Ideology* (Berkeley: University of California Publications in the Social Sciences, 1943; reprint, New York: Howard Fertig, 1971); and Spragens, *The Irony of Liberal Reason* (Chicago: University of Chicago Press, 1988).

26. For the Catholic understanding of freedom and how it differs from the liberal understanding, see Maritain, *Freedom in the Modern World,* tr. Richard O'Sullivan, K.C. (New York: Gordian Press, 1971); and "The Conquest of Freedom," in *The Social and Political Philosophy of Jacques Maritain: Selected Readings,* ed. Joseph W. Evans and Leo R. Ward (Notre Dame, Ind.: University of Notre Dame Press, 1976), 10–27.

27. *Dei Verbum,* 8, 754.

28. For some helpful suggestions as to the differences between the understanding of religious liberty contained in *Dignitatis* and that defended by the liberal tradition, see Francis Canavan, S.J., "The Catholic Concept of Religious Freedom as a Human Right," in *Religious Liberty: An End and a Beginning,* ed. Murray, 65–80.

29. For an account of this spirit and substance by one of this century's seminal Catholic thinkers, see Maritain, *Scholasticism and Politics* (New York: Macmillan, 1940), especially 56–117.

30. On this point, see Kenneth L. Grasso, "A Special Kind of Freedom," in *Building the Free Society,* 117–26.

4

Religion as Moral Duty and Civic Right: *Dignitatis Humanae* on Religious Liberty

Kenneth R. Craycraft Jr.

In the main, religious persons in America embrace the religious liberty principles of the American Founding.[1] Many, if not most, Catholics see Vatican II's *Dignitatis Humanae*[2] as consonant with that. None other than John Courtney Murray, S.J., in fact, has said that the "object or content of the right to religious freedom, as specified both in the *Declaration* and in the American Constitutional system, is identical."[3] And Father Murray explains that the final content of *Dignitatis* owes much to the contribution of the American bishops. "It is apparent from their interventions that the American bishops made important theoretical contributions toward the illumination of the principle" of religious liberty in the *Declaration.*[4]

But Francis Canavan, S.J., has noted that Murray, despite having been one of the chief authors and despite his public optimism, was not altogether satisfied with the *Declaration on Religious Liberty,* especially on one very key point: religious liberty being linked with the idea of the freedom of conscience.[5] In a symposium chaired by Murray, Canavan critiqued *Dignitatis* for not paying sufficient attention to the juridical aspect of rights, and giving too much emphasis to an abstract right of conscience.[6] Murray thanked Canavan for being " 'much too kind' " in his remarks, and later, in an introduction to the proceedings of the conference, pointed out his essential agreement with

Canavan's criticism of *Dignitatis:* "With a critical eye," says Murray, Canavan "sees its argument deficient—as indeed it is—through a failure to fully appreciate the political dimension of the issue."[7] This leads Canavan to suspect that "Murray put the best face he could on the final version of the *Declaration on Religious Freedom* and was in fact less content with it than he let on."[8]

This vignette is instructive in that it shows Murray's ambiguity about even this, his greatest accomplishment (and indeed one of the most significant achievements in the Roman Catholic Church in the twentieth century). And there is good reason to have ambiguous feelings about the document, since it is not always clear what moral or theological principles are at work in its argument. Murray said shortly after the council that the course of development between Pius IX's *Syllabus of Errors* and *Dignitatis* needed to be explained by theologians.[9] "Like all developments," says Murray, "this one will initiate a further progress in doctrine, that is, a new *impostazione* of the doctrine of the Church on the problem of Church and State, as it is called, in order to restore, and to perfect its own sense of, the authentic tradition."[10] A reading of Murray's own reluctant commentary[11] on the *Declaration* demonstrates that this is no mean feat, even for its primary author. Its undeniable ambiguity makes it difficult indeed to give a definitive and final understanding of the council's intention.[12]

The following essay makes no pretense of solving the problem of theological development in the *Declaration*. Nor is it intended to account for the development of the *Declaration* itself.[13] In fact, my interpretation of *Dignitatis* makes the problem of development less of a problem than Murray contends.[14] This might itself be considered ironic, as I also argue that my interpretation is consistent with (and, indeed, is enlightened by) Murray's own reflections on the meaning of *Dignitatis*. That is, while leaving aside the use or abuse of the *Declaration* since the council, I argue that its fundamental understanding of religious freedom, including most importantly a robust defense of the freedom of the Church and its denial of the moral right of error, is more continuous with the "traditional" view than is often asserted.[15]

This is not to deny that certain tensions exist in *Dignitatis,* and that these tensions may well be irresolvable. The very notion of "rights" employed here and in other recent offical Church documents is problematic at best. The Church has adopted a language that may be irreconcilable with its more ancient and basic claims about man and his relationship to God.[16] It is not my intention to attempt to resolve these tensions, as I am not sure they are resolvable. Rather, I am attempting to read *Dignitatis* according to the dominant and fundamental principles at work there.

Historical Consciousness and Human Dignity

While not mentioning the phrase, the very first sentence of *Dignitatis* is an expression of the Church's acknowledgment of the modern understanding of consciousness as necessarily related to historical contexts—of "historical consciousness."[17] Murray understands this to be *the essential element* in the Church's "new" understanding of religious liberty.[18] And while this acknowledgment on the part of the Church might be understood as a radical departure from the tradition, and a problematic capitulation to "modernism," the onus of the *Declaration* is precisely to dispel this understanding. That is, the council did not attempt to deny the reality of historical consciousness with all its legitimate implications. It did attempt to deny, however, that this implies the impossibility to know and articulate objective religious and moral truth.[19] In Murray's words,

> In the 19th and early 20th centuries, the movement away from the classical mentality toward historical consciousness came to an immediate term in modernism, that compendium of all heresies. The Church rejected this term, flatly and uncompromisingly. This was altogether necessary. Unfortunately, however, the Church also rejected the movement itself. This was not altogether necessary, as now we know. Happily the *Declaration* on Religious Freedom signified the acceptance of the movement.[20]

That is, the Church came to accept it as a fact of human existence that human knowledge and understanding of truth are conditioned by history, but rejected the idea that this entails that truth is relative.[21] The practical implication of this is that the Church recognized, in principle, the legitimacy of changing human consciousness as a source of information for Church teaching.[22]

The truth newly conscious in the mind of man with which the Church is mainly concerned in *Dignitatis* is the idea of the dignity of the human person.[23] With this individual dignity comes the sense that all men's actions should be free of coercive power by individuals and associations. That is, mankind has become universally aware of the necessity of freedom from coercion in making moral decisions, and has universally begun to assert this right to freedom in political society. This consciousness and its incumbent demands are concerned primarily with religious and spiritual matters, because they are matters that have to do with a "sense of duty."[24] This demand is concerned especially with "the free practice of religion in society."[25]

But unlike liberal political theory, *Dignitatis* situates religious freedom not in the right of a free conscience, but in the duty of a conscience objectively bound by the obligation to seek and embrace truth. "All men are bound to seek the truth, especially in what concerns God and his Church, and to embrace it and hold on to it as they come to know it."[26] It is important to draw this distinction carefully. The council has declared not only that one is obliged to embrace the truth when found, but also that the conscience is bound by an obligation to seek that truth until it is found and embraced. "The Sacred Council likewise proclaims that these obligations bind man's conscience. . . . It leaves intact the traditional Catholic teaching on the moral duty of individuals and societies towards the true religion and the one Church of Christ."[27] That is, the idea of a conscience radically free from any encumbrance other than those it chooses for itself[28] is rejected. As a creature of God, man's conscience is bound by an obligation to seek the truth of God's revelation, which obligation is issued by God. "God calls men to serve him in spirit and in truth," says *Dignitatis*. "Consequently they are bound to him in conscience."[29] Man is bound not by the "duty" to shun all duties (as is James Madison's unencumbered self[30]), but rather by a duty to seek and to know the truth of the Gospel. This obligation is the source of each man's dignity as a human person, which dignity ought to be "immune from coercion on the part of individuals, social groups and every human power," and thus entails a "right to religious freedom."[31]

This dignity is founded not in the autonomy of human conscience, but in the truth that obliges human conscience. The Church recognizes a universal awareness of human dignity, and thus of freedom, but places this dignity in its proper foundation of an obligation to seek and to know the truth. Dignity is rooted not in freedom, but in obligation and responsibility.[32] And because every person is bound by this obligation, every person's dignity is to be respected by all earthly powers. "It is in accordance with their dignity," the *Declaration* continues, "that all men . . . are both impelled by their nature and bound by a moral obligation to seek the truth, especially religious truth. . . . But men cannot satisfy this obligation in a way *that is in keeping with their own nature* unless they enjoy . . . immunity from external coercion."[33] Man's obligation is the source of his dignity; his dignity in turn is the basis for his political or civic right to religious liberty.

Since obligation is the source of dignity, it follows that full dignity comes in full obedience.[34] The dignity of man is in accord with his nature, and is thus perfected as man more consistently acts according to his nature.[35] This might be thought of as a distinction between *ontological* dignity and *moral* dignity. Ontological dignity is of the essence of man as a rational, reflective, and therefore *responsible* creature. It is this essential dignity that is to enjoy immunity from coercion by other people or by the state. But man's moral dignity may be forfeited. A murderer, for instance, loses his moral dignity: he is imprisoned, his rights are severely restricted, and in some cases, he is killed by the state. Thus, man is more perfect—more in accord with his own nature—when he uses his ability to reflect and choose to choose rightly. His moral dignity is compromised and his ontological dignity misused when he chooses badly.

Though he does not use the terms, Murray hints at such a distinction when he says, "Though the *Declaration* deals only with the minor issue of religious freedom in the technical secular sense, it does affirm a principle of wider import—that the dignity of man consists in his responsible use of freedom."[36] The responsible use of freedom is, of course, obedience to truth. Or as Murray says elsewhere, "The dignity of man is formally identified with his free fidelity to the imperatives of the conscience that is rightly . . . formed."[37] But, though this dignity is fully and perfectly realized only when one obeys the obligation to embrace the truth, one who has not done so is still immune from coercion because of the dignity that inheres in the responsibility itself. Human dignity is found "not in the subjective attitude of the individual but in his very nature" as a creature who is bound to seek the truth.[38] Though the disobedient person is not acting perfectly in accord with his or her nature, this shortcoming is multiplied when that person's dignity is not respected by human powers.[39]

Civic Rights in the Juridical Order

It is only after establishing the primacy of obligation to seek and embrace truth as the source of human dignity that *Dignitatis* affirms a *right* to religious liberty. "Everybody has the duty and consequently the right to seek the truth in religious matters."[40] But this right is not a human right *coram Deo;* it is only a civic, legal, and political right. Even though the phrase "human right" is never used in the *Declaration,* most commentators (Murray included) refer to it as having established religious freedom as a human right.[41] But of course it cannot be a human right in the sense of an inalienable right residing in the very essence of man, else the duty to form one's conscience in a very particular way and to embrace a very particular claim of truth is contradicted. The civic right of religious liberty emerges precisely out of the *obligation* before God to conform one's conscience to truth; the existence of coercive government causes man to assert certain rights against the state that his obligation to seek the truth not be impeded. Therefore, it is a political, not a "prepolitical" right; it does not exist in nature, but is asserted against coercive government.

Duty of Conscience and the Limited State

Thus is laid a much stronger and surer foundation than the liberal one for religious liberty. And though the benefit of this teaching extends to all people, it is a distinctly Christian argument, and it implies that the Church is free to *make* such an argument against the state; the Church is free to pronounce to the state what its limits are.[42] Man's sacred obligation before God, an obligation rooted in transcendent truth, relativizes the scope and concentration of the authority of the state. The liberal denial of this sacred obligation and the incumbent denial of the freedom of the Church *qua* church make the state immune from the necessity of protecting religious liberty when the interests of the state are threatened by it.

For Madison, Jefferson, and the First Amendment, the one religious truth is that religion is mere opinion, and so no one is harmed if mere opinions are somehow abridged when necessary. This is especially true if an opinion asserts itself in political life against the liberal religious truth-claim that religion is mere opinion. Conventional political obligation trumps religious obligation. Against this idea, *Dignitatis* affirms that man "is bound to follow this conscience faithfully in all his activity so that he may come to God, who is his last end." Man's religious obligation creates a juridical–legal right against the state, and therefore relativizes the authority of the state.

As noted above, Francis Canavan was disappointed that this argument was not made more strongly and more clearly in *Dignitatis*. The argument the *Declaration* does make, "which proceeds from the obligation to follow conscience to a rather elaborate series of rights that collectively constitute religious freedom," does not seem to be able to carry the "full weight that is put on it." Thus, the Church's commitment to religious freedom "might have had a stronger intellectual underpinning if it had devoted more attention to the nature of a just political and legal order in society."[43] As it is, says Canavan, the argument for religious liberty in the *Declaration* is too abstract; it does not sufficiently consider concrete political existence in the modern liberal world. It ought to have carried out more systematically the assertions in the preamble — that a sense of religious duty, translated into human dignity, demands civic, legal, and political freedom from coercion. This line of argument "is neglected in favor of an abstract ethical argument."[44] Canavan's reasoning would make the case stronger in *Dignitatis* that these rights are civic or legal rights derived from duties, rather than first-principle natural or human rights. The *Declaration* itself intimates this conclusion, but there is no sustained discussion of the crucial point, namely, "the right of the human person to religious freedom must be given such recognition in the constitutional order of society as will make it a civil right."[45]

Murray lends evidence that Canavan's understanding of *Dignitatis* is the proper one, both by citing it approvingly and by explaining what he means by the idea of a "human right" to religious liberty. He does not mean a "prepolitical" right inhering in man qua man, but rather a right necessitated by the "relation between people and government. This is the order of human rights and the order in which the principle of freedom obtains in its full validity."[46] In Murray's usage, human rights are juridical tools used to maintain peace and to protect the grace-bound conscience from intrusion by external coercive measures. "Therefore," says Murray, "in its juridical sense as a human right, religious freedom is a functional or instrumental concept."[47] Thus, for Murray, a "human" right is not a subjective prepolitical claim against all other individuals, but rather a civic or legal right, afforded to each and every human being, as a result of his or her duty-based dignity. It is the universal assertion of an identical objective claim against the state. The "function of religious freedom as a legal institution embodying a civil right" is "to assure full scope for the manifold manifestations of freedom in religious matters."[48] The ends pursued under the protection afforded by these civic rights "are of the meta-juridical order. They are . . . remote from direction or control by any forces of the juridical order."[49] How the pursuit of these ends is protected is a question of political exigency.

Murray's position "does not propose the legal institution of religious freedom as a constitutional ideal, an abstract thesis, conceived a priori, under abstraction from historical-social reality."[50] This statement is closely related to Murray's mature understanding of the thesis-hypothesis doctrine of church–state relationship (what Murray calls the "First View"). While it is clear that Murray thought that this line of reasoning is not practicable in the modern situation, it is not at all clear that he abandons the theological legitimacy of it in some political situations. For Murray, the thesis-hypothesis argument is not wrong, it is "archaic." That is, under the exigencies of modern, liberal constitutional government, the theory simply cannot work; it has been rendered superfluous by historical circumstance. Thus, the current "task is to discern the elements of the tradition that are embedded in some historically conditioned synthesis that, as synthesis, has become archaistic."[51] The thesis-hypothesis doctrine was the correct and true answer to a question that is not asked any longer, and so we must find the abiding principle that informed that true answer and apply it to modern questions. It is not rejected because the Church has become more "mature"; rather it is put aside because the political-social situations it addressed no longer exist.

Thus, the Second View (the view here being explicated), does not, in principle, reject the confessional Catholic state. As Murray notes,

> The Second View does not denounce the Church or the Republic of Ecuador for a violation of religious freedom in 1862. More in general, in judging all past or present realizations of the Catholic state, so called, the historical situation needs to be considered. The historical institutions of establishment and intolerance are to be judged *in situ. They might well be judged valid in situ.* The function of the law,

said the Jurist, is to be useful to people. These institutions might well have been useful to the people, in the condition of the personal and political consciousness of the people at the time. This was Leo XIII's judgment. It would be anachronistic to judge it.[52]

Thus, the Second Vatican Council declared, "If because of the circumstances of a particular people special civil recognition is given to one religious community in the constitutional organization of the state, the right of all citizens and religious communities must be respected as well."[53] Murray makes a very carefully worded comment on this passage in a note to his translation. The council did not condemn in principle the institution of a confessional state since "a respectable opinion maintains that the institution is compatible with full religious freedom." But neither did the council wish to canonize such institution since "a respectable opinion holds that establishment is always a *threat* to religious freedom."[54]

Neither Murray nor the council reject, in principle, the legitimacy of the confessional state. Murray, in fact, makes the crucial point that it is just as much a theological error to say that "the notion of religious freedom as a human right [is] a piece of theological–ethical theory, arrived at by a process of abstract argument, in a vacuum of historical, political and juridical experience,"[55] as to affirm the thesis–hypothesis doctrine in such a vacuum. Religious freedom is not a per se good for Murray; it is an exigent one.

Church as Judge of All Politics

This points up the more general truth that the Catholic Church has no particular political theory of its own. The Church reserves—indeed strongly asserts and protects—the right to stand in judgment of the moral and legal principles of all regimes, but it makes no suggestion of a particular kind of regime. Moreover, it adjusts its teaching according to the particular regime that it finds itself in, affirming principles that are in accord with right, condemning those that are not, and at all times protecting its own freedom to make such judgments. It is precisely the historical contingency of political regimes that make it a danger for the Church to identify with any particular one, or with any at all. Prescriptive identification with any kind of political regime poses the danger of the Church's being unable to keep the critical distance necessary to make the judgments it must always make.

Thus, for Murray, the right of religious liberty is a juridical right, based upon the exigencies of historical consciousness, and he thinks that *Dignitatis* agrees. The right of religious liberty is a "technical question of public care of religion by the public power, as a theological, ethical, political, legal and jurisprudential question."[56] It is a right developed in response to "the exigencies of the personal and political consciousness" of the twentieth century.[57] Similarly, Murray explains that *Dignitatis* has a narrow, specific task and a "very modest scope": the document is concerned only with the "juridico-social order."[58]

In the metajuridical order—in that theoretical Eden before the first city with its coercive laws was founded by the first fratricide—the conscience has no rights, only duties.[59] "In the face of truth itself, no man can assert a 'right,' " Murray explains, "nor can he claim 'freedom' from the moral order and its imperatives."[60] Man's duty *qua* man is to accept the objective truth and to conform to its imperatives. "In other words, in the face of what is true and good, no man can claim to be completely free; he is obliged to accept the truth and to do what is right and good."[61] For Murray, "human rights" are really juridical, civic or legal rights; *coram Deo,* the conscience has no rights; it has no claim against truth.[62] Thus, *Dignitatis* never uses the phrase "human rights" at all; when Murray uses it, he means the universal possession by each person of the duties that constitute his or her dignity, and thus of the freedom to exercise that duty.[63]

The Freedom of the Church in the Liberal City

Perhaps the greatest methodological distinction between the liberal theory of religious freedom and the Murray/Vatican II theory is the *subject* of religious liberty. In the former, religious liberty resides in the conscience of each individual; neither the Church nor God may bind a person's conscience and still call it "free." A church is merely a spontaneous voluntary assemblage of like-minded, radically free atomic persons.[64] In the latter, religious liberty is primarily and essentially seated in the Church, as the free people of God.[65] Murray understands this as entailing the twin claims of the Church as being the ultimate spiritual authority over mankind, and for all men to have unrestricted access to the salvation the Church offers.[66] Of course, both of these claims imply the overarching claim that the Church is free to define itself and its mission, and that this freedom supercedes the freedom of any political regime.[67] Vatican II affirms this principle, even while trying to protect the civic freedom of those outside the Church.

The first sense of the Church's freedom is announced at the very outset of *Dignitatis,* although it was inserted very late.[68]

> The sacred Council begins by professing that God himself has made known to the human race how men by serving him can be saved and reach happiness in Christ. We believe that this one true religion continues to exist in the Catholic and Apos-

tolic Church, to which the Lord Jesus entrusted the task of spreading it among all men.[69]

Therefore, the relative freedom of man in forming his conscience "must pay careful attention to the sacred and certain teaching of the Church. For the Catholic Church is by the will of Christ the teacher of truth."[70] Freedom inheres in the one true Church as it proclaims the truth of the gospel; the relative freedom of the individual consists in his not being prevented from embracing this truth, nor, insofar as the only authentic expression of faith is one free from coercion,[71] in being coerced to do so. But even this personal freedom is properly ordered only when it is directed toward the "sacred and certain teaching of the Church." People abuse their natural freedom by not heeding this teaching; and thus their full, authentic moral freedom is not attained. Moreover, just as individual liberty is founded in man's duty to God, so the Church's political liberty is founded in its duty to propagate the gospel. "It is her duty to proclaim and teach with authority the truth which is Christ and, at the same time, to declare and confirm by its authority the principles of the moral order which spring from human nature itself."[72] This is a divine duty, which cannot be legitimately abrogated by any human power, and it is a duty the perimeter of which the Church alone may define.

Thus, the first order of any political community should be to protect the Church as it carries out its mission; the claims and prerogatives of the Church are always precedent.

> The freedom of the Church is the fundamental principle governing relations between the Church and public authorities and the whole civil order. . . . As the spiritual authority appointed by Christ the Lord with the duty imposed by divine command, of going into the whole world and preaching the Gospel to every creature, the Church claims freedom for herself in human society and before every public authority. The Church also claims freedom for herself as a society of men with the right to live in civil society in accordance with the demands of the Christian faith.[73]

It is impossible to say that the council is calling for mere tolerance here. The premise of the assertion of freedom is that the Catholic Church is the repository of religious truth and the guardian of moral truth; its freedom in society is based upon its possession of truth, and therefore its freedom is precedent to the freedom of any other institution or individual. Obviously, other religious traditions may not make the same claim; the Church's claim to truth is exclusive.

Thus in his commentary on his translation of *Dignitatis,* Murray distinguishes between the object of the right—religious liberty in society—and the *foundation* of that freedom—the Church's possession of truth. As to the foundation of the right, the Catholic Church claims freedom from coercive interference in her ministry and life on grounds of the divine mandate laid upon her by Christ Himself. . . . It is Catholic faith that no other Church or Community may claim to possess this mandate in all its fullness. In this sense, *the freedom of the Church is unique, proper to herself alone,* by reason of its foundation.[74]

Thus any relative, contingent allowance of liberty to individuals or institutions, broad as it may be, must never be at the expense of the Church. In *Dignitatis,* the Church has indeed expanded the bounds of liberty that it will prudentially sanction, but it has not budged from the central claim that animated such popes as Gregory XVI and Leo XIII, namely that the Church alone has an absolute and unqualified claim of freedom, and that all other freedom is defined and delimited by its own claim.

But it must be noted that this is not a different type of claim than the liberal one, which insists (as it must) that the freedom of the Church is contingent upon the *state's* definition, grounding, and delimitation of that freedom. And the fundamental principle in these things is that neither this church nor any church possesses truth. The state alone possesses the most important religious truth, namely that religion is mere private opinion; dissenting claims of religious freedom may be made only within the boundaries that this entails.

Thus, just as liberalism recognizes its role in caring for the well-being of its establishment of irreligion, the Church makes a counterclaim that a properly ordered state must care for the well-being of its claim of religious truth. "When the principle of religious freedom is not just proclaimed in words or incorporated in law but is implemented sincerely in practice, only then does the Church enjoy in law and in fact those stable conditions which give it the independence necessary for fulfilling her divine mission."[75] This is the freedom of the Church, and it is contrasted with the freedom of individuals, whether Christian or not.

At the same time the Christian faithful, in common with the rest of men, have the civil right of freedom from interference in leading their lives according to their conscience. A harmony exists therefore between the freedom of the Church and that religious freedom which must be recognized as the right of all men and all communities and must be sanctioned by constitutional law.[76]

Thus, as the fundamental principle, freedom of the Church is not a mere immunity, as it is with freedom of individuals. Rather, the Church's freedom is a positive claim of privilege based upon its possession of religious truth. In contrast, the civic rights of all individuals are claims (based upon the dignity of the human person) against the potentially coercive power of the state. By making the contrast between freedom of the Church and freedom of religion, the *Declaration* takes the same ambivalent attitude toward pluralism that Father Murray takes in *We Hold These Truths*.[77] Pluralism is a fact; it cannot be done away with, and indeed *should not* be done away by coercive means. But neither should this lamentable pluralism be at the expense of the authentic freedom of the one true Church, which, after all, is in the world to offer true liberty to all mankind.

Cura Religionis

Since liberating truth subsists in the Church, *Dignitatis* insists that the state has a positive role in guarding its freedom in such a way that it is not hindered in its mission. The state must not merely grant the Church negative immunity, but must positively foster an atmosphere in which it enjoys the maximum opportunity of carrying out its mandate. "The civil authority, the purpose of which is the care of the common good in the temporal order, must recognize and look with favor[78] on the religious life of its citizens."[79] Christ is the one true end of mankind, and so the state must establish and protect a state of affairs in which man may most likely come to know this end. On the other hand—and again as a concession to the inevitability of the secular, pluralist state—the state may not make a judgment about the content of religious teaching. If the state "presumes to control or restrict religious activity it must be said to have exceeded the limits of its power."[80] In order to protect its own freedom and to establish the conditions by which it may best carry out its mission, the Church calls for the state to foster all religious teaching, while judging none. But this is based neither upon the rights of individuals, nor a denial of the right of the Church to delimit government.

Murray tries to clarify what this means by saying that the modern secular state is no longer *defensor fidei,* nor is it concerned with the *cura religionis,* if by that is meant that it defends a particular faith and cares for a particular confession. On the other hand, "the highest value that both state and society are called upon to protect and foster is the personal and social value of the free exercise of religion."[81] Since the state has the duty to assist people in choosing and living well (according to *Dignitatis*), it naturally follows that the state ought to foster the conditions under which the highest good—to know Christ—may be attained.

Thus, while this sounds something like the "nonpreferentialist" or "accommodationist" school of First Amendment interpretation, the difference is actually very great since the foundation of the *Declaration*'s teaching is the freedom of the Church for the sake of propagating the gospel, not the freedom of individual conscience for the sake of the security of the regime. Under the founding principles, the American regime always reserves the right to judge the content of a religious claim in order to determine its fitness and legitimacy. And it must always condemn a claim—and thus the religion that makes it—

that the state ought to be guided by the teaching of the church, or that the church may presume to dictate how its members ought to act in the executive, legislative, or judicial chamber, or that the church's members must recognize their primary (or sole) allegiance to the moral teaching of the church, regardless of its effect on "civic peace" as defined by the regime. That is, the state must jealously guard its mandate *not* to foster the conditions under which religious opinion flourishes in public and political life, since such opinion is divisive and injurious to "civil order."

Thus, when Murray says, "to affirm freedom of religion in society is to affirm the value of religion in and for the secular society,"[82] he cannot be talking about American society. In American political institutions, the final cause of religious liberty is religion's *danger* to the regime, not its value.[83] By dividing the sects and weakening their authority in the name of freedom of conscience, we secure the peace. When peace is threatened by religious liberty, or when one uses one's religious liberty to proclaim his or hers as the only true religion, for the sake of the regime this liberty must be abridged. As the Catholic Church defines it in *Dignitatis,* however, religious liberty is a constant reminder of the contingency of the state's claims, and the derivative nature of its authority. Therefore, the liberal state must reject the Catholic Church's own definition of itself, and it must insist that the Church subscribe to the state's definition and delimitation.

Thus the *Declaration* laments the fact that, while many states go as far as to make constitutional provision for religious liberty, "the public authorities themselves strive to deter the citizens from professing their religion and make life particularly difficult and dangerous for religious bodies."[84] It is the cruelest but most appropriate irony that this condition in America is typified by that archtypically American Catholic, President John F. Kennedy,[85] who in his famous 1960 speech in Houston, renounced the authoritative claims of his church, and proclaimed the authority of the American Constitution to be absolute, normative, and all-encompassing. "I do not concede any conflict to be remotely possible," said Kennedy, because he had already subscribed to the normative religious opinions of the state. For Kennedy, freedom of religion consists in complete surrender to the state's definition and delimitation of religion. Anything else is, well, un-American.

Conclusion: The Impossibility of Religious Liberty

Is this a call, then, for a new confessional state? No. While I affirm (with *Dignitatis*) that the legitimacy of such a state cannot be ruled out in principle,[86] it is not a practical suggestion in the modern secular liberal context. Mine is the more modest call for Catholic theologians to have a more cautious and circumspect reading of the First Amendment in particular and liberalism in general than many today have. From the political and theological left, to the political and theological right, the American idea of religious freedom is hailed as the universally valid theory, one which the Church ought to champion and all people ought to embrace. It is my contention that this is to embrace and celebrate a moral and political system that was designed to erode authentic commitment to revealed religion, especially as represented by the Roman Catholic Church. The extent to which we embrace this theory of religion is the extent to which we jeopardize the freedom of the Church to exercise its divine mandate to propagate the gospel as it sees fit.

By revisiting the letter, rather than the "spirit," of Vatican II's Declaration on Religious Liberty, we find a more sure foundation for an authentic and humane theory of religious liberty; one which recognizes the freedom of the Church not only for its own benefit, but because its teaching about man and society is more capable of securing and maintaining human freedom. Not to affirm a rigorous theory of the freedom of the Church is to jeopardize human freedom in all its varied raiment.

Notes

1. See, for example, Richard John Neuhaus, "A New Order of Religious Freedom," *First Things* 20 (February 1992): 13–17; George Weigel, *Freedom and Its Discontents* (Washington, DC: Ethics & Public Policy Center, 1991), especially chapters 1 and 2: "Religious Freedom: the First Human Right," 7–24; and "Catholicism and Democracy: The Other Twentieth-Century Revolution," 25–52. And examples abound of calls to apply the same teaching *within* the Church. See, for instance, Eugene C. Bianchi and Rosemary Radford Ruether, eds., *Toward a Democratic Catholic Church* (New York: Crossroad, 1992), especially chapters by Charles Curran, "What Catholic Ecclesiology Can Learn from Official Catholic Social Teaching," 94–112; John A. Coleman, S.J., "Not Democracy but Democratization," 226–47; and "Conclusion," by the editors, 248–60. See also Dennis McCann, *New Experiment in Democracy* (Kansas City, Mo.: Sheed & Ward, 1987); and John A. Coleman, *An American Strategic Theology* (New York: Paulist, 1982).

2. All citations of the English translation of *Dignitatis Humanae* are from Austin Flannery, O.P., ed., *Vatican II: The Conciliar and Post Conciliar Documents,* Study Edition (Northport, NY: Costello, 1987), 799–812, and are cited as *Declaration.* The section number will be followed by the page number.

3. Murray, "*Declaration* on Religious Freedom: Commentary," *American Participation in the Second Vatican Council,* Msgr. Vincent A. Yzermans, ed. (New York: Sheed & Ward, 1967), 668. (Hereafter cited as Murray, "Commentary.")

4. Ibid. Murray himself is too modest to take the credit for his own direct contribution to the *Declaration*. For an account of this role, see Donald E. Pelotte, S.S.S., *John Courtney Murray: Theologian in Conflict* (New York: Paulist, 1975), 81ff.; and Michael Novak, *The Open Church* (New York: Macmillan, 1964), 256–81. After the *nihil obstat* was given to the penultimate schema, according to Novak, "the applause that thundered through St. Peter's was by far the loudest and most enduring of the second session. . . . Somewhere in the tribunes, John Courtney Murray may have been smiling, and perhaps recognizing 'one or two' of the phrases" (281). Pelotte concludes his chronology by saying, "More than anyone else, Murray was responsible for the best parts of the final *Declaration*" (Pelotte, 99). Pietro Pavan, who himself had no small role in the development of the *Declaration,* has said that among those who played a part in forging the document, "there is no doubt, one man always stood out, not so much because of his physical stature but much more because of the nobility of his mind: John Courtney Murray" (Pietro Pavan, "Ecumenism and Vatican II's *Declaration on Religious Freedom,*" *Religious Freedom: 1965 and 1975,* ed. Walter J. Burghardt, S.J. [New York: Paulist, 1976], 38).

5. As shown above, Murray objects to this idea even before the Vatican Council. See *We Hold These Truths: Catholic Reflections on the American Proposition* (New York: Sheed & Ward, 1960). Hereafter this work will be cited as *WHTT*. As he saw it, the purpose of chapter 9 of *WHTT* is to challenge "the validity of the supra-political tenet upon which modernity staked the whole success of its political experiment. This tenet . . . was that the individual conscience is the sole ultimate interpreter of the moral order (and of the religious order), and therefore the sole authentic mediator of moral imperatives to the political order" (213).

6. Francis Canavan, S.J., "Murray on Vatican II's *Declaration* on Religious Freedom," *Communio* 9 (1982): 404. Canavan, commenting on the original critique, says, "Respect for conscience, on which we have been inclined to rest the case for religious freedom at least since John Locke's *Letter Concerning Toleration,* will not, in my opinion, sustain an adequate theory of religious liberty" (404). That the *Declaration* began as a section of the decree on ecumenism, and therefore concentrated on the *moral* aspect of religious liberty, might help to explain why it never attained the full legal–juridical emphasis that Canavan (wisely) wishes it had.

7. Murray, "Preface," *Religious Liberty: An End and a Beginning,* ed. John Courtney Murray, S.J. (New York: Macmillan, 1966), 9. Canavan's critique appears in this volume as "The Catholic Concept of Religious Freedom as a Human Right," 65–80.

8. Canavan, "Murray on Declaration," 405.

9. Murray says: "It was of course the most controversial document of the whole Council, largely because it raised with sharp emphasis the issue that lay continually below the surface of all the conciliar debates. The notion of development, not the notion of religious freedom, was the real sticking-point for many of those who opposed the *Declaration* even to the end. The course of development between the *Syllabus of Errors* (1864) and *Dignitatis Humanae* (1965) still remains to be explained by theologians" ("Religious Freedom," *The Documents of Vatican II,* Walter M. Abbott, S.J., ed. [New York: America Press, 1966], 673).

10. Murray, "The *Declaration* on Religious Freedom," Franz Böckle, ed., *War,*

Poverty, Freedom: The Christian Response, Concilium 15 (New York: Paulist, 1966), 3. (Hereafter cited as *Concilium 15.*)

11. "It would be disastrous to suppose that our major task at the moment is simply to do commentaries on the conciliar texts," he wrote in 1966. "This work of explanation and justification," he continued,

> does indeed have to be done, in order to insure that the themes explicitly treated by the Council are understood. But to stop with this would be to return theology to its pre-conciliar state, in which the theologian had been forced to abdicate his high function and to become simply a commentator on the latest magisterial utterance. Such a return to the past would be a contradiction of the intention of the Council. The Council did not aim to turn the Church in upon itself—to make it the complacent auditor of its own voice. The Council's intention was to bring the Church into courageous confrontation with the new moment of history (Murray, "The Declaration on Religious Freedom: Its Deeper Significance," *America* [April 23, 1966]: 592).

See also Donald E. Pelotte, S.S.S., *John Courtney Murray: Theologian in Conflict* (New York: Paulist, 1975), 101, citing a 1966 letter from Murray to Paul Weber, S.J.: " 'I myself have given up the idea of writing a history of the *Declaration on Religious Freedom*. I have done six articles on various theoretical aspects of the declaration and I am frankly tired of the whole subject.' "

12. I am not as sanguine, therefore, as Father Murray that the *Declaration* "did no more than clear up a historical and doctrinal *équivoque*" (Murray, "Deeper Significance," 592).

13. For accounts of this dramatic development, see Gregory Baum, "*Declaration* on Religious Freedom—Development of Its Doctrinal Basis," *The Ecumenist* 4 (September–October 1966): 121–26; Pietro Pavan, "Ecumenism and Vatican II's *Declaration on Religious Freedom," Religious Freedom: 1965 and 1975,* ed. Walter J. Burghardt, S.J. (New York: Paulist, 1976); and Murray, "The *Declaration* on Religious Freedom: A Moment in Its Legislative History," in Murray, ed., *Religious Liberty: An End and a Beginning* (New York: Macmillan, 1966). For a book-length history of the development, see Richard J. Regan, S.J., *Conflict and Consensus: Religious Freedom and the Second Vatican Council* (New York: Macmillan, 1967).

14. In an interview after the council, Murray was asked how *Dignitatis* represents authentic development. "That is a complicated question," he replied. "Its answer, I think, is not yet entirely clear. In his final *relatio,* Bishop de Smedt, himself, stated that this issue is a task remaining for the theologians after the Council. No development of doctrine can be understood until the term of the development has been reached" (Edward Gaffney, "Religious Liberty and Development of Doctrine: An Interview with John C. Murray," *The Catholic World* 204 [1967]: 278). For an account of de Smedt's *relatio,* see Henri Fesquet, *The Drama of Vatican II,* tr. Bernard Murchland (New York: Random House, 1967), 776ff.

15. See, for instance, J. Leon Hooper, S.J., *The Ethics of Discourse* (Washington, DC: Georgetown, 1986).

16. For the best account of this tension and its probable insolubility see Ernest L. Fortin, A.A., " 'Sacred and Inviolable': *Rerum Novarum* and Natural Rights," *Theological Studies* 53 (1992): 203–33.

17. Although Canavan complains that while the idea is stated the *Declaration* falls somewhat short in not more fully elaborating this principle. *Dignitatis* might better "have situated the argument for religious freedom in the stream of history. Without abandoning the idea of human nature as a moral norm or denying the need to found human rights on the objective moral order, it would have recognized more clearly that human nature unfolds itself—and therefore progressively recognizes its duties and rights—only in the course of time" (Canavan, "The Catholic Concept," 79).

18. Indeed, he thought historical consciousness to be necessary for all moral and philosophical argument and understanding. Such argument "has to be informed by historical consciousness, by an awareness that demands inherent in the nature of man manifest themselves and come to recognition in history, under the impact of developing human experience." Echoing a theory as old as Aristotle, Murray says, "Good moral philosophy, like all good philosophy, must begin with man's historical experience and undertake to discern in it the intentions of human nature, the rational imperatives that rise from the depths of the concrete human person, the dictates of reason that claim affirmation as natural law" (Murray, "Religious Freedom," Murray, ed., *Freedom and Man* [Washington, D.C.: Georgetown, 1965], 137–38).

19. For the best account of this problem, see John Lukacs, *Historical Consciousness: or The Remembered Past,* 2d ed. (New York: Schocken, 1985). Lukacs discusses what he calls "participant knowledge" as the proper way to understand historical consciousness.

20. Murray, "Deeper Significance," 592. Elsewhere, Murray explains the distinction between "classicism" and "historical consciousness." The former "designates a view of truth which holds objective truth, precisely because it is objective, to exist 'already out there now' (to use Bernard Lonergan's descriptive phrase)." The latter, "while holding fast to the nature of truth as objective, is concerned with the possession of truth, with man's affirmations of truth, with the understanding contained in these affirmations, with the conditions . . . of understanding and affirmation, and therefore with the historicity of truth and with progress in the grasp and penetration of what is true." For a very long time the Church resisted because "the insight into the historicity of truth and the insight into the role of the subject in the possession of truth were systematically exploited to produce almost every kind of pernicious 'ism,' into the destruction of the notion of truth itself—its objective character, its universality, its absoluteness" (Murray, *Concilium* 15, 11).

21. The council understood its role as merely drawing upon the objective body of truth of the tradition, and applying it to the "new things" of modern existence. The council observes modern "aspirations" and "with a view to declaring to what extent they are in accord with the truth and justice, searches the sacred tradition and teaching of the Church, from which it draws forth new things that are always in harmony with the old" (*Declaration,* 1, 799).

22. In one sense, this is not such a new idea. St. Augustine's *City of God* is a primer in the Christian use of history as a tool for theological reflection. But as Canavan warns,

"Unless we are prepared to subscribe to the liberal myth of progress, or to affirm with Hegel that the real is the rational and the rational is the real, we cannot assume that every belief that emerges in the historical consciousness of modern man affirms a genuine human value and establishes a valid human right" (Canavan, "The Catholic Concept," 68).

23. Murray explains that this idea was not present in *Dignitatis* until the third (and final) schema. See, *An End and a Beginning,* 37.

24. *Declaration,* 1, 799.

25. *Declaration,* 1, 799. In a footnote to his translation, Murray says that this prologue has to do with "man's aspiration to live as a free man under a limited government which puts no obstacle to his pursuit of truth and virtue, and, in particular, leaves him unhindered in the free exercise of religion in society. (Happily, the *Declaration* adopts the classical phrase which the Founding Fathers likewise adopted when framing the First Amendment in 1791)" (Murray in Abbott, 676).

26. *Declaration,* 1, 800.

27. *Declaration,* 1, 800.

28. For an excellent critique of such an idea, see Michael Sandel, "Freedom of Conscience or Freedom of Choice?" *Articles of Faith, Articles of Peace,* ed. Os Guinness (Washington, D.C.: Brookings, 1990), 74–92.

29. *Declaration,* 11, 807.

30. See Kenneth R. Craycraft Jr., "James Madison, Religion & Liberal Irony," unpublished paper as part of Ph.D. dissertation, Boston College, 1993.

31. *Declaration,* 2, 800. See below for a fuller discussion of this order: obligation precedes dignity which precedes rights (of a very specific kind).

32. As Pietro Pavan, explains, "This is certainly indicative of a very great dignity—to bear by nature the primary responsibility for one's eternal destiny in such a manner as to be unable to renounce such a responsibility" ("The Right to Religious Freedom in the Conciliar Declaration," *Religious Freedom, Concilium* 18, eds. Neophytos Edelby and Teodoro Jiménez-Urresti [New York: Paulist, 1966], 44).

33. *Declaration,* 2, 801 (emphasis added).

34. "The dignity of man arises also from his relationship to truth" (Pavan, "Right to Religious Freedom," 44).

35. Murray, *An End and a Beginning,* 40–41.

36. Murray, Abbott, 674.

37. Murray, *An End and a Beginning,* 21.

38. *Declaration,* 2, 801.

39. Elsewhere, Murray affirms that "rights" cannot be founded on error, but only on truth. But the foundational truth upon which a juridical order is founded is that people possess a certain dignity, and therefore a certain immunity from coercion. "The dignity of the person is a basic constituent element of the objective moral order, the order on which society itself and its laws and processes must be based. Beginning, therefore, with the dignity of the human person, the argument begins in the objective order of truth and moves wholly in it" (Murray, *Freedom and Man,* 138).

40. *Declaration,* 3, 801.

41. Murray's use and understanding of the phrase is discussed below.

42. This is pronounced in Romans 13, where St. Paul explains that government is

God's minister. If government is the minister of God, then it is derived from, rooted in, and defined and delimited by God through his more direct minister on earth, the Church. "Two there are," indeed, but the prince exercises his authority under the higher authority of the Church.

43. Canavan, "The Catholic Concept," 79.

44. Ibid., 80.

45. *Declaration*, 2, 800.

46. Gaffney, "Development of Doctrine," 280. In *WHTT*, Murray states explicitly: "The Catholic rejects the religious position of Protestants with regard to the nature of the church, the meaning of faith, [and] the absolute primacy of conscience" (51).

47. Murray, *An End and a Beginning*, 29.

48. Ibid.

49. Ibid.

50. Murray, *The Problem of Religious Freedom*, 99.

51. Ibid., 102.

52. Ibid., 102–3.

53. *Declaration*, 6, 804.

54. Abbott, 685, n. 17 (emphasis added). It is important to note that these two respectable opinions are completely compatible. A confessional state may allow a great deal of religious liberty for those outside the Church; but this freedom would be restricted in such a way that the official religion would not, and it would always feel that its freedom is precariously founded. But this situation is no different than the one established by the United States Constitution. Those who do not subscribe to the official religious opinions may still enjoy a rather broad immunity, but it is always subject to the judgment of the state's own need for order and protection, and thus always subject to severe restriction.

55. Murray, *The Problem of Religious Freedom*, 20–21.

56. Ibid., 104.

57. Ibid., 100.

58. Murray, *Concilium* 15, 3. Murray continues, "The Declaration therefore does not undertake to present a full and complete theology of freedom" (ibid., 4). Of course, as noted above, Murray is not clear about the main focus or concern of *Dignitatis*. But if one must be singled out, it seems that it is this one. Where *Dignitatis* is not as focused on the juridical question, Murray seems to wish it were.

59. Much earlier in his career, Murray was less reticent to use the phrase of "rights of conscience," but even then he still maintained the fundamental rule of conscience is duty to God. "The first effect of conscience is a binding, and not . . . a freeing" (Murray, "Freedom of Religion: I. The Ethical Problem," *Theological Studies*, 6 [June 1945]: 255). Before God "conscience has no rights," he says, "but only the duty of unlimited obedience to God's known truth and will" (263). While he uses the modern locution of "rights" of conscience, the first order is obligation: "In order to determine these rights, we have first to formulate the obligations of conscience, from which rights flow" (263). Rather than rights being the moral foundation for discussion of conscience, rights are only the logical derivative of the duty of conscience. "Conscience has rights because it has duties; its freedoms are measured in terms of its bounds." This duty translates into

five obligations, the first of which is that "man has the obligation to search for the truth about God and God's purposes for man . . . and to accept it when found" (263).
60. Gaffney, "Development of Doctrine," 280.
61. Ibid.
62. This is precisely the argument of *Dignitatis*, which is summed up nicely by A. F. Carrillo de Albornoz:

Es simplemente absurdo pensar que el hombre posea esta libertad en cuanto es *criatura de Dios*, or que pueda reivindicarla delante de su Creador y Señor. Para empezar, no se puede decir que el hombre tenga derechos respecto de Dios. Al contrario, el hombre tiene la gravísima y suprema obligación de obedecer a Dios, de aceptar plenamente su revelación, y de seguir fielmente el camino señalado por El para la salvación del género humano. Sería pues una lamentable confusión creer que la libertad religiosa civil aquí proclamada [in *Dignitatis*] tiene la menor relación con el indiferentismo y naturalismo antirreligiosos del siglo XIX, según los cuales la libertad religiosa era presentada como la completa autonomía e independencia de la razón human y del hombre respecto de Dios y de su santa voluntad. . . . Consecuencia de lo anterior es que el hombre, que tiene libertad religiosa in el fuero externo civil, es decir, en cunato es ciudadano, *no la tiene* en el fuero interno moral, o en cuanto es sujeto de obligaciones morales (Carrillo de Albornoz, La Libertad Religiosa y El Concilio Vaticano II [Madrid, 1966], 55, 57).

See also Leo XIII, *Libertas*, 20 June 1888, 30; 18. "It is absurd to say that all ideas have equal rights, since all ideas are not equally rooted in reality; some are rooted in unreality and therefore are false." This and other citations are from Joseph Husslein, S.J., ed. *Social Wellsprings: Fourteen Epochal Documents by Pope Leo XIII* (Milwaukee: Bruce Publishing Co., 1940).
63. Thus, as Murray explains in a note to his translation of *Dignitatis*,

The issue of religious freedom arises in the political and social order—in the order of the relationship between the people and government and between man and man. This is the order of human rights, and in it the principle of freedom is paramount. However, man's life is also lived in another order of reality—in the spiritual order of man's relationship to what is objectively true and morally good. This is the order of duty and obligation. In it a man acts freely indeed, but under moral imperatives, which bind in conscience. No man may plead "rights" in the face of the truth or claim "freedom" from the moral law (Murray in Abbott, 676, n. 3).

64. "A church then," explains Locke, "I take to be a voluntary Society of Men, joining themselves together of their own accord, in order to the publick worshipping of God, in such a manner as they judge acceptable to him, and effectual to the Salvation of their Souls" (John Locke, *A Letter Concerning Toleration*, ed. James H. Tully [Indianapolis: Hackett, 1983], 28). And Madison explains: "Religion consists in voluntary acts of individuals, singly or voluntarily associated" (James Madison, "Detached Memoranda," ed. Elizabeth Fleet, *William and Mary Quarterly* 3 [1946]: 559).

65. Here is a case where Murray is either profoundly wrong or profoundly "appropriative" in his reading of the American idea. "Neither the *Declaration* nor the American Constitution affirms that a man has a right to believe what is false or to do what is wrong. This would be moral nonsense" (Murray in Abbott, 678, n. 5). While Murray is certainly correct that this is moral nonsense, it is just such nonsense that is established by the First Amendment. As understood by its chief author, James Madison, the First Amendment must mean either that there is no such thing as a false religious opinion, or that if there is such a thing, there is no moral obligation to embrace it. Murray might be correct, therefore, that the First Amendment does not represent such moral nonsense as the rightness to believe falsehood; but this is only because the First Amendment institutionalizes the idea that there is no such thing as religious falsehood (except a claim of religious truth that denies the sovereignty of the individual conscience), which from a Catholic point of view is the very institutionalization of falsehood.

66. See *WHTT*, 201.

67. "The private and public acts of religion by which men direct themselves to God according to their convictions transcend of their very nature the earthly and temporal order of things" (*Declaration*, 3, 802).

68. See Regan, *Conflict and Consensus,* 164; Pelotte, 99; Pavan, "Ecumenism and Religious Freedom," 23. Pelotte says that the insertion of such language after the final approval "weakened the *Declaration* and left it somewhat ambiguous." But the opposite is true; the document is strengthened in its affirmation of the truth-claim of the Church, and by reaffirming these claims, it makes *Dignitatis* all the more clear in what it means by a right to religious liberty.

69. *Declaration*, 1, 799.

70. Ibid., 14, 811.

71. Ibid., 10, 806.

72. Ibid., 14, 811.

73. Ibid., 13, 810.

74. Abbott, 682, n. 9.

75. *Declaration*, 13, 810.

76. Ibid.

77. "The truth is that American society is religiously pluralist," he says. "The truth is lamentable; it is nonetheless true" (*WHTT*, 74). And, "Religious pluralism is against the will of God. But it is the human condition; it is written into the script of history. It will not somehow marvelously cease to trouble the City" (*WHTT*, 23).

78. It must look with favor, rather than "indifference."

79. *Declaration*, 3, 802. See also John XXIII's *Pacem in Terris,* 63: "It is also demanded by the common good that civil authorities should make earnest efforts to bring about a situation in which individual citizens can easily exercise their rights and fulfill their duties as well"; 57: "We judge that attention should be called to the fact that the common good touches the whole man, the needs both of his body and of his soul. Hence it follows that the civil authorities must undertake to effect the common good by ways and means that are proper to them; that is, while respecting the hierarchy of values, they should promote simultaneously both the material and the spiritual welfare of the citizens"; and 59: "Men, however, composed as they are of bodies and immortal souls, can

never in this mortal life succeed in satisfying all their needs or in attaining perfect happiness. Therefore all efforts made to promote the common good, far from endangering the eternal salvation of men, ought rather to serve to promote it."

80. *Declaration,* 3, 802.

81. Murray, *Concilium* 15, 9.

82. Murray, "Deeper Significance," 593.

83. As Madison wrote to Jefferson, "When indeed Religion is kindled into enthusiasm, its force like that of other passions is increased by the sympathy of a multitude. But enthusiasm is only a temporary State of Religion, and while it lasts will hardly be seen with pleasure at the helm [of government]. *Even in its coolest State, it has been much oftener a motive to oppression than a restraint from it*" (Madison to Jefferson, Oct. 24, 1787, in Madison, *The Writings of James Madison,* 9 vols., ed. Gaillard Hunt [New York: Worthington, 1900–1910], V: 28–29).

84. *Declaration,* 15, 811–812. This is another echo of *Pacem in Terris,* where John XXIII objects that the merely contractual idea of the state is not sufficient to protect people's freedom: "It is of course impossible to accept the theory which professes to find the original and unique source of civic rights and duties, of the binding force of the Constitution, and of a government's right to command, in the mere will of human beings, individually or collectively" (78).

85. William Lee Miller sums up the irony of Kennedy's presidency:

The first member of the ancient Church of Rome, the intellectual bastion of the perennial philosophy of Natural Law and the major institutional opponent of the skeptical, reductionist, relativist, and pragmatic philosophies of modernity—of the Enlightenment, of "liberalism," even at one point "Americanism"—turned out to be the first man of a thoroughly modern "pragmatic" temper to occupy the White House. Kennedy's own outlook was not that of the perennial philosophy rooted in Aristotle and Aquinas, the tradition of Reason with a capital letter, of objective Truth and of received Dogma; it was instead a markedly empirical, skeptical, unideological, thoroughly in tune with the "technical reason" that the best of Catholic thinkers find a limitation of the age. (Miller, *The First Liberty: Religion and the American Republic* [New York: Knopf, 1987], 287).

86. Against Walter Burghardt, S.J., who suggests that "the genuinely confessional state is not in accord with Catholic doctrine" since such a state could not "grant equal rights to those who do not share the faith of the vast majority" ("Critical Reflection," *Religious Freedom: 1965 and 1975,* 72). The argument of *Dignitatis* is primarily concerned with the right of the Church to define herself and to act according to that definition, not primarily with the rights of individuals. The Church is not in the rights-granting business, even when it is officially tied to the state. *Dignitatis* is concerned about the rights of individuals only insofar as the modern liberal state has the tendency to deny these rights. More importantly, it is concerned with liberalism's intrinsic denial of the Church to be herself free.

5

Subsidiarity: The "Other" Ground of Limited Government

Christopher Wolfe

I recently participated in a conference on Catholicism and religious liberty attended by a variety of scholars, Catholic and non-Catholic. In the course of our discussion, we turned to the question of various grounds for limited government in the Catholic tradition, and some of us mentioned the principle of subsidiarity. Several scholars in the group, intelligent and well-read in political theory, interrupted to ask what subsidiarity was, never having heard of it.

This anecdote reflects a great failure of American Catholics, since it shows how ineffective they have been in making the riches of the Church's social teaching known to their fellow citizens. Worse yet, I suspect that many Catholics would likewise be puzzled by a reference to subsidiarity. That is very unfortunate, because Catholics in America thereby lose an opportunity to make a valuable contribution to our country's well-being. Subsidiarity, I want to argue, is a more satisfactory foundation for ideas of limited government than what the American tradition of political thought (drawn largely from Locke) offers.

This essay will reflect on some American notions of limited government, focusing on a contemporary form of liberalism that is particularly dangerous. It will then briefly describe the principle of subsidiarity and give several examples of it, trying to suggest why subsidiarity is a better ground for limited government than the more fashionable liberal alternative.

Americans and Limited Government

Americans have always been attached to the concept of limited government. At the time of its writing, the American Constitution was strikingly innovative in the extent of its concern to restrict the powers of the new national government (by enumerating those powers and by imposing some explicit limitations on them) and to provide for internal checks as well, by separating the various branches of the new government and establishing a series of checks and balances between them. This limitation on the powers of government, in fact, became in time one of the principal criticisms directed at it. Walter Bagehot, for example, argued in *The English Constitution* (1867) that the American Constitution was extremely defective and that it was saved from catastrophe only by the quality of American citizens:

> The Americans now extol their institutions, and so defraud themselves of their due praise. But if they had not a genius for politics; if they had not a moderation in action singularly curious where superficial speech is so violent; if they had not a regard for law, such as no great people have yet evinced, and infinitely surpassing ours,—the multiplicity of authorities in the American Constitution would long ago have brought it to a bad end. Sensible shareholders, I have heard a shrewd attorney say, can work *any* deed of settlement; and so the men of Massachusetts could, I believe, work *any* Constitution.[1]

I think Bagehot was wrong about the American Constitution, but he was certainly right to note that Americans have placed a heavy emphasis on dividing and limiting the powers of government. What he failed to see was the connection between the form of government and the American traits that he admired. One aspect of that connection is the topic of this paper.

What were the sources of the founders' insistence on limited government? There were many. Some commentators have seen in the political thought of the founding a kind of secularized Calvinism, emphasizing the corruption of human nature and the necessity, therefore, of never *relying* on its better elements.[2] Recent historical studies of the Revolution and of early American history have focused attention on various strands of "republican" thinking and the English "Country Party" opposition, with their deep suspicion of "corruption" in government.[3] In addition to these powerful theoretical reasons supporting liberty, the founders of American government faced the simple fact of the pluralism of American beliefs, especially in the area of religion, which caused certain questions to be placed outside the sphere of politics, according to certain "articles of peace."[4]

Despite the importance of these sources, however, John Locke should still be considered the most significant intellectual influence on the formation of the

American regime.[5] Locke's political philosophy asserts that men in a state of nature are endowed with that fundamental desire for self-preservation that is the first law of nature, and that each man has the "executive power" to enforce that law. This state of nature turns out to be a not particularly secure or happy form of life—though Locke is not quite as blunt as Hobbes, who calls it "solitary, poor, nasty, brutish, and short." Men must form a social contract by which they give up the executive power to enforce their right to self-preservation and create a government for specifically limited purposes, namely, to protect life, liberty, and property. The foundation for liberty, then, is the desire for self-preservation and its corollaries (especially property, understood in a broad sense) and the limitation of legitimate governmental concerns to the protection of these rights.

Of course, many Americans were not simply Lockeans (much less Hobbesians) in their attitude to government, as is evidenced by various elements of American law that were not explicable on a Lockean understanding. The common law, for example, with its roots in medieval Christian constitutionalism, and the (mostly Protestant) Christianity of most Americans, with the various moral teachings associated with it, were also important elements of the regime.[6] Nonetheless, the Lockean individualist principles in the long run proved to be the most influential, especially because of their impact on the early leaders of our nation. Our political culture has therefore tended to stress rights over duties, the individual pursuit of happiness over absorption in communal undertakings, and a moderate but relentless effort to acquire material well-being over the development of spiritual faculties.[7] The great question is whether such a political culture can sustain itself successfully over time, and that is a question American government confronts starkly in the twentieth century.

America has continued to commit itself to the principle of limited government over the past two hundred years, but the character of that commitment has changed in important ways. Most obviously, the twentieth century has seen the rise of the liberal welfare state. The concern for equality that in the early years of American government was associated primarily with the limited purpose of preventing government from creating inequality was transformed, as government became a positive vehicle for the establishment of greater equality. Especially under the leadership of Franklin Roosevelt during the Great Depression and World War II, the scope and purposes of government broadened dramatically. American conservatives fought the establishment of the welfare state, and continue to view it grudgingly, but American public opinion has been so committed to its maintenance that a string of Republican presidents (including one as conservative and distrustful of "big government" as Ronald Reagan) has presided over its continued expansion rather than contraction.

But twentieth-century Americans have witnessed an even more important phenomenon—one that has further limited governmental power on specific issues, but in a way that, in my opinion, actually leads to a more powerful and dangerous form of government power. This phenomenon is a liberal legal philosophy of libertarianism, acting under the banners of government "neutrality," "nondiscrimination," "privacy" (personal autonomy), and equality.[8]

This "antiperfectionist liberalism" contends that government may never base any action on the argument that one way of life is superior to another. All ways of life (at least insofar as they are tolerant of other ways of life) are to be treated equally. Government in principle is to be "neutral" on the question of normative human ends or purposes. Law and morality are to be kept separate. This push for a general principle of government neutrality is viewed as a logical extension of strict government neutrality with respect to religious questions.

The implications of this new libertarian principle are many and substantial. Let me point out just a few. First, its roots are found in a philosophy that is sceptical about any knowledge of human ends, and this inclines libertarians toward a general scepticism about whether human beings can obtain objective knowledge about the nature of reality. Under this dispensation, even our fundamental political principles are relativized. For example, freedom of speech can no longer be defended as the founders defended it—as an essential means to maintaining a free political system.[9] Nor can it even be defended in classical nineteenth-century style, as John Stuart Mill argued in *On Liberty,* on the grounds that freedom of thought and discussion is the most effectual method of obtaining the truth.[10] Freedom of speech—or, better, freedom of expression—is justified instead as another form of self-actualization.[11] The only "public orthodoxy" is that there is no public orthodoxy. Inculcating libertarian constitutional principles thereby becomes a way of teaching Americans to be relativists: there are no fundamental truths.[12] (Of course, there is no perfectly consistent way of achieving a neutral teaching without fundamental truths. Ultimately, every form of education encourages some way of life or another, together with its "fundamental truths," even if they are not so denominated. Even relativism has its fundamental truth that there is no truth, or at least no truth known with certitude.)

Second, freedom of action is to be broadly protected, in line with Mill's "harm" principle.[13] Unless a person directly and tangibly harms another, his action is his own concern and no coercive restrictions upon him are justified. Traditional efforts to legally regulate morality (e.g., laws prohibiting or restricting pornography, divorce, fornication, adultery, prostitution, abortion, sodomy) must give way to an emerging right to "privacy," or more accurately, personal autonomy. Under this dispensation, no-fault divorce and abortion on demand (or something close to it) have become the law of the land.[14] In fact, according to this view, government cannot discriminate on the basis of moral principles in its funding of various activities. For example, when government decides to fund art and childbirth, it must also be willing to subsidize pornographic works and abortion if it is to remain nondiscriminatory.[15]

Third, freedom of religion can no longer be based on the duty of each creature to worship the Creator as his beliefs dictate, as Madison argued in his *Memorial and Remonstrance.*[16] In fact, freedom of religion does not distinguish between religion and irreligion, since separation of church and state demands absolute government neutrality on the topic.[17] (This makes it very difficult to explain, however, why the founders bothered to single out *religious* speech and action for special protection, rather than letting them be subsumed under freedom of speech and privacy rights.) Under new views of church–state separation, when government funds activities (most notably education, but also health care and day care) it should keep those activities insulated from religion.[18]

This new libertarianism claims to be a realization of the principle of government neutrality, but in fact it constitutes strong government support for one particular way of life, one that is secularized and sceptical, hostile to revealed religion and to traditional morality. Its ultimate value is self-actualization, though it denies that there are any objective standards for determining the content of this self-actualization. It is not clear what foundation this ultimate norm has or could have—it is simply posited.[19]

While this new legal philosophy has gained considerable power in contemporary intellectual circles, including law schools, and exercises a corrosive effect on older mores and legal doctrine, it has never attained dominance to the point where it could simply sweep away older ideas and influences. Nonetheless, it aims to do so and has manifested growing power.[20] Its victory would constitute an overthrow of the traditional American political and legal order. And yet, would it truly be an overthrow at all? One question that must be asked is whether it is a corruption of the political philosophy on which American government was founded, or whether it might not be in some important respects a working out of some of the logical implications of the principles dominant in that philosophy.

It is important to remember once more that the principles of the American political order were not perfectly unitary and coherent. It was not a simply "Lockean" regime, and it was certainly not simply a regime based on principles of medieval constitutionalism. It was a combination of these and others. Indeed, the very strength of the American regime has been its balanced character. Made for a modern pluralist society, its fundamental principles were basically Lockean, but it also contained a healthy admixture of "premodern" elements, especially derived from its common-law roots and from the predominance of Christian morality in American society.[21]

Contemporary liberal movements can be viewed as attempts to "purify" the American regime of its nonliberal elements. For example, traditional church/ state separation in America was compatible with a generalized support for religion, without discrimination between different sects.[22] That is why the Declaration of Independence could say that we are endowed with inalienable rights by our "Creator" and why a 1952 Supreme Court decision could say that our political institutions "presuppose a Supreme Being."[23]

But modern Supreme Court doctrine has come to demand complete neutrality on religious questions, including the question of religion versus irreligion. If today's Supreme Court still, somewhat incoherently, maintains some accommodation of religion, the tendency among legal intellectuals is toward a radical privatization of religion, a "naked" public square.[24] In its extreme forms, this amounts to a virtual disenfranchisement of believers. For example, some have argued that moral opinions, such as those opposing abortion and homosexual acts, are essentially religious, and that laws based on them would therefore violate the First Amendment prohibition of establishment of religion.[25]

The Court has also created a doctrine of "privacy" rights that has been a powerful weapon against laws that limit personal autonomy in the name of traditional understandings of moral duties (e.g., regarding abortion). It has, fortunately, refused to work out fully the logical implications of its doctrine, most notably in its refusal to strike down a state prohibition of homosexual acts in *Bowers v. Hardwick* (1986). But it has not done this in a particularly convincing fashion, basing its reticence to go further on a simple majoritarianism. In the absence of more principled limits, it may only be a question of time before the logic of personal autonomy works itself out.

But if those more traditional elements that are being removed from the mixture of principles on which the country was based were essential for the health of the regime, próviding a balance to liberal emphasis on rights by their concern for duties derived from nature, then the process of purifying liberalism may end by destroying it.

The Principle of Subsidiarity

The foregoing analysis suggests that any notion of limited government based on purely Lockean or libertarian principles should give us real cause for concern. This should lead us to ask what might be a safer basis for the idea of limited government. That basis (a richer and fuller as well as safer one) can be found in Catholic social thought, in the principle of "subsidiarity."

Catholic social thought, especially as formulated since the Second Vatican Council, is governed by one fundamental principle, the dignity of the human person.[26] This, in turn, rests on the twin pillars of the principles of solidarity and subsidiarity.[27] Solidarity emphasizes the priority of the common good above all parties, ideologies, or partial interests in society. All persons are obligated to contribute to the common good at all its levels. Hence, the Catholic Church is opposed to all forms of liberal individualism. But subsidiarity emphasizes that the common good is to be pursued in a particular way, one that has much in common with traditional notions of limited government.

The classic definition of subsidiarity was given by Pope Pius XI in his encyclical *Quadragesimo Anno* (1931):

> As history abundantly proves, it is true that on account of changed conditions many things which were done by small associations in former times cannot be done now save by large associations. Still, that most weighty principle, which cannot be set aside or changed, remains fixed and unshaken in social philosophy: Just as it is gravely wrong to take from individuals what they can accomplish by their own initiative and industry and give it to the community, so also it is an injustice and at the same time a grave evil and disturbance of right order to assign to a greater and higher association what lesser and subordinate associations can do. For every social activity ought of its very nature to furnish help to the members of the body social and never destroy or absorb them.[28]

Political and social tasks ought to devolve upward toward larger communities only when they cannot be performed adequately by lower ones, beginning with that most fundamental unit of human community, the family. The Church's social teaching is thus opposed to all forms of collectivism.

This is a fundamental principle, not merely a useful rule of thumb. Note the force with which Pius XI spoke: He refers to "that most weighty principle," acting against which is "gravely wrong," "an injustice," "a grave evil and disturbance of right order." Such a principle holds out hope of being a very solid foundation for limited government. But what are its own foundations?

Unlike the tendency in American political thought toward an "antiperfectionist" view of liberty, the foundations of subsidiarity are not merely negative. The foundations of subsidiarity, this is to say, go beyond the simple fear that higher political authorities will abuse their power. The reasons are deeper and more powerful, more principled, because they would apply even in the case of a good ruler and not merely in the "accidental" case of a bad one.[29] They reflect the primacy of the person over things in the Church's social teaching.

The goal of the political community is the common good, and that means preeminently the good of the citizens of whom the community is composed. The highest good of politics is not some external product of the political community's action, such as a higher level of goods and services, but the quality of the common life of the citizens, which in turn is dependent on the qualities of their souls. The most important "product" of a good polity is good citizens. Whatever government undertakes to do, therefore, should be done with a view to its impact on the development of its citizens as virtuous human beings.

But human virtue depends on free choice: virtue lies, not just in the performance of certain actions, but in the disposition of the will to perform good actions. Thus, government should consider not just that "something good ought to be done" for people, but that it be done, to whatever extent possible, by the person or persons for whom it is a good. In that way, the community attains not only the particular good aimed at, but also the additional good of the development of the citizens themselves, the different talents and capacities and faculties that citizens bring into play by their own efforts to secure the particular good.

A corollary of this reasoning is that, even when higher communities must play a role in achieving some good, they ought to do so, to the extent possible, by fostering and seconding the initiative and efforts of lower communities, rather than by simply substituting for those efforts. The principle of subsidiarity governs not only whether higher communities should intervene, but also the ways in which they should intervene.

This is the reason why Catholic social thought—despite what some American conservatives have feared and some American liberals have hoped—is profoundly "antistatist." For example, while the Church acknowledges that the state has greater responsibilities under modern economic circumstances than it had in the past,[30] there is a permanent disposition to prevent the state from drawing too much activity into its vortex. This explains the Church's criticism of even moderate socialism (i.e., socialism shorn of its exclusive materialism and the doctrine of class struggle).[31]

So far I have emphasized the way in which subsidiarity fosters the talents and abilities of the citizens. Let me add another ground for subsidiarity that may be of peculiar concern in modern pluralist societies. There is a broad realm of legitimate differences of political opinion, as the Church has specifically recognized in *Gaudium et Spes*.[32] Within that area of the legitimate autonomy of temporal affairs, where there is no moral principle that demands that things be accomplished in this or that specific way, it would seem desirable to minimize the occasions when people must live under rules with which they disagree. It would seem worthwhile to maximize a people's subjective satisfaction in this area of moral freedom—both for its own sake and for the stability this satisfaction contributes to political arrangements.

In general this can be done most effectively by contracting the sphere of decision making, that is, by decentralization. An oversimplified example makes the point. Assume that Americans are divided roughly equally on the question of whether seat belts or air bags are the better means of preventing traffic fatalities with a minimum of inconvenience and expense. If there is a single, national decision on the question, about half of Americans will be unhappy being governed by that result. If, however, opinion is not spread around the country in a perfectly even way—that is, if there are greater pockets of pro–seat belt opinion here and of pro–air bag opinion there—then it is likely that decentralized decision making will yield different rules in different states, with fewer citizens having to live under the rule they dislike.

Moreover, this line of reasoning suggests another traditional advantage of decentralization: in conditions of uncertainty, the possibility of different rules being made by different political subunits provides an opportunity for experimentation and comparison of results.[33] The lower the unit of decision making—the greater the dispersal of authority—the more variety, and the more experimentation and information can be obtained. Other things being equal, that would be desirable. ("Other things being equal" involves at least two factors. First, we are talking here about matters where there is no unambiguous moral imperative, a moral principle that holds always. Second, we are assuming that the function at issue can be performed *adequately* by lower levels of community.)

Two Examples of Subsidiarity

This discussion can be developed by looking at two different examples of subsidiarity—one historical, the other practical. First, I want to point out how subsidiarity is strongly reflected in the thought of one of the most famous commentators on America: Alexis de Tocqueville. Second, I will point out how it is part of our daily experience in that most fundamental of human institutions, the family.

Tocqueville

In his discussion of the advantages of democracy in America, Tocqueville contends especially that democracy's greatest advantage is the stimulus it gives to every kind of societal activity. This ceaseless agitation that democratic government has introduced into the political world influences all social intercourse. I am not sure that, upon the whole, this is not the greatest advantage of democracy; and I am less inclined to applaud it for what it does, than for what it causes to be done.

It is incontestable that the people frequently conduct public business very ill; but it is impossible that the lower orders should take a part in public business without extending the circle of their ideas, and quitting the ordinary routine of their thoughts. . . .

When the opponents of democracy assert that a single man performs what he undertakes better than the government of all, it appears to me that they are right.

. . . Democratic liberty is far from accomplishing all its projects with the skill of an adroit despotism. It frequently abandons them before they have borne their fruits, or risks them when the consequences may be dangerous; but in the end, it produces more than any absolute government; if it does fewer things well, it does a greater number of things. Under its sway, the grandeur is not in what the public administration does, but in what is done without it or outside of it. Democracy does not give the people the most skilful government, but it produces what the ablest governments are frequently unable to create; namely, an all-pervading and restless activity, a superabundant force, and an energy which is inseparable from it, and which may, however unfavorable circumstances may be, produce wonders. These are the true advantages of democracy.[34]

Democratic life, says Tocqueville, is an example of the benefits derived from resisting the temptation to centralize power. By leaving so much freedom to individuals to conduct their own affairs, democracy gives the incentives and means for self-development.

Tocqueville returns to the same theme in the conclusion of the second volume of *Democracy in America*, where he warns against democratic tendencies toward the concentration of government power:

It would seem that the rulers of our time sought only to use men in order to make things great; I wish that they would try a little more to make great men; that they would set less value on the work and more upon the workman; that they would never forget that a nation cannot long remain strong when every man belonging to it is individually weak; and that no form or combination of social polity has yet been devised to make an energetic people out of a community of pusillanimous and enfeebled citizens.[35]

Tocqueville's sensitivity to the importance of individual citizens developing their capacities is one factor in his great emphasis on decentralization (especially decentralized administration), and it is also reflected in his discussion of the importance of political and civic associations in America as well.[36]

Tocqueville represents an older tradition of political science that understood the close connection between the form of the regime and the character of its citizens. He is a healthy antidote to tendencies in America to think that only ancient forms of government shaped the character of their citizens. Modern forms of government tend not to do so as self-consciously (they seek to protect the individual's "pursuit of happiness," as the Declaration of Independence says), but they cannot avoid doing so. Modern democracies, in fact, are sometimes defended on the ground that, unlike ancient governments, they do not try to shape character—they are "tolerant" of different ways of life. But even modern democracies shape a way of life (tolerance itself is, after all, a way of life). It is better to defend a given modern democracy, like our own, on the ground that it shapes character well and on the ground that the defects encouraged by it are a worthwhile price to pay for its benefits.[37]

The Family

The most immediate and practical arena in which we can see the operation of subsidiarity as a principle of community life is the experience we have in the family. Family life is an area where men and women naturally learn to be sensitive to the indirect effects of the exercise of authority.

If the first and only principle of family life were that all work is to be done as perfectly as it can be done, then all the work would end up being done by parents, who are, after all, capable of doing jobs better than their children. But good parents understand—not without some trepidation—that this would be disastrous for the true ends of the family.

I say "not without some trepidation," because there are few words that can strike greater terror into the heart of a young father as he heads out to paint the back of the house than "Daddy, can I help?"! The "help" of young children, of course, results in a longer and more difficult job. They must be prepared (dressed properly in dirty clothes), set up with their own paintbrushes, and assigned an area to work. Their unending questions must be answered, their spills cleaned up, and their work (with all its gaps and splotches) typically needs to be redone.

And yet a father who, in light of these facts, generally insisted on doing all the work himself would be a worse father for that. (I make the necessary allowances that some jobs he must always do himself and others he may sometimes need to do alone.) By focusing exclusively on the ease and quality of the paint job, he would fail to accomplish his primary task of raising his children and fostering the development of their character and abilities. The educative impact on the children in doing such chores, in the long run, is likely to be of much greater importance than the task itself narrowly considered. One is tempted to say that the father ought to consider this if only out of self-interest, given that someday he can hand the older child a paintbrush and go take a nap. Unfortunately, it seems sometimes that the abilities developed in the child by his working around the house before age thirteen suddenly disappear or become inoperative at that age, for a period of approximately five years called "adolescence"! (Actually, they are just finding new arenas outside the family in which to employ those and other abilities!) The more important ground for involving the children in activities is not self-interest, but the long-term goal of developing the children's talents and good habits.

Conclusion

Subsidiarity, then, may not be as alien to Americans as some might be tempted to think. We have reason to see it in the indirect benefits of our own political system and in our daily family lives. But irrespective of how easily Americans can understand it, it is essential that they do so. Subsidiarity is a much safer and richer ground for limited government than the better known grounds Americans may think of more instinctively.

Subsidiarity is not rooted in a political theory that assumes that human beings are asocial by nature and that government is an artificial construct, a phenomenon made necessary by the defects of man—somewhat regrettable, but necessary. It does not portray limited government as necessary simply because of the "bad" side of man. It sees man as a *naturally* political being, who achieves his good through natural communities (political as well as familial) and not just voluntary contractual arrangements. Subsidiarity is thus capable of combining a high regard for freedom with a more positive and generous conception of the role of government. This reflects the fact that subsidiarity is not "just" a principle of liberty. It is a more comprehensive criterion rooted in the common good. It acknowledges both the essential contributions that government makes to the common good and the desirability of limiting government as far as circumstances permit. Subsidiarity also enables us to avoid certain evils of individualism. Because of its context in a theory of the common good, it supports a view of human life that harmonizes the individual and communal aspects of life more easily. Among other things, this view encourages citizens to be active members of the community (or rather various communities). It resists a certain democratic tendency noted by Tocqueville for the individual to withdraw into a small circle of family and friends, neglecting participation in the life of the political community, and thus making it easier for government to fall into unfit hands.[38]

Individualism is also problematic because it is a kind of myth, in the pejorative sense of that term. The individualist thinks of himself simply as a free agent who makes decisions independently, and ironically that may lessen his capacity to do so. While it is true, of course, that human beings do ultimately have the power of free will, it is also true that they are profoundly affected by what goes on around them, by the ideas and ideals that are dominant in their families, among their friends and acquaintances, and in society at large. There is a danger that genuine freedom may be curtailed if we are not sensitive to the ways in which this happens. (Nothing is more ironic than the adolescent absolutely determined to be his own person, the sturdy individualist who seeks to free himself from the domination of parents, only to join his peers in lockstep in any fashion that happens along.)

If we understand the principle of subsidiarity, and especially the primary grounds for it—that it helps us to develop our own abilities and talents rather than to rely on others to do things for us—it makes us sensitive to the relationship between our form of government and our own character. That is an extremely important lesson for citizens of a liberal democracy to learn, if they truly want to control their own destiny. In our own day, for example, it will help them to see that modern legal philosophies based on a pursuit of radical autonomy are illusions, since they too create and foster a particular way of life, shape a certain character—a character that may often leave people enslaved to various human passions.

Subsidiarity thus goes beyond negative and individualistic justifications of liberty, and gives a better account of how limited government is rooted not merely in the defects of people (especially government officials) and their disagreements (the fact of pluralism), but in the positive goals they ought to strive for in community life as well.[39]

Notes

1. Walter Bagehot, *The English Constitution* (Garden City, NY: Dolphin Books [Doubleday and Co.], no date), 255.

2. Richard Hofstadter, *The American Political Tradition* (New York: Vintage [Random House], 1948), chap. 1.

3. Forrest McDonald, *Novus Ordo Seclorum* (Lawrence: University Press of Kansas, 1985); see also Robert Shallope "Republicanism and Early American Historiography," *William and Mary Quarterly,* 39 (1982): 334.

4. John Courtney Murray, *We Hold These Truths* (New York: Sheed and Ward, 1960).

5. On this point, see Thomas Pangle, *The Spirit of Modern Republicanism* (Chicago: University of Chicago Press, 1988), especially part 1.

6. Murray (above, note 4) rightly notes the medieval roots of some aspects of the American political order, although I believe he considerably overstates them. Alexis de Tocqueville points out the extremely important influence of Christianity, especially its moral precepts, in *Democracy in America* (New York: Alfred A. Knopf, 1945).

7. Mary Ann Glendon discusses the effect of our individualistic political vocabulary on our national life and discourse in *Rights Talk* (New York: Free Press, 1991).

8. Representative advocates of this new legal philosophy are Ronald Dworkin, "Liberal Community," in 77 *California Law Review* 479 (1989) (although the foundation of Dworkin's broad libertarianism is not liberty itself, but a certain understanding of equality), David A. J. Richards, *Sex, Drugs, Death, and the Law* (Totowa, NJ: Rowman and Littlefield, 1982), and Bruce Ackerman, *Social Justice in the Liberal State* (New Haven: Yale University Press, 1980).

9. For a good presentation of the more limited understandings of free speech found in the thought of those on whom the founders relied, see Francis Canavan, *Freedom of Speech: Purpose as Limit* (Durham, NC: Carolina Academic Press, 1984).

10. John Stuart Mill, *On Liberty* (Indianapolis: Hacket Publishing Co., 1978), especially chap. 2, "Freedom of Thought and Discussion."

11. For example, see David A. J. Richards, *Toleration and the Constitution* (New York: Oxford University Press, 1986).

12. Perhaps the classic proponent of this view in American legal thought is Oliver Wendell Holmes. He wrote in his dissent in *Lochner v. N.Y.* that "a Constitution is . . . made for people of fundamentally differing views," and he refers there (echoing some extrajudicial writings on natural law) to "the accident of our finding certain opinions natural and familiar, or novel" (198 U.S. 75–76 [1905]). His deeply ingrained relativism is also reflected in free speech cases, e.g., his dissents in *Abrams v. N.Y.* (250 U.S. 624–31 [1919]) and *Gitlow v. N.Y.* (268 U.S. 672–73 [1925]).

13. Mill, *On Liberty,* especially chaps. 1 and 4.

14. The origin of the modern privacy right in American constitutional law is in *Griswold v. Conn.* (381 U.S. 479 [1965]) and its best-known exemplar is *Roe v. Wade* (410 U.S. 113 [1973]), which prohibited attempts to limit abortions in the interest of fetal life until the last trimester, and even then protected abortion rights in cases of threats to maternal life or health (including mental health).

15. The Supreme Court refused to accept that argument regarding abortion in *Maher v. Roe* (432 U.S. 464 [1977]), subjecting itself to harsh criticism from commentators (e.g., Laurence Tribe, *Constitutional Choices* [Cambridge: Harvard University Press, 1985], 243–45). The art example obviously refers to the recent debate regarding National Endowment for the Arts funding of controversial projects (antireligious and homoerotic art in particular).

16. The "Memorial and Remonstrance" may be found in *The Mind of the Founder,* ed. Marvin Meyers (New York: Bobbs-Merrill Co., 1973), 8–15.

17. *Everson v. Board of Education* (330 U.S. 1 [1947]).

18. For example, the Court had restricted public aid to religiously affiliated schools substantially (*Lemon v. Kurtzman* 403 U.S. 602 [1971]), although no one on any side of the issue would contend that it has acted consistently in this regard.

19. See Russell Hittinger, "Liberalism and the American Natural Law Tradition," 25 *Wake Forest Law Review* 429–99 (1990).

20. One thinks, for example, of the plurality opinion in *Planned Parenthood v. Casey,* which reaffirmed what it calls the central holding of *Roe v. Wade.* Justices Sandra Day O'Connor, David Souter, and Anthony Kennedy hardly seem to be wild-eyed radicals, but they could author the following sentence: "At the heart of liberty is the right to define one's own concept of existence, of meaning, of the universe, and of the

mystery of human life." But if individuals really are free to define the mystery of human life, then *Dred Scott* can be resurrected and no one can argue with Nazi definitions of Jews and Slavs. When "moderate" justices uncritically invoke the vocabulary of radical autonomy, the situation looks bleak.

21. Some have gone so far as to argue that the founders intended to create a "mixed regime," e.g., Paul Eidelberg, *The Political Philosophy of the American Constitution* (New York: Free Press, 1968), while others have argued that they meant to create a "democratic republic," e.g., Martin Diamond, *The Founding of the Democratic Republic* (Itasca, IL: F.E. Peacock Press, 1981). I believe that both views (especially the former) are overstated, and that the best description is found in a phrase from Justice Joseph Story's *Commentaries on the Constitution of the United States:* the United States is a "balanced republic," i.e., a republic or representative democracy with an admixture of certain nondemocratic features (Boston: Little, Brown, and Co., 1873), vol. II, 419.

22. Gerard Bradley, *Church-State Relationships in America* (New York: Greenwood Press, 1987).

23. In *Zorach v. Clauson* (343 U.S. 306 [1952]).

24. Richard John Neuhaus, *The Naked Public Square* (Grand Rapids, MI: W.B. Eerdmans Publishing Co., 1984).

25. See, for example, Justice Harry Blackmun's dissent in *Bowers v. Hardwick* (92 L.Ed.2d 140, 159 [1986]).

26. *Gaudium et Spes (Pastoral Constitution on the Church in the Modern World),* chapter 1, in *Vatican Council II: The Conciliar and Post Conciliar Documents,* ed. Austin Flannery (Northport, NY: Costello Publishing Co., 1975), 903.

27. Sacred Congregation for the Doctrine of the Faith, *Instruction on Christian Freedom and Liberation,* no. 73 (Boston: St. Paul Editions, 1986), 47.

28. Pius XI, *Quadragesimo Anno,* no. 79, in *The Church and the Reconstruction of the Modern World,* ed. Terence P. McLaughlin (Garden City, NY: Doubleday/Image, 1957), 246–47. There is not much written on subsidiarity in English. The best piece I am familiar with is Johannes Messner, "Freedom as a Principle of Social Order: An Essay in the Substance of Subsidiary Function," in *The Modern Schoolman* 28, no. 2 (January 1951): 97–110. John Finnis also explains and employs the notion of subsidiarity in his *Natural Law and Natural Rights* (Oxford: Clarendon Press, 1980), chapt. 6 and 7.

29. Authority is not based only on people's defects, but flows from human nature itself. See Yves Simon, *The Philosophy of Democratic Government* (Chicago: University of Chicago Press, 1951), chap. 1.

30. Besides the very paragraph in which the principle of subsidiarity was articulated by Pius XI (above, note 26), see John XXIII, *Mater et Magistra,* nos. 54, 59–67 (Boston: St. Paul Editions, 1961), 18–22.

31. See, for example, Pius XI, *Quadragesimo Anno,* nos. 113–26 (McLaughlin, 258–63) and Paul VI, *Octogesima Adveniens,* nos. 31–34 (Washington, DC: United States Catholic Conference, 1971), 16–18. To keep things in perspective, note that the Catholic Church has treated "liberalism" (a term that includes many American conservatives) in a parallel way: it has been critical of liberal ideology and also of milder forms of liberalism. On these issues, see my "The Vatican as Nobody's Ally," *This World* no. 4 (Winter 1983): 63.

32. *Gaudium et Spes,* nos. 36, 76, in *Vatican Council II,* ed. Flannery, 935, 984–85.

33. The most famous quote in American constitutional law on this point occurs in Justice Brandeis's concurrence in *New State Ice Co. v. Liebmann:* "It is one of the happy incidents of the federal system that a single courageous State may, if its citizens choose, serve as a laboratory; and try novel social and economic experiments without risk to the rest of the country" (285 U.S. 311 [1932]).

34. Tocqueville, 251–52.

35. Ibid., 329

36. For Tocqueville on decentralization, see vol. 1, chap. 5 (especially 85–97) and chap. 16 (especially 271–72); on voluntary associations, see vol. 2, book 1, chaps. 5 and 7, and book 4, chap. 7 (especially pp. 323–24).

37. One of the finest discussions of the effects of modern government on character can be found in Martin Diamond's "Ethics and Politics: The American Way," in *The Moral Foundations of the American Republic,* ed. Robert H. Horwitz (Charlottesville, VA: University Press of Virginia, 1977). I think Diamond may be optimistic, however, to the extent that he believed that even these limited virtues (e.g., somewhat lower and commercial forms of honesty, frugality, liberality, industriousness, and justice, rooted in acquisitiveness rather than avarice) will flourish without the support of religion.

38. Tocqueville, vol. 2, book 2, chap. 2 (98–99).

39. Some proponents of a broad modern form of autonomy (one divorced from an understanding of the end or goal of human life) do try to justify it as a way of fostering self-actualization. (In this they are faithful disciples of John Stuart Mill, who does the same thing in *On Liberty,* chap. 3, "Of Individuality, as One of the Elements of Well-Being.") Without a view of human ends, however, they cannot provide a persuasive ground on which to assert that any human action contributes to self-actualization more than any other, except by falling back on purely conventional arguments.

6

Catholic Social Thought, the City, and Liberal America

Jean Bethke Elshtain

The horizon for this essay is framed by the notion of subsidiarity, drawn from Catholic social thought; the history of "the city" as a site of public rather than exclusively individual freedom; and the current state of a particular liberal society—our own. I begin with this third concern, which translates into a focus on the fate of *civil society,* by which I mean "the many forms of community and association that are not political in form: families, neighborhoods, voluntary associations of innumerable kinds, labor unions, small businesses, giant corporations, and religious communities."[1] When we think of civil society, we think of networks of voluntary associations and the obligations they involve. Some may cavil at the notion that such associations are not "political," but theorists of civil society would insist, in response, that this network and the many ways we are nested within it, lie outside the formal structure of state power.

It is by now a familiar lament that all is not well with us; that something has gone terribly awry with the North American version of market-modernity. The man and woman in the street speak of a loss of neighborliness; of growing fear and suspicions; of the enhanced pressures, sexual, commercial, contractual, upon the young. Things used to be better, and easier, they say. Now there is not enough time to be a parent and a citizen and a worker. All the evidence is consistent on the score. Explanations for our discontents vary, as do prescriptions for a cure. But analysts from left and right alike speak of an erosion in a

97

sense of civic responsibility and the entrenchment of a brittle conviction of everyone for themselves.

Recent surveys, for example, offer a profile of apathy and alienation among the young, to which one must add the rising tide of violence that threatens to engulf whole sections of American youth. Since 1975, murders committed by juveniles have increased three times; rape two times; robberies five times. In 1989, the House Committee on Children, Youth and Families reported a "national emergency" of growing violence by and against youth, with homicide now the leading killer of black males ages 15–24 and the leading crime among black youths in the same age bracket. On what might be called the female side of the ledger, matters are similarly critical. Nearly one in four American infants is born to an unmarried mother, six times the rate of the 1950s. This litany could go on for pages. The continuing decline of voter turnout, the drop in charitable contributions, the desocialization of life as measured by declining contacts with parents, siblings, and neighbors, and the skyrocketing rate of professed diminution of social trust are other sad indicators.[2]

Most often identified as the source of such troubles is a breakdown of our basic institutions—families, churches, neighborhoods, schools. One group of strong communitarians wants to restore these institutions to the robustness and definitiveness they once had, or so their story goes. Others seek solutions by turning to the state, to more and better welfare programs. Some statist politicians and philosophies go so far as to design programs and policies aimed at destroying particular local loyalties and identities in favor of a prescriptive universalism. There the matter is joined—and checkmated: localists versus universalists, on one reading of the situation; individualists versus communitarians, on a second. My approach offers a third option, one that focuses on the mediating institutions of civil society in a way that, ideally, nurtures both rights *and* responsibilities; that sees persons as irreducibly social; and that locates such persons in the overlapping relations, public and private, of civil society. That this approach is profoundly at odds with the dominant rights-based, individualist thrust of contemporary American culture is the case I shall make in order to foreground my own speculative musings about an alternative.

Consider Tocqueville's classic, *Democracy in America,* as our entry point into American liberalism.[3] Tocqueville praised the practices of American democracy but feared for America's fate. In his view, American democracy freed individuals from the constraints of older, undemocratic structures and obligations, but also unleashed atomism, individualism, and privatization. Tocqueville's fear was not that this invited anarchy; rather, he believed that the individualism of an acquisitive bourgeois society would engender new forms of social and political domination. Individual disentanglement from the web of overlapping social bodies invites the tyranny of mass opinion and centralized political authority. The lure of private acquisitiveness would spawn political apathy and invite democratic despotism. Once the social webs that held persons intact disintegrated, the individual would find himself or herself isolated and impotent, exposed and unprotected. "The organized force of the government," the centralized state, would move into this power vacuum.

This is pretty bleak stuff. But Tocqueville also insisted that American democracy had the means to avoid this fate, to effectively respond to atomization and disassociation. The cure could be found in *political* liberty, remnant of a civic republican tradition that stresses civic participation, and the moral ethos of religious identity that invites social responsibility. Tocqueville noted the many voluntary political and beneficent associations in which Americans participated. Their flourishing went hand-in-hand with effective power at municipal and state levels.

Nineteenth-century America was a society whose ideals bred simultaneous strengths and weaknesses. Though a new world freed from the orthodox and corporate constraints of the old, American democracy faced not only the prospect of liberty with equality, but also the danger that over time privatized individualism accompanied by a gradual drift toward centralization could issue in the "soft" despotism that Tocqueville warned against. Tocqueville's political hope rested in a society honeycombed by multiple, voluntary political associations—civil society—checkmating tendencies toward coercive homogeneity.

If this is where we were, on one of the great "readings" of America as a civic culture, where are we? In the danger zone presaged by Tocqueville, it seems. Our public discourse is increasingly dominated by a doctrine I tag "ultraliberalism."[4] I distinguish ultraliberalism from the liberal tradition, for liberalism is not of a piece. Although I believe the sources for a political renewal are present in contemporary American liberalism, I also find these civic wellsprings under pressure to succumb to the combined force of market-modernity, including an increasingly dismal, violent anticivic culture. This is a worry. If I am even partially correct, it means that the version of liberalism that dominates our public life and our media's constructions of that life has become self-defeating. For the priorities and doctrines it deploys serve as vehicles and rationalizations for newer modes of social control, including deeper dependency of the self on antidemocratic bureaucracies and modes of social engineering, and the continued stripping away of the last vestiges of personal authority (construed as domination) and traditional identities (construed as irrational and backward).

What makes ultraliberalism run? The foundational motor that moves the system is a particular notion of the self. There is no single, shared understanding of the self that grounds all forms of liberal theorizing. The transcendental subject of Kant's deontological liberalism, for example, is a being at odds with the prudential calculator of Bentham's utilitarianism. Ultraliberalism's vision of self flows from seventeenth-century contractarian discourse, doctrines linked to the names of Hobbes and Locke (very different thinkers, to be sure). Contractarianism of an atomistic sort posits the self as given, prior to any social order—ahistorical, unsituated, a bearer of abstract rights, an untrammeled chooser in whose choices lie his (and initially this character was a "he") freedom and autonomy.

One uneliminable feature of atomism, then, is "an affirmation of what we would call the primacy of rights."[5] Although atomism ascribes primacy to rights, it denies the same status to any principle of belonging or obligation. Primacy of rights has been one of the important formative influences on the political consciousness of the West. We remain so deeply immersed in this universe of discourse that most of us most of the time unthinkingly grant individual rights automatic force: in our political debates rights are trumps. Atomism makes this doctrine of primacy plausible by insisting on the "self-sufficiency of man alone or, if you prefer, of the individual."[6] Closely linked to the primacy of rights is the central importance atomists attach to a version of freedom—not freedom as that free domain within which citizens debate and struggle to achieve goods in common that are not reducible to self-interest alone—but freedom to constitute and choose values for oneself. In making this notion of freedom of choice an absolute, atomism "exalts choice as a human capacity. It carries with it the demand that we become beings capable of choice, that we rise to the level of self-consciousness and autonomy where we can exercise choice, that we not remain mired through fear, sloth, ignorance, or superstition in some code imposed by tradition, society, or fate which tells us how we should dispose of what belongs to us."[7]

Solidified by market images of the sovereign consumer, this atomistic self was pitted against the self of older, "unchosen" constraints. The atomist picture of freedom is an overreaching *Bildung* that valorizes a market model of choice. It is so deeply entrenched that we modern (or postmodern, as the case may be) Americans tend to see the *natural* condition or end of human beings as one of self-sufficiency. At least this is what we are told; this is the vision that saturates the cultural air we breathe. Atomism's absolutizing of choice and its celebration of radical autonomy cast suspicion on ties of reciprocal obligation or mutual interdependence and help to erode the traditional bases of personal identity and authority in families and civil society alike. Once choice is made absolute, important and troubling questions that arise as one evaluates the writ over which individual right and social obligation, respectively, should run are blanked out of existence. One simply gives everything, or nearly so, over to the individualist pole in advance.

Clearly, the cluster of assumptions I have characterized signify much more than currents of thought. They point to habits and dispositions, to actions and ways of being. In *The True and Only Heaven,* Christopher Lasch tells the tale in this way. In the eighteenth century, the founders of modern liberalism embraced an argument that posited human wants and needs as infinitely expandable. It followed that an indefinite expansion of the productive forces of economic life were needed in order to satisfy and continually fuel this restless and relentless cycle of needs-creation. This ideology of progress was distinctive, Lasch claims, in exempting its world from the judgment of time. This ideology led to an unqualified and, for Lasch, altogether unwarranted optimism that a way of life could persist untarnished, undamaged, and without terrible pressure in an unlimited kind of way.

This progressivist ideology has been, in my view, the joint property of various liberalisms and conservatisms since its historic birth. Its leading twentieth-century purveyors, however, have primarily been those on the left who celebrated a political philosophy of growth, meaning in practice, "more and better" consumerism. Glorification of the consumer was necessary to sustain the (desired) conclusion that underconsumption resulted in declining investment. No real alternative to the culture of productivity, then, can be found in most left-wing ideologies generated *within* a culture of liberal individualism framed by the story of progress. Promoting a brittle present-mindedness, the idea of progress weakens our capacity to think intelligently about the future and undermines our ability to make intelligent use of the past: thus Lasch.[8]

I take this critique to be similar to John Paul II's criticism of "liberal capitalism" in his encyclical on social concerns, *Sollicitudo Rei Socialis.* Rejecting the smugness of the teleology of progress, John Paul scores a phenomenon he calls "superdevelopment," which is "an excessive availability of every kind of material goods for the benefit of certain social groups." Superdevelopment, in turn, "makes people slaves of possession" and of immediate gratification, with no other horizon than the multiplication or continual replacement of the things already owned with others still better. This is the so-called civilization of "consumption" or "consumerism," which involves so much "throwing away" and "waste."[9]

The "sad effects of this blind submission to pure consumerism," John Paul continues, is a combination of materialism and relentless dissatisfaction as the "more one possesses the more one wants." Aspirations that cut deeper, that speak to human dignity within a world of others, are stifled. John Paul's name for this alternative aspiration is "solidarity," not "a feeling of vague compassion or shallow distress at the misfortunes of so many people" but, instead, a determination to "commit oneself to the common good; that is to say, to the good of all and of each individual because we are really responsible for all."

Through solidarity we see "the 'other' . . . not just as some kind of instrument . . . but as our 'neighbor,' a 'helper' (cf., Gn. 2: 18–20), to be made a sharer on a par with ourselves in the banquet of life to which all are equally invited by God."[10] The structures that make possible this ideal of solidarity are the many associations of civil society "below" (it is difficult not to spatialize this imagery) the level of the state.

To the extent that John Paul's words strike us as forbiddingly utopian or hopelessly naive, I submit, we have lost civil society. So concludes Alan Wolfe in his important book, *Whose Keeper? Social Science and Moral Obligation.* Wolfe updates Tocqueville, apprising us of how far we have come down that dangerous road to an excessive individualism requiring immense centralization of political and economic power. Wolfe speaks directly to our discontents. We citizens of liberal democratic societies understand and cherish our freedom but we are "confused when it comes to recognizing the social obligations that make . . . freedom possible in the first place."[11] This confusion permeates all levels, from the marketplace, to the home, to the academy.

Our moral crisis is manifest in the irony of a morally exhausted left embracing rather than challenging the logic of the market by endorsing the relentless translation of *wants* into *rights*. Although the left continues to argue for taming the market in a strictly economic sense, it follows the market model where social relations are concerned. The left considers any restriction of individual "freedom" to live any sort of lifestyle an unacceptable diminution of choice. On the other hand, many conservatives love the untrammeled (or the less trammeled the better) operations of the market in economic life but call for a restoration of traditional morality, including strict sexual scripts for men and women, in social life. Both rely either on the market or the state "to organize their codes of moral obligation" when what they really need is "civil society — families, communities, friendship networks, solidaristic workplace ties, voluntarism, spontaneous groups and movements — not to reject, but to complete the project of modernity."[12]

Wolfe reminds us that early theoreticians of liberal civil society were concerned to limit the sphere of capitalist economics by either assuming or reiterating a very different logic, the moral ties that bind in the realms of family, religion, voluntary association, community. The market model, Adam Smith insisted, should not be extended as a metaphor for a process of all-encompassing exchange. Were we to organize "all our social relations by the same logic we use in seeking a good bargain," — and this is the direction we are pushed by the atomist, contractarian project — we could not even "have friends, for everyone else interferes with our ability to calculate conditions that will maximize self-interest."[13]

Nor is the welfare state as we know it a solution to the problems thrown up by the operations of the market. The welfare state emerged out of a set of ethical concerns and passions that ushered in the conviction that the state was the "only agent capable of serving as a surrogate for the moral ties of civil society" as these began to succumb to market pressures.[14] But over forty years of evidence is in and it is clear that welfare statism as a totalizing logic erodes the social ties that make social solidarity and a commitment to justice possible. Government can strengthen moral obligations but cannot substitute for them. As our sense of particular, morally grounded responsibilities to an intergenerational web falters and the state moves in to treat the dislocations, it may temporarily "solve" delimited problems broadly defined, but these solutions, over time, may serve to further thin out the skein of obligation. Eventually, popular support for the welfare state plummets. A politics of resentment, evident in tax evasion, black markets, proliferation of asocial behavior (constituting a form of revolt against an intrusive and abstract "caregiver") flourishes in its stead. Wolfe's primary case in point is Sweden where what Jurgen Habermas calls a "therapeutocracy," a world in which "professional expertise comes increasingly to substitute for family autonomy," is everywhere in evidence. Just as the family has corroded in Sweden, so have all other intermediary social bodies.[15]

Wolfe understands, as did Tocqueville, that a social crisis is also an ethical crisis. Although he presents no menu of policy options, Wolfe calls for a "third perspective on moral agency different from those of the market and the state," one that will "allow us to view moral obligation as a socially constructed practice negotiated between learning agents capable of growth on the one hand and change on the other."[16] This is strikingly similar to Daniel Hollenbach's "pluralist-analogical understanding of the common good and human rights." Hollenbach recognizes, as does Wolfe, that social and institutional change is not only inevitable but needed "if all persons are to become active participants in the common good, politically, economically and culturally."[17] Wolfe does not deploy the language of common good but he does call upon "obligation" to others as a form of "genuine freedom." We cannot rely on either markets or states to make us decent or to create a decent society. Wolfe rightly fears we are in peril of "losing the gift of society."

At this point, Catholic social thought makes contact with the nonatomistic theory of liberal civil society—with such thinkers as Tocqueville.[18] Latter-day Tocquevillians and Catholic social thinkers share the hope that our social practices are richer and reflect greater sociality than current atomistic liberal doctrine allows. Perhaps, they muse, most of us most of the time do not govern our lives by principles of exchange, despite the totalizing logic of contractarians and hard-line individualists (including, alas, one powerful school of feminism). Liberalism historically has been a notoriously unshapely thing, open to many assessments, interpretations, definitions, permutations, and possibilities.

Perhaps, just perhaps, there is a distinction to be made between how we are compelled to talk, given the dominant rhetoric of individualism, and how, in fact, we act as members of families, communities, churches, and neighborhoods. Perhaps. But surely it is the case that our social practices are under extraordinary pressure. What might be called the unbearable lightness of contemporary liberalism in fact disguises a heavy hand that swats back more robust notions of an explicitly social construction of the self. I have in mind here not an antinomy that poses individualism against a strong, collective notion of the good, but a less stark, less dichotomous set of possibilities. Tocquevillians and Catholic social thinkers indebted to the principle of subsidiarity offer up conceptual possibilities not locked into binary opposites and allow us to pose such questions as: Is there any longer the possibility for the existence of multiple *civitati* not wholly dependent upon, nor brought into being by, the state? What are the possibilities for reanimating these civic entities, including the city as a home for citizenship and solidarity, in order to stem the individualist-market tide? Is there available to us an understanding of rights tied to a social rather than atomistic theory of the self? Does this understanding really have any purchase on our current self-understandings and social practices?

These are but a few of the concerns I will put into play as I turn to a discussion of Catholic social thought and subsidiarity. The easiest question to tackle is the alternative understanding of rights imbedded within Catholic social thought (whether this alternative is among the repertoire of civic possibilities we contemporary Americans can call up is another question). Lisa Sowle Cahill insists that in the Christian view generally, persons are creatures for whom rights are the counterparts of duties. *Pace* "natural rights" liberalism, there is no claim to personal goods, "which are prior to social relationships and obligations."[19] Rights are grounded in an ontology of human dignity, but this dignity of the self cannot be dehistoricized and disembodied from the experience of human beings as creatures essentially, not contingently, related to others.

The modern social encyclicals of Leo XIII, Pius XI, John XXIII, Paul VI, and John Paul II "affirm much more strongly the importance of the individual and, as Thomas never did, of his or her rights."[20] But these rights are not "spoken of primarily as individual claims against other individuals or society. They are woven into a concept of community which envisions the person as a part, a sacred part, of the whole. Rights exist within and are relative to a historical and social context and are intelligible only in terms of the obligations of individuals to other persons."[21] This understanding of persons steers clear of the strong antinomies of individualism versus collectivism. Catholic social thought does *not* offer a "third way," as if it were simply a matter of hacking off bits and pieces of the individualist/collectivist options and melding them into a palatable compromise. Rather, Catholic social thought begins from a fundamentally different ontology from that assumed and required by individualism, on the one hand, and statist collectivism, on the other—assumptions that provide for *individuality* and rights as the goods of persons in community, together with the claims of social obligation.

Thus Pope John XXIII argues that society must be ordered to the good of the individual and that good is achievable only in solidarity with others, in cooperative enterprises tailored to an appropriate human scale. This version of individuality makes possible human unity as a cherished achievement and acts as a brake against coercive uniformity.[22]

Or take these words from the U.S. Bishops' Pastoral Message on the economy: "The dignity of the human person, realized in community with others, is the criterion against which all aspects of economic life must be measured." All economic decisions must be judged "in light of what they do *for* the poor, what they do *to* the poor and what they enable the poor to do *for themselves*."[23] The bishops draw upon the principle of subsidiarity when they speak of the "need for vital contributions from different human associations," considering it a disturbance of the "right order" of things to assign to a greater and higher association what a "lesser" association might do. In this way institutional pluralism is guaranteed and "space for freedom, initiative and creativity on the part of many social agents" is made possible.[24] Hollenbach calls this "justice-as-participation," noting that the bishops' contribution to the current, deadlocked "liberal/communitarian debate" lies in the way justice is conceptualized "in terms of this link between personhood and the basic prerequisites of social participation."[25]

Summing up subsidiarity, Joseph A. Komonchak lists nine basic elements: (1) The person has priority as origin and purpose of society; (2) The human person is essentially social with self-realization coming through social relations—the principle of solidarity; (3) Social relationships and communities exist to provide help to individuals and this "subsidiary" function of society does not supplant self-responsibility, but augments it; (4) "Higher" communities exist to perform the same subsidiary roles toward "lower" communities; (5) Communities must enable and encourage individuals to exercise their self-responsibility and larger communities must do the same for smaller ones; (6) Communities are not to deprive individuals and smaller communities of their rights to exercise self-responsibility; (7) Subsidiarity serves as a principle to regulate interrelationships between individuals and communities, and between smaller and larger communities; (8) Subsidiarity is a formal principle that can be embodied only in particular communities and circumstances; (9) Subsidiarity is a universal principle, grounded in a particular ontology of the person.[26] Subsidiarity thus favors Tocqueville's associative version of democracy at its best and works to exclude "unnecessary centralization and suppression of self-government" by favoring the construction of society "from below up."[27] Subsidiarity is a theory of and for civil society that refuses stark alternatives between individualism and collectivism.

My hunch is that most Americans share the "principle of subsidiarity" without calling it that or positing it in any formal sense. Surely most Americans believe that federal government, for the most part, encourages families, neighborhoods, associations, even cities and states to try to work things out as much as possible for themselves. Opinion polls show, repeatedly, that Americans favor some rough and ready association of rights with responsibilities.

So what has happened? Are we faced with the prospect of the loss of civil society, the drying up of the wellsprings of sociality? To offer a partial answer to that question, one that yields a set of proposals for social and political transformation that build upon subsidiarity and that turn on a conviction that civil society is a precious gift we are in danger of losing, I make what may appear, at first, to be a rather strange move. I return, briefly, to Aristotle and to the concept of "the city," going on to track the fate of the city in American political thought and history. I do this in the recognition that if we fail to create civic homes for citizens, we will become more and more homeless, more and more civically bereft. None of us can be a "universal" citizen. We must begin in our own backyards.

Book 3 of Aristotle's *Politics* opens with the question, "Whatever is the city?" (in some translations, "What is the nature of the *polis?*"). Aristotle offers throughout the *Politics* a strongly teleological appreciation of the city as the supremely authoritative association that encompasses all others, as well as a caution against speaking of "the city" in the abstract, for there are many cities, many ways to create this public entity. Our own roots for the words "city" and "citizen" derive from the Latin "civitas," but the ideas of the city and citizen go back to the *polis* and *polites* of ancient Greece. The city was public by contrast to the private, which belonged to a particular individual (or was even construed as a condition of privation) rather than being the property of a country or locality, that which was in common.

Classical western political thought arose out of this form of city-thinking, structuring our theorizing about the civic. The city was a particular setting. It had to transcend the household—hence, the discussion with which Aristotle opens his *Politics* in Book 1, distinguishing between household and city. Self-sufficiency was a requirement for city life. The citizen shared honors and burdens, rights and responsibilities: he deliberated and ruled, but he could also be called upon to forfeit his life for that of the civic body. (The citizen was a "he" and a minority of "he's" at that.)[28]

The ancient city ended in empire, first Macedonian, later Roman, and Cicero's lament over the grave of the Roman republic echoes still through the years: "We have lost the res publica." We've now got to add another ingredient to this already rich mulch, one that brings us closer to our contemporary target. I refer to the medieval city, an entity quite different from its classical counterpart, constituted in and through an amalgam of ideas derived from Roman law, Germanic tribal codes, and, of course, Christianity with its combination of suspicion of any political formation, yet its insistence, ever more exigent following the twelfth-century revival of Aristotle in the West, that communal entities are necessary to sustain some common good and to achieve certain earthly possibilities, including justice.

In his classic work, *Die Stadt,* Max Weber extols the medieval city as a site of freedom, a free domain.[29] "*Stadt luft macht frei.*" This free domain was available to anyone within its boundaries. As the city developed throughout the medieval period, although nested within larger social formations (the very loosely structured Holy Roman Empire, the interlaced episcopates and bishoprics of the Church), it forged its own political independence. It was, in important respects, an autonomous polity. The city was both fortification and market, but to be a real city, juridical independence was required.

Citizenship in the city got construed along familialized lines or, perhaps better put, was dominated by fraternal metaphors. Members were bound to one another by oaths. In matters respecting landownership, markets, and trade, citizens served as jurymen adjudicating cases affecting their own. Such legal establishments, writes Weber, originated or emerged either through settled practice or specific constitutive charters granted by medieval kings who thereby relinquished much of their right—or writ—to interfere in city affairs. For our purposes, the most salient feature of this city is the ideal of citizenship construed as a mode of genuine sharing in political rule.

A particular structure of belief is implicated in all of this. The narrative of city origins in the medieval period is that the city derives from human free will. Citizenship is a "complex relation of rights and duties to a body conceived as a public possession, and a relation to one's fellow citizens as one's own."[30] Let me add that women were more in than out of this picture. The great pioneer of social history, Eileen Power, apprises us of the fact that a medieval woman held a "full share . . . in private rights and duties" and lived a life that "gave her a great deal of scope."[31] Involved in trade guilds, women worked, marketed, hunted, and tended animals, and went on pilgrimage. Sharp cleavages between civic and "private" persons did not exist. These categories, in their modern form, congealed only with the triumph of the nation-state.

Cities established their own communal rules and their power to do so was part of a cluster of shared recognitions in the medieval period. Patriotism was local. All inhabitants shared in the peace of the city. Over time, however, the evolution of free-flowing capital (hence the notion of exchange as not town-bound) and the emergence of what I have called the "political theology of the Protestant nation-state," eroded the autonomy of cities in Europe. State sovereignty, as a kind of secular mimesis of God as ultimate law giver whose commands must be obeyed and whose power to judge is absolute, triumphs. Social divisions between home life and public life, peace and war, family and state, were sealed. As the greatest theorist of the state as triumphant *Kriegstaat*, Hegel, formulated it, the immediacy of desire is contrasted with the power of universal life achievable *only* in and through the state in war (for the male citizen, of course).[32] The city is small potatoes in this abstract Hegelian scheme of things.

If you have borne with me in this *grande jeté* across several millennia, perhaps you are ready to emigrate with me, conceptually and historically, to the shores of the New Land. There we shall explore what America, as a political space and as an idea, did to (and with) this complex heritage as American men and women constructed their own civic ideals. The argument will take us down two tracks, one conceptual, the other legal, both historical. Carrying with them ideas about the city from Europe, the men and women of America intermingled with their commitment to "natural right" a bit of civil republicanism as well as a theology of the covenant. They wavered between trust and skepticism in their attitudes toward self-governance and, in turn, asked themselves what sort of governance was appropriate to the new democratic person. A town? A city? A small republic? A large, territorial nation–state?

Thomas Jefferson, you may recall, feared the propertyless, potentially anarchic mobs of the big cities of Europe as much as he detested highly centralized government. The communal ethos of the city-ideal inherited from the Middle Ages seems not to have touched Jefferson in large part because he shared Enlightenment disdain for all things medieval, all things Catholic. For Jefferson, civic virtue, or the hope for such, reposed in the robust souls of independent, landed yeomen–farmers. Suspicion of the city was bred in the bones of our stalwart civic forebears. The city was often construed as a site of decivilization rather than as a site for civility and citizenship.

Reenter Tocqueville. Acknowledging the "utility of an association with his fellow men," the Tocquevillian citizen

> is free and responsible to guard alone, for all that concerns himself. Hence arises the maxim, that everyone is the best and sole judge of his own private interests, and that society has no right to control a man's actions unless they are prejudicial to the common weal or unless the common weal demands his help. This doctrine is universally admitted in the United States. . . . I am now speaking of the municipal bodies.

Tocqueville extols the New England township as a "strong and free community."[33] Tocqueville's reading prevailed in part because it offered such a powerful contrast between the spirit of the free township and, alternatively, the dangers of undifferentiated mass opinion and an overly centralized, European-style government.

But the Jeffersonian cloud—the fear that cities could easily become ulcers on the body politic, sites of squalor, vice, areas of darkness—hovered. For many American thinkers, the city posed a problem rather than presaged a possibility. Views of the city as a site of disorder came to prevail in the minds of Progressive reformers in the early twentieth century. (A big dose of anti-immigrant, anti-Catholic prejudice got incorporated into their analyses of problems and their prescriptions for change, which, almost invariably, involved stripping cities of genuine power.) A unified political system, so held the reformist–centralizers, was necessary to deal with the factions of the city, and state control of cities came to be seen as a defense rather than a restriction of freedom and got encoded as such in American constitutional law. The city as a real civic space was lost—the city as a site that needs to be administered by states—and the state triumphed.

Lewis Mumford tags this development a form of "growth by civic depletion," as independent organs of communal and civic life other than the state are slowly extirpated or allowed to persist only in shadowy forms.[34] We wind up, at present, with a picture of the city as a place where the search for wealth predominates and civic possibilities stagnate, prompting Thomas Bender, in an essay "The End of the City?" to write: "In current political discourse the city has no legitimate existence prior to or superior to the claims of the market. There is no political justification of the city."[35] The faltering of our commitment to a flourishing civic life beneath the level of the state—and I name that civic life "city" given the theoretical and historical purchase of the term—is one constitutive feature of those enumerated discontents with which this essay began.

Now to the legal track, for that will lead us, finally, back to subsidiarity and to our central themes. Gerald Frug, in a provocative essay "The City as a Legal Concept," traces the way the law has contributed to the "current powerlessness of American cities." He argues that "our highly urbanized country has chosen to have powerless cities, and that this choice has largely been made through legal doctrine."[36] Here is the story Frug tells.

American liberal thought and practice have no robust way to thematize entities intermediate between the state and the individual. The city as a "corporation" remains ambiguous, an anomaly within liberalism because it cannot be construed as public or private in a simple sense, and liberalism turns on strong demarcations, or the presumption of such, between public and private. In *Dart-*

mouth v. Woodward (1819), the Supreme Court used the public/private distinction to insist that all public corporations were *founded* by government. Justice Joseph Story's concurring opinion was particularly important in embedding a particular understanding of the public/private distinction for corporations into American political, social, and economic life, leaving implications for the cities and their autonomy somewhat murky.

But all murkiness vanishes with Chancellor Kent's *Commentaries on American Law,* published seventeen years after the Dartmouth College case, where we find the assertion, presented as a given that need not be argued, that cities are "created by the government," that they are brought into being rather than being independently incorporated, and that any power they have is derivative. The most important American treatise on municipal corporations, John Dillon's *Treatise on the Law of Municipal Corporations,* published in 1872, called for rational, objective governance of cities, staffed by a professional elite, as citizens of cities might be capricious and untrustworthy. State power over cities is "supreme and transcendent." Finally, in *Hunter v. City of Pittsburgh* (1907), the nails are pounded into the coffin and city autonomy is buried. The language in this holding is strong and unrelenting:

> The State . . . at its pleasure may modify or withdraw all [city] powers, may take without compensation [city] property, hold it itself or contract the territorial area, unite the whole or a part of it with another municipality, repeal the charter and destroy the corporation. All this may be done, conditionally or unconditionally, with or without the consent of the citizens, or even against their protest. In all these respects the State is supreme, and its legislative body, conforming its action to the state constitution, may do as it will, unrestrained by any provision of the constitution of the United States.[37]

This case corresponded with the attack by "good government" reformers on immigrant city politics and the quest for efficient, businesslike management to curb the evils of the city. Political science joined the parade by assuming state control as a given.

Frug goes on to offer an argument *for* recovery of city power, hence for the possibility that the principle of subsidiarity might have some real civic "bite." This argument rests on the presumption that cities have served historically and might serve again as "vehicles to achieve purposes which have been frustrated in modern American life. They could respond to what Hannah Arendt has called the need for 'public freedom' — the ability to participate actively in the basic societal decisions that affect one's life."[38] Absolute self-determination, whether for individuals or the institutions of civil society in an epoch dominated by state formations is, of course, a fantasy. But Frug suggests that there remains some room to maneuver in recapturing a notion of public freedom that exists in tension with liberal constructions of "individual" and "the state," hence requires softening or reconfiguring those constructions.

If the notion of subsidiarity, central to Catholic social thought, is to have any real purchase in dealing with our current discontents, it must be tied to notions of effective power. This becomes a very complicated proposition when one gets down to brass tacks. But that the law must be adapted is central. Writes Pierre Rosanvallon, a European theorist of civil society:

> Our own particular individualist-cum-statist legal framework provides no scope for the existence of any other form of grouping that may come into being within civil society. . . . The definition of positive alternatives to the welfare state requires, on the one hand, that segments of civil society (neighborhood groups, mutual aid networks, structures for running a community service, and so forth) be recognized as legal subjects and enjoy the right to establish rules independent of state law.

Such associations come into being all the time, Rosanvallon argues, but their situation is "extremely precarious" in light of state law and encroachment. Thus, progress "towards a . . . less rigid society means that the law must become pluralist."[39]

Similarly, Frug insists that, having lost structured guarantees of genuine power at municipal and state levels, we must work to restore such guarantees. He reminds us that, under the terms of an early New York City charter in 1730, New York had effective power over property. This autonomy enabled it to "shape its own identity independent of state control; its status as a property owner gave the city its power." That power, in turn, could be effectively deployed to require social responsibility of property owners. The city could, and did, impose conditions requiring those who purchased land to engage in *pro bono* construction of streets and docks, and so on.[40] Updated to the present, Frug proposes some half-dozen ways in which cities could increase their power, and citizens their effective democratic enfranchisement. I will not present the list here. Suffice it to say that Frug, along with many other contemporary legal scholars, is calling both for a new politics and a "new language" that "nurtures equality and mutual respect rather than deference to professional expertise."[41]

I take the Catholic bishops, in their pastoral on the economy, to be up to something very similar. The call is not for some utopian vision of participatory democracy but for a more effective, more authentic form of democracy embodied in genuinely viable, overlapping social institutions. Here critical political theory, Tocquevillian moments, and Catholic social thought come together to challenge hegemonic liberalism at its most rigid, in its overly abstract, overly legalistic conceptualizations of individual and state, private and public.

At the conclusion of *Public Man, Private Woman,* I articulated a vision of an "ethical polity." I wrote:

Rather than an ideal of citizenship and civic virtue that features a citizenry grimly going about their collective duty, or an elite band of citizens in their public space cut off from a world that includes most of us, within the ethical polity the active citizen would be one who had affirmed as part of what it meant to be human a devotion to public, moral responsibilities and ends.[42]

I called my ideal one that preserves "a tension between spheres and competing ideals and purposes."

At the conclusion of *Women and War,* I gave my citizen a name—the Chastened Patriot—drawing away from those nationalist conceptions of citizenship that have terrorized our century, to a civic character who is capable of modulating the rhetoric of high civic purpose in light of her recognition of multiple loyalties and responsibilities and her awareness of the way loyalty to the nation can shade into excess. This Chastened Patriot constitutes men and women as citizens who share what Hannah Arendt calls "the faculty of action," responsible action to and for others as well as oneself. This citizen is skeptical about the forms and claims of the sovereign state. He or she understands that there are other possibilities within our reach, multiple ways to understand and to achieve power, to engage in civic activity.

But my Chastened Patriot needs a civic home. The space that might sustain her is the city as a metaphor of encompassable civic space, not quite the shining city set on a hill, but certainly not the ugly, menacing, unruly city we have come so much to fear and call increasingly upon the "police powers of the state" to control. This city as an imagined civic place is a site in which diversity is recognized and commonality is a cherished achievement. Is this city a worthy ideal? I have argued, yes, and sketched the historical, legal, political, and religious ideals and concepts that can be called upon to help call her into being. I am reminded, in closing, of the words of "an old master of medieval history" cited at the conclusion of Peter Brown's "Preface" to his small masterwork, *The Cult of the Saints.* They go like this: "Above all, by slow degrees the thoughts of our forefathers [and foremothers!], their common thoughts about common things, will have become thinkable once more. There are discoveries to be made; but also there are habits to be formed."[43]

Notes

1. David Hollenbach, S.J., "Liberalism, Communitarianism, and the Bishops: Pastoral Letter on the Economy," in *The Annual of the Society of Christian Ethics,* ed. D. M. Yeager (1987), 30.

2. Stephen Knach, "Why We Don't Vote—or Say Thank You," *Wall Street Journal,* 31 December 1990.

3. I draw on my essay, "Citizenship and Armed Civic Virtue: Some Critical Questions on the Commitment to Public Life," in Charles H. Reynolds and Ralph B. Norman, *Community in America* (Berkeley: University of California Press, 1988), 47–55.

4. Whether our practices follow suit in some total sense is a question I take up below.

5. Charles Taylor, "Atomism," in *Power, Possessions and Freedom: Essays in Honor of C. B. McPherson*, ed. Alkis Kontos (Toronto: University of Toronto Press, 1969), 39.

6. Ibid., 41.

7. Ibid., 48.

8. I summarize points drawn from Christopher Lasch, *The True and Only Heaven: Progress and Its Critics* (New York: W.W. Norton, 1991).

9. Pope John Paul II, "Sollicitudo Rei Socialis," *Origins* 17, no. 38 (1988): 650.

10. Ibid., 654–55.

11. Alan Wolfe, *Whose Keeper? Social Science and Moral Obligation* (Berkeley: University of California Press, 1989), 2.

12. Ibid., 20.

13. Ibid., 30.

14. Ibid.

15. As well, all modern liberal welfare states increasingly transfer funds, not from rich to poor, but to the middle classes. Those who most need help get very little of it.

16. Ibid., 220.

17. David Hollenbach, "A Communitarian Reconstruction of Human Rights: Contributions from the Catholic Tradition," in *Catholicism and Liberalism*, ed. R. Bruce Douglass and David Hollenbach (Cambridge: Cambridge University Press, 1994), 139.

18. Many of the most important theorists of civil society today are Central Europeans—Adam Michnik, Vaclav Havel, George Konrad—but discussion of their work is beyond the scope of this essay.

19. Lisa Sowle Cahill, "Toward a Christian Theory of Human Rights," *Journal of Religious Ethics* 8 (Fall 1980): 278.

20. Ibid., 284.

21. Ibid.

22. Pope John XXIII, "Ad Petri Cathedram," in *The Encyclicals and Other Messages of John XXIII* (Washington, D.C.: TPS Press, 1964), 24–26.

23. U.S. Catholic Bishops Pastoral Message and Letter, "Economic Justice for All: Catholic Social Teaching and the U.S. Economy," *Origins* 16, no. 24 (1986): 415.

24. Ibid., 422–23.

25. Hollenbach, "Liberalism, Communitarianism, and the Bishops," 34.

26. Joseph A. Komonchak, "Subsidiarity in the Church: The State of the Question," *The Jurist* 48 (1988): 301–2. I have recast Komonchak's principles in my own language.

27. Ibid., 326–27.

28. The darker side of the story of civic birth is one I tell in *Women and War* (New York: Basic Books, 1987), in my discussion of the tradition of "armed civic virtue." I have a rather different tale to tell here.

29. Max Weber, *The City,* trans. and ed. D. Martindale and G. Neuwirth (New York: Collier Books, 1958).

30. Nancy Schwartz, "Communitarian Citizenship: Marx and Weber on the City," *Polity* 17, no.3 (1985): 548.

31. Eileen Power, "The Position of Women," in C. G. Crump and E. F. Jacob eds., *The Legacy of the Middle Ages* (Oxford: Clarendon Press, 1948), 432–33.

32. Hegel's "state" is most fully elaborated in the *Philosophy of Right* (London: Oxford University Press, 1973).

33. Alexis de Tocqueville, *Democracy in America,* vol. 1, ed. Phillips Bradley (New York: Vintage Books, 1945), 67.

34. Lewis Mumford, *The Culture of Cities* (New York: Harcourt, Brace and Co., 1938).

35. Thomas Bender, "The End of the City?" *Democracy* (Winter 1983): 8.

36. Gerald Frug, "The City as a Legal Concept," *Harvard Law Review* 93, no. 6 (1980): 1058–59.

37. Ibid., 1062–63.

38. Ibid., 1068.

39. Pierre Rosanvallon, "The Decline of Social Visibility," in *Civil Society and the State,* ed. John Keane, (London: Verso, 1988), 204–5.

40. Gerald E. Frug, "Property and Power: Hartog on the Legal History of New York City," *American Bar Foundation Research Journal* 3 (1984): 674.

41. Gerald E. Frug, "The Language of Power," *Columbia Law Review* 84, no. 7 (1984): 1894.

42. Jean Bethke Elshtain, *Public Man, Private Woman: Women in Social and Political Thought* (Princeton: Princeton University Press, 1981), 351.

43. Peter Brown, *The Cult of the Saints* (Chicago: University of Chicago Press, 1982), xv.

7

Moral Truth, the Common Good, and Judicial Review

Gerard V. Bradley

The cardinal features of Catholic Social Thought (CST), it is commonly supposed, are the two extensively treated in this volume: subsidiarity and (a distinctive understanding of) the "common good." The leading instruments of CST are, it is further supposed, the great "social encyclicals" beginning with *Rerum Novarum* and including (most recently) *Centesimus Annus*. The most controverted questions in CST are likely thought to be the possibility of a Catholic "third way" (between capitalism and socialism) in political economy, and the contemporary meaning and application of traditional "just war" theory,[1] especially including the (im)morality of maintaining a nuclear deterrent.[2] The leading domestic questions addressed by CST pertain to distributive justice, whether capital punishment may ever be morally approved of, and what the law of abortion in a pluralistic society should be.

These are all "social" questions in a classic sense: they concern the scope and exercise of public authority and have to do with norms governing vast institutions—markets, armies, states. But this account of CST, sound as far as it goes, can seriously mislead. It suggests by negative implication that in the Catholic tradition of moral reflection there is—as in most contemporary secular political theories—a sharp divide between the "public" or "social" morality of collective or governmental affairs and some "private" morality governing the conduct of individuals. But Catholic moral reflection is not so divided. CST is continuous with private morality. The same *basic* norms govern all human choices. There is no separate public morality in the Catholic tradition.[3]

CST is not only organically united to Catholic moral teaching, simpliciter. The backbone of Catholic moral teaching — the exceptionless negative moral norms like those against intentionally killing the innocent — is also CST's backbone. As Pope John Paul II wrote in *Veritatis Splendor,*

> These [exceptionless negative moral] norms in fact represent the unshakable foundation and solid guarantee of a just and peaceful human coexistence, and hence of genuine democracy, which can come into being and develop only on the basis of the equality of all its members, who possess common rights and duties. When it is a matter of the moral norms prohibiting intrinsic evil, there are no privileges or exceptions for anyone.[4]

The purpose of this paper is to explore some implications of treating *Veritatis Splendor* (*VS*), particularly its affirmation of the exceptionless negative moral norms, as a social encyclical.[5] In the first three sections of this paper I try to validate CST's entry visa, so to speak, against three basic challenges to the type of natural law theory that *Veritatis Splendor* defends. In the remaining sections I sketch the trajectory of the teaching on exceptionless norms into the realm of law, especially constitutional law, in contemporary America.

Let me meet a fundamental objection at the outset. Someone might object: *Veritatis* is inapplicable to our nonconfessional, pluralistic state because it presents a theological or sectarian doctrine. This view, however, is mistaken. *Veritatis* does not hold that knowledge of God is a necessary condition for coming to know the principles of the natural law, including the exceptionless norms. Besides, the Pope's rejection of a voluntarist account of ethics could hardly be clearer in *VS,* and it means that the norms of the natural law do *not* bind by dint of their origin in a superior will. I concede straightaway that a longer argument is reasonably in order to adequately support these claims about *Veritatis Splendor*. That argument, which I am confident can successfully be made, is for another occasion. But CST should not be *epistemologically* barred from the public square of a pluralistic democracy like ours.

Weinreb's Deontological Challenge

The first challenge is that of Harvard law professor Lloyd Weinreb. In his contribution to a recent collection of essays on natural law theory, Weinreb investigates the present state of relations among freedom, rights, and natural law theory.[6] After a brief summary of the role of rights in pre–twentieth-century natural law theories, he opines that, "[i]n contemporary philosophy . . . there is scarcely any connection, substantial or formal, between natural law and rights."[7] That is because, according to Weinreb, natural law thinking has not flourished outside the Catholic Church. (Weinreb apparently thinks the Church has not much influenced "contemporary philosophy.") Natural rights discourse, under the rubric of "human rights," *has* flourished, and Weinreb does admit that there is a "genuine, strong connection" between it and natural law. Since Weinreb is not Catholic, does not believe in any normative natural order, and has been highly critical of (for instance) John Finnis's reliance upon self-evident practical principles, the natural law half of this equation calls for close scrutiny.

Weinreb defends a "deontological" theory of rights, one which swings entirely free of conceptions of the human good, save (arguably) for the good of human freedom itself. For him rights are "in a rather special way constitutive of human freedom, and that is what rights are and all that they are."[8] Weinreb ties rights to "responsibility," but responsibility turns out to be difficult to distinguish from freedom, and therefore from rights. For Weinreb, responsibility attaches to a person when we identify him as an actor. His decision is the source of the conduct in question. Then we hold him "responsible" for his "choice," implying that prior occurrences did not determine the action fully. Precisely because persons are constituted by choices, responsibility attaches to choices; rights, Weinreb insists, are "the sufficient ground of responsibility" because they are the signs of freedom.

These circular locutions turn out, in Weinreb's construction, to be strategic contrivances. They constitute the best available (if unsatisfying) answers to some urgent questions. "How," Weinreb asks, "in a concrete case can we ever convincingly dissociate a person's conduct from the not self-determined circumstances that account for his being the person he is?"[9] The problem is no longer as solvable as it traditionally was. As Weinreb interprets the classical and Christian approaches, they relied upon a "normative natural order." "[N]either of these solutions," he maintains, "offers much to the intellect unaided by faith, and they do not figure much in current philosophic discussions."[10] Thus,

> whereas they asserted that the natural order is *not* morally arbitrary and is therefore compatible with individual responsibility, it is asserted now, with no greater plausibility, that *although* the natural order *is* morally more or less arbitrary, it is compatible with individual responsibility. The former assertion threatens the foundations of our understanding of the natural order; the latter assertion threatens the foundations of moral order.[11]

Weinreb rejects such a "normative natural order." The problem is, the alternatives he thinks available are still dictated by it. Without nature's norms, there are none. After Hume, there is no moral order.

Now what? "Rather than taking individuals 'as they are' and seeking to explain how, so constituted, they can be regarded as personally responsible, one might begin at the other end, and ask what are the conditions of self-determination (or freedom or autonomy), that have to be met to validate the idea of personal responsibility and moral reasoning generally."[12] Rights are simply "specifications of this morally constituted individual." They enable us to "mediate between" determinism and freedom, conceptions "not dissolved" but "contained, in suspension, as it were, within it."[13] It seems that "rights" is seductively emblazoned upon a pennant strung between the horns of a dilemma, and we are supposed to grasp it and proceed. "Rights" is the emblem of morality, a waysign declaring "Freedom at Work Here!"

What does all this have to do with natural law? Weinreb says (extravagantly and wrongly, in my view) that natural law theory as it is ordinarily understood—identifying certain goods and general requirements of right choosing—has nothing to do with rights. Understood differently, as by Weinreb, it can serve as a spare pennant. "Natural law" affirms moral reality, the reality of freedom, and thus of rights and responsibility. Somehow, the language of natural law confirms our wavering faith in something—freedom, responsibility— we seem to *need* to believe, but do not have good reason to believe. Natural law, it turns out, obscures (from us?) our fideism.

Weinreb cautions that traditional natural law does not furnish an additional argument for "moral responsibility." (By that he means rights or morality.) But no one thought otherwise. Every natural law theory concerns itself with rectitude in choosing. That humans do choose, that some states of affairs owe their existence to—are caused by—human decision is presupposed. Some natural law theorists have developed (effective) arguments for the reality of free choice.[14] But those arguments are not themselves "natural law theories." Natural law theorists may also encounter hard cases in which decision so mixes with other causes that responsibility is debatable. But so do other theorists.

The position on morality defended in *Veritatis Splendor,* for example, presupposes that persons can and commonly do make free moral choices, and that these choices define one's character. In *Veritatis Splendor* the Pope points out that many prevalent moral theories are incompatible with this presupposition. How so? Free choice must be an uncaused decision to adopt one of two or more incompatible options. But consequentialism denies that possibility: it proposes to guide choice by identifying the single best option, that which contains the most of some common metric (good, pleasure, wealth). But once such an option is identified, the others lose all rational appeal. Choosing one of the other (undeniably inferior, all things considered) options would therefore be explainable only by stupidity or some overweening subrational drive. In other words, one could not choose *for a reason,* but (still) choose *wrongly.*

Weinreb concludes on a still more peculiar note. "Does it matter. . . .

[w]hether morality is real?" The question has "an unfamiliar if not distinctly peculiar, ring."[15] Weinreb is not asking whether objective moral norms exist. For him, they certainly do not. What he is asking is whether freedom exists. Weinreb places little stock in one promising response: human beings do not doubt that they exercise free will and prove it to themselves every day. He goes on to wonder about "the universe," and whether *it* is "moral" or "determined."

Arkes, Natural Rights, and Natural Law

My conversation partner in this part is one of America's leading constitutional theorists, Hadley Arkes. *His* conversation partner is Cicero, particularly as Cicero explores "naturalism."[16] American debtor-relief legislation supplies the factual background. In Arkes's view, these laws took property from A and gave to B without justification. The taking was therefore arbitrary. The principle of natural justice offended was mentioned by Justice Samuel Chase in *Calder v. Bull,* and it was the central tenet of turn-of-the century substantive due process. Cicero's expression of it: "what is the meaning, he asked, of an abolition of debts, except that you buy a farm with my money; that you have the farm and I have not the money."[17] For Cicero (and for Arkes) "behind the power of statutes and edicts was the natural law, which gave us the measure of the things that were right or wrong, just or unjust."[18]

In *Beyond the Constitution,* Arkes examined the effect of natural injustice upon the validity of legislation when brought before courts upon a constitutional challenge. (He opined that such laws were unconstitutional.) In this essay the natural injustice of laws introduces for Arkes a "thorny" and "enduring" question in moral philosophy: "the *tension* between the right and the expedient" [my emphasis]. If there are exceptionless moral norms, do they invariably apply to and thus constrain the statesman?

Arkes does not claim Cicero solved this problem, "which stands at the center of natural rights and the claims of moral truth."[19] But Cicero did mark off "a path of argument" different from and more illuminating than those familiar to us. Arkes takes us down that path, mixing (but never blurring) Cicero and Arkes in an enlightening discussion of a question that might be phrased, are there exceptionless moral norms for the statesman? That is, is the teaching of *Veritatis Splendor* (and, indeed, the whole tradition summed up there) sound?

Arkes says that "the ontological standing of the 'social body' becomes the centerpiece in Cicero's naturalism" because it dissipated much of the "tension." The personified polity possesses a sixth sense for natural justice, an intuitive awareness of the ruinous consequence of injustice. Not often do genuine conflicts between expediency and right arise. "The rules of justice . . . [are] so plainly drawn, so bound up with the commands of equity, so accessible to people of ordinary intellect, that [they] could be counted on to produce their palpable effects as soon as they were violated."[20] ("Nature herself has placed" even in the ears of the uncultivated "a power of judging.")

Very occasionally we must choose between the categorical and the expedient. Arkes offers examples: Suspend habeas corpus to preserve constitutional government? Die as free men rather than live as slaves? Poison Hitler to end the War? Arkes knows these are not all equally compelling examples, and none is the most compelling imaginable. We *can* (and probably should) poison Hitler, suspend habeas corpus, and (in some circumstances) die free, all without trespassing upon moral absolutes.

But, Arkes says, "what if it were possible to preserve a constitutional government by engaging in acts of genocide?"[21] *That* puts the question squarely. *Veritatis Splendor* (following here *Gaudium et Spes*) counts "genocide" among those acts that may *never* be uprightly performed.[22] Neither Cicero nor Arkes offers an unequivocal answer. Neither embraces the papal position; neither, this is to say, is heard to say that nothing whatsoever can make genocide a morally permissible choice. As I understand Arkes's reading of Cicero, Cicero implied that the problem was not solvable. By "not solvable" Cicero appears to have meant that there are, in the end, *no* categorical rules, no exceptionless moral norms. The mature statesman knows it. Cicero's prince might, in principle, do *anything*. Were this recognition elevated to a public doctrine, however, lesser persons (the multitude as well as second-rank statesmen) would misuse it as a license.

Arkes's own voice is more tentative. He concludes that "[t]here are layers, then, beyond layers." "Principles may have to be suspended from one case to another, but there may be deeper principles that tell us when principles are to be suspended."[23] Let me take the more Ciceronian view of Leo Straus (a view to which Arkes alludes[24]) as an influential standard contemporary view. In *Natural Right and History,* he finally exempted the statesman from the rules of morality.

> The common good consists in what is required by commutative and distributive justice or by other moral principles of this kind or in what is compatible with these requirements. But the common good also comprises, of course, the mere existence, the mere survival, the mere independence, of the political community in question. Let us call an extreme situation a situation in which the very existence or independence of a society is at stake. . . . In such situations, and only in such situations, it can justly be said that the public safety is the highest law. A decent society will not go to war except for a just cause. But what it will do during a war will depend to a certain extent on what the enemy—possibly an unscrupulous and savage enemy—forces it to do. There are no limits which can be defined in advance, there are no assignable limits to what might become just reprisals.[25]

This extraordinary license is not limited to foreign affairs, as if incinerating Dresden or Hiroshima were the only kinds of exceptions. Strauss continues,

> But war casts its shadow on peace. The most just society cannot survive without "intelligence," i.e., espionage. Espionage is impossible without a suspension of certain rules of natural right. Considerations which apply to foreign enemies may well apply to subversive elements within society. Let us leave these exigencies covered with the veil with which they are justly covered.[26]

Can the veil be pierced? Is the "tension" one that may be resolved cognitively? If so, somewhere down the line we should be able to get a grip on the principles that determine the exceptions to (other) principles. Taken that far, we would ask if the "expedient" was transparent for a consequentialist moral theory. If so, there is no tension between the right and the expedient because the expedient is the right. But because consequentialism is unsound, the "tension" returns. If a more traditional moral theory is retained—one holding to exceptionless moral norms—the dilemma (though not the anguish) disappears. Because, as St. Paul taught, it is better to suffer injustice than to perpetrate it, we must refrain from every direct attack upon a basic human good, including human life. No one may deliberately take the life of one innocent.

Statesmen wield public authority but they (like every other person) must avoid complicity in injustice. The "social body" metaphor tends to obscure this requirement of practical reason (just as it caused St. Thomas's account of capital punishment—wherein he likens it to a person amputating a diseased limb to save the body—to derail). The device points to one subtle but significant difference between natural rights and natural law theories. Natural rights theory is primarily about the relationship of coercive public authority and individuals. Natural law theory is about rectitude in all human choosing, both the choices made by public authority, and also those of private persons in everyday affairs. Thus, natural law is primarily an account of the individual moral life, and of just relations between persons. Organized political authority ("the state") debuts quite late in the picture, and introduces no qualitatively different conception of the problems presented to the theorist.

Boyle on the Morality of Traditions

The social body metaphor for the politically organized community may lead to affirmation of one moral absolute: self-preservation. An individual or a social unit *in extremis* may do *anything* necessary to survival. This position is abetted by recent developments in epistemology. What if moral knowledge is entirely dependent upon a particular tradition of inquiry? What if we can only know within a particular historical community? How then could we reasonably hold that certain moral norms hold good for everyone everywhere?

Joseph Boyle has recently defended natural law's claim of universality against formidable questioning by ethicists of traditions like Bernard Williams and Alasdair MacIntyre.[27] "Virtue ethics" is probably the best known of these tradition-based ethics. It may be distinguished from natural law theory at an operational level; that is, virtue ethics moderates (in extreme examples, rejects) natural law's subject matter—choices and actions—in favor of habits, or what kind of life to live, or what kind of person to be. The "ethics of traditions" (which includes but is not limited to virtue ethics) may also be distinguished from natural law theory foundationally. It *may* focus on acts and choices, as does natural law theory, but it questions (or rejects) the universal knowability claimed for basic principles of natural law. Perhaps the quickest way to grasp these differences is to contrast starting points and boundaries. For natural law theory, the ground is rationality as such; more exactly, human choices and the *intelligible* goods realized in them. For the ethics of traditions (including virtue ethics), the starting-point is a particular community and the values instantiated in its life. Can the reasoning person, as such, get a grip on the moral life? Or, must that person first be situated within a particular community?

Boyle argues that these alternative accounts share much common ground. Virtues *do* play an important role in the moral life for natural law theorists. Because temperance and courage, for examples, integrate emotions, they allow reason to direct moral decision making. But, Boyle says, reason, not the virtues, is the source of the principles of moral life. Additionally, natural law theory is tradition dependent in two significant ways: language (a cultural product) shapes inquiry (including moral inquiry); and, natural law theorists self-consciously develop a tradition of thought stretching back through Aquinas to Aristotle.

Boyle maintains that recognition of these forms of tradition-dependence does not undermine universal moral norms. Is it reasonable, he asks, to believe that the moral life can be lived entirely within a particular community? He believes that it is. The moral life includes a capacity for critical reflection upon a community's practices. Someone in every community will eventually think critically about the truth of conventional values. This questioning cannot be satisfied solely by purifying the tradition from within, by ordering it more coherently. Thus, if the more extreme virtue theorists are right, serious moral criticism is impossible. Yet moral criticism seems an inescapable component of the moral life. Since virtue theorists seek to give a satisfying account of the moral life, their argument falters.

Boyle next addresses more potent evidence against natural law's claim of universality: "the extent and depth of the moral diversity which is known to exist."[28] Though natural law theory is compatible with some moral diversity and can explain the presence of still more, its claim to universality "may [still] seem," in Boyle's words, "implausible, and, indeed, false."[29]

What, exactly, does "universality" mean here? It means that basic principles of morality are *accessible* to all persons, at least to those with sufficient ability to understand the relevant concepts. That is a familiar claim of natural law theorists. But, according to Boyle, they *also* are "apparently, universally known."[30] I am not sure that this claim has so regularly been made, though Aquinas said something very similar. But, having made it, Boyle now (seemingly) holds that people know things that they evidently do not know.

The most courageous and original part of Boyle's essay explains why natural law theory is wed to this twofold universality. The concept of human dignity within the natural law tradition presupposes the moral self-criticism made possible by it. Holding persons responsible for wrongful actions depends upon the claim, too.

Boyle has space only to introduce the main points of a defense. He is not talking about all persons' articulable knowledge. Like the principle of non-contradiction, basic moral principles may only be implicitly held. The defense, in my view, may also need to exhibit the precise deformity in morally repugnant acts like Aztec human sacrifices, acts that weigh heavily as evidence against universality. Human sacrifice is indeed immoral, but it is not pointless. It is sincerely thought to serve the good of friendship with God or the gods. But the Aztecs pursued this good unreasonably—and they acted immorally—because they pursued this good by means of an attack on another good, human life, not to mention the goods of fairness, friendship, and human solidarity.

The Aztec practices undoubtedly sustained the judgments that friendship with God and human life are both basic goods. They are. The precise difficulty with the sacrifices, then, was their authors' mistaken belief that there was a hierarchy among these goods, so that the good of religion justified a direct attack upon the good of human life.

In any event, Boyle concludes by soberly reporting that rival moral theories are now so well thought out, articulated, and defended that no knock-down argument against them can be expected. The hard work, he says, will begin with further explication and defense of a natural law theory's reliance upon "self-evidence," and the "foundationalist epistemology of which it is a part."[31]

Moral Norms and Human Rights

The pertinent teaching of *Veritatis* is this: the exceptionless negative moral norms form the backbone of any coherent account of inalienable human rights, including the right not to be intentionally killed, the right not to be lied to by public officials, the right to be free of treatment as a subhuman thing or piece of property (the secure moral basis for prohibition on slavery, as well as the foundation for evaluating various reproductive technologies whereby a human person is at least initially brought into existence with the status of a manufactured *thing*).

Lloyd Weinreb is therefore mistaken in holding that the natural law tradition is or has been unconnected to natural rights. Nevertheless, many of our era's leading legal and political theorists—Rawls, Dworkin, Stout, Rorty, Richards among them—continue to claim that natural law doctrines, if they become reasons for action by public authority, are inimical to civil liberties. A brief sketch of some features of the type of natural law theory defended in *Veritatis Splendor* that limit the power of government in favor of citizens' freedom enables us to see the erroneous character of this claim.

The exceptionless negative moral norms protect irreducible aspects of human flourishing, or basic goods. These norms thus *entail* rights against public authority. The leading example of this is religious freedom. The Second Vatican Council taught in *Dignitatis Humanae* that individuals enjoy a right to immunity from coercion in matters religious. That is because, as the entire tradition made clear (even if its full implications were not always appreciated and acted upon), "man's response to God in faith must be free." No one "is to be forced to embrace the Christian faith against his own will."[32] *This* affirmation is consistent with the council's affirmation of the "traditional" doctrine on "the moral duty of men and societies toward the true religion and toward the one Church of Christ."[33] It is, then, the very *nature* of religion and its status *as* a basic good that *sustains* religious liberty. As Robert George recently explained it, "Communion with god . . . is not communion unless it is the fruit of a *choice* to enter into a relationship of friendship, mutuality, and reciprocity. Any attempt by government to coerce . . . even *true* religious faith and practice will be futile, at best, and is likely to impair people's participation in the good of religion."[34]

The tradition stretching back through Aquinas, George points out, never held that civil law could or should reproduce morality as such, that it could and should enforce all moral obligations as such. Whether those entrusted with legislative authority for the common good should pass *this* or *that* law depends (even if the action prohibited by the law *is* truly immoral) upon a host of contingent prudential considerations. What are they? Criminal laws must be tailored to the moral character of the people *as is,* lest we bear the consequences of imposing burdens on people that they simply cannot bear. Toleration is often the better policy, depending on considerations including the need to limit governmental power, to discourage underworld cartels and secondary crimes against innocent parties. (Just think of how our current drug laws affect rates of burglary, robbery, and other property crimes.)

Another consideration is the real possibility that an excessive zeal on the part of those in power to surprise vice will issue in the suppression of valuable activities. Too much morals legislation, moreover, may well engender a kind of servile attitude among citizen-subjects, at the expense of opportunities to build genuine friendships and valuable communal bonds. Indeed, the common judgment of the tradition is that law cannot in any direct or immediate sense make people moral. In the words of Robert George, the tradition's most articulate recent defender, laws cannot "in any direct sense" make people moral because laws can (only) compel outward behavior, not internal acts of the will. Laws cannot compel people to realize moral goods because moral goods are "reflexive": one *cannot* participate in such goods save by choice. Legislators concerned with the moral soundness of the people have compelling reason *not* to eliminate every opportunity for choice, and hence for immorality.

Natural Law Tradition and the Constitution

The common charge—that a thick account of the good, characteristic of natural law theory as found in *Veritatis Splendor,* is incompatible with familiar civil liberties—is a caricature. Since the law of such civil liberties in our society is so largely a matter of judicial interpretation of the federal constitution, I should like in these concluding parts to trace the path of the natural law tradition into the constitutional corpus.

Turning to that corpus, the defender of the natural law tradition as instantiated in *Veritatis* finds this paradox: the language and substance of natural rights and natural justice (and, occasionally natural law) inhabits opinions arguing *in favor of* abortion, sodomy, suicide, pornography, contraception—all positions *inconsistent* with the moral tradition. Further, it is rather the *critics* of these decisions, by and large, who speak positivistically of law, and tend to deride natural law, when they mention it at all. The hallmark of these theories of judicial review—prototypically, "originalism"—seems to be Hugo Black's notion that natural law has *no* role in constitutional interpretation. Constitutional law is entirely a matter of drawing conclusions from conventional legal materials. Courts never *make* law. They *find* and apply it. As Justice Scalia wrote in the 1989 *Michael H.* case, "[a] rule of law that binds neither by text, nor by any particular, identifiable tradition is no rule of law at all."[35] More recently, Scalia pointedly questioned Harry Blackmun's renunciation of the death penalty, chiding Blackmun for referring "often" to "intellectual, moral and personal" perceptions[36] but never to "the text and tradition of the Constitution." According to Scalia "[i]t is the latter rather than the former that ought to control."[37]

In the dominant conservative polemic against decisions like *Roe v. Wade,* friends of the moral tradition take aim at judicial philosophizing, which they brand "imposition" of "personal preferences" by unelected, robed guardians. But the constitutional theorist cannot (and the clear-headed originalist does not) rule out, a priori, the possibility of judicial philosophizing. Sometimes sound constitutional law depends entirely upon sound unrestricted practical reasoning. Perhaps the clearest example is one that both Blackmun and Scalia deny. They think that "person," as used in the Fourteenth Amendment's Equal Protection Clause, should be defined by reference solely to conventional legal materials.

There is abundant historical evidence for the proposition that, as used in the Fourteenth Amendment, *person* refers to whoever *really*—metaphysically, morally—*is* a person. In any event, to the extent originalists hold that unrestricted practical reasoning is irrelevant to constitutional adjudication, they are quite mistaken. Not only is "finding" the right norm sometimes a philosophical endeavor, *applying* it to present circumstances always involves a kind of lawmaking—albeit not "legislative" but interstitial in character—which should be done on a sound philosophical footing. To the considerable extent that originalists traffic in skeptical rhetoric (as if where the "law" runs out, judicial "value preferences," which cannot be rationally vindicated, begin), they undermine confidence in the legitimacy of these inevitable philosophical components of adjudicatory practice.

Originalism and Natural Law Theory

Natural law has more to do with constitutional adjudication than the conservative critics of the court allow. Natural law also has less to do with constitutional adjudication than liberals claim. In my view, a refined originalism captures these insights and is the best methodology for constitutional construction by courts. This refined originalism presupposes a wider account of practical reason and of what constitutes genuine human flourishing, but also distinguishes legal reasoning from unrestricted practical reasoning. The former is an institutionalized and restricted version of the latter. Much of it will be arcane, completely technical. That is basically why we have lawyers: to mediate this specialized discourse to, and to make sure it serves, ordinary people.

Though "enactment" is central to originalism, originalists are not the "positivists" their critics say they are. Originalism presupposes no positivist theory of law. Originalists do not claim that law, including constitutional law, is beyond normative evaluation. Nothing in a sound originalism denies that there are natural or inalienable rights, some of them secured in the Bill of Rights. Originalism presupposes no voluntarist theory of moral obligation on the part of contemporary judges, legislators, or citizens to obey the will of the founders.

This misplaced criticism—that originalists must be "positivists"—presumes (in order to be a criticism rather than just an observation) that positivism is defective. Positivism *is* defective if by "positivism" one means the command theory of law associated with Austin, and (or) moral skepticism. Some contemporary positivists entertain such presuppositions; others do not.

I concede straightaway that some originalists have invited this criticism. Some originalists may even be positivists in the Weberian, morally skeptical sense. Chief Justice Rehnquist is a good candidate. I doubt that Judge Bork is, though he usually writes as if he is. Some moral skeptics are legal positivists, as Arkes asserts, but many legal positivists (H. L. A. Hart, Neil MacCormick) are not. Many academic originalists—myself included—not only reject positivism but count themselves within the natural law tradition.

Originalists insist upon the proper autonomy of law, including constitutional law, from unrestricted practical reasoning. Put a bit more decisively, positivism (like natural law theory) is *not* a theory of constitutional interpretation. Originalism *is*. There may be some differences between the focal point of natural law theory and the focal point of positivism, but neither is or purports to be a technique for resolving disputed questions of the law of a particular political community (say, the United States) at a particular time (say, now).

The important question—the one that *does* distinguish originalists (who may be natural law or natural rights theorists) from most of their critics—is to what extent judges ought to invalidate legislation on the basis of principles of natural justice not discoverable in (or inferable from) the constitutional text. Originalists insist that *this* is a prudential question, *not* one whose answer is entailed by natural justice. Reasonable persons—anticipating the kinds of individuals who would sit on the bench, the intrinsic limits of the adjudicatory setting, the need for impartially administered justice and the inevitable diversity of views over the demands of practical reason, among other factors—might differ on whether to have judicial review at all. Such an arrangement offends no tenet of natural justice. And, in light of *Dred Scott, Plessy, Lochner,* and *Roe,* we might well wish the Framers had done so. The main point is this: no deduction *from* the existence of natural rights (or natural law or natural justice or any other account of political morality justified by critical reason) *to* judicial review is possible.

A sound originalism insists that whether or not judges should engage in unrestricted reasoning depends upon the positive law. Does the positive law direct judges to go outside conventional sources—authorities—to determine the truth of the matter? If so, a good "positivist" judge will engage in natural law reasoning. If not—and, if the positive law stipulates, for example, that "person" is a legal term of art including only human individuals born and still living, together with some fictional "persons" like corporations—then the judge has no jurisdiction to add the unborn to the list of persons according to the truth of the matter. Of course, such a stipulation may be unjust, and fail to bind in conscience. It is still the positive law.

Unjust Laws and Judicial Review

Let us finally consider the question: can a judge who believes in natural law render judgment in accord with positive law even when the positive law in question is unjust?

According to natural law theorists, judges are under the same obligations of truth telling that the rest of us are under. If the positive law is in conflict with the natural law, the judge may not lie about it. If his or her duty is to give judgment according to the positive law, then he or she must either (1) do so or (2) recuse himself or herself. If the judge can give judgment according to immoral positive law without rendering himself or herself formally or materially complicit in any way in its immorality, and without giving scandal, then he or she may licitly do so (though he or she may also licitly recuse himself or herself). One *formally* cooperates in another's wrongful act when one participates in the immoral act in such a way that it becomes one's own. In the case of abortion, one formally cooperates when one performs abortions, or acts to encourage, counsel, facilitate, or make abortions available. One is formally complicit in the injustice of abortion when one votes for a candidate even partially on the basis of his or her proabortion positions. The same is true when a legislator votes for legislation even partially for the purpose of making abortion available.

One *materially* cooperates in another's wrongdoing when one's acts help to make that wrongdoing possible, although one does not *intend* that wrongdoing. Material cooperation in abortion takes place when *one does not will* that an abortion happen, or that the unborn be left unprotected from abortion, but where one's actions—although motivated by another purpose—nevertheless help to make an abortion possible.

The point is that a conscientious judge must know what he or she thinks is unjust and he or she must know why. The problem with the "value imposition," "personal preference" stance of judicial conservatives is that it renders this knowledge either impossible or inert in the face of majoritarian will. That is, if it is all a matter of feelings, then the solitary judge *will* defer to the multitude. The available options seem to be a Holmesian "I'll follow the majority to hell," or the incoherent explanation offered by Blackmun.

The judge who refuses to give judgment in accord with an unjust positive law does not pursue a personal agenda, or opt out of an unpleasant duty through an implicit conscience clause. This is not mere conscientious objection. It is rather about the right not to be complicit in grave injustices. The recusant judge acts *for* the common good by not giving effect to the positive law. In my view, Catholic jurists have been much too insensitive to these questions, perhaps to the point of giving scandal.

Even in cases where the judge conscientiously concludes that he or she *may*, without immoral complicity and without giving scandal, give judgment according to the law, he or she might well do what Justice Scalia has regularly done: affirm forthrightly the moral truth of the matter, albeit in dictum. In *Minnick v. Mississippi*,[38] for example, Scalia defied a generation of pundits, judges, and commentators (including all his conservative brethren) by asserting that a suspect's voluntary confession served not only state (or police) "interests" but the good of the suspect! In *Barnes*,[39] Scalia alone treated the ban on lewd dancing as a true morals law. For him, lewd dancing *is* immoral, and is therefore prohibited to protect the character of citizens, especially that of the dancer-in-the-buff.

We need more philosophical analysis of a slightly different type. Scalia has begun this work as well. He rightly saw in the *Cruzan* "right-to-die" case that the issue in most cases like it is not "letting die,"[40] but killing: suicide (assisted or not) and homicide. He then went to the conventional legal authorities, and found that, according to them, no one has a right to take innocent life, even if the life is one's own. There was even more philosophical work to do in the *Cruzan case*. Justice Stevens claimed in support of a "right to die" that the state must remain "neutral" about choices to discontinue medical treatment as well as basic nursing care. But Stevens's argument for neutrality was hardly neutral.[41] It rested upon philosophical dualism, which treats the body as the instrument of the "person," identified with the experiencing consciousness.

Notes

My presentation has benefited from reading John Finnis's as yet unpublished paper, "Is Natural Law Theory Compatible with Limited Government?" and by (especially with regard to parts 4, 6, and 7) conversations with Robert George.

1. See, e.g., G. Weigel, *Tranquilitas Ordinas: The Present Failure and Future Promise of American Catholic Thought on War and Peace* (Oxford: Oxford University Press, 1987).

2. See John Finnis, Germain Grisez, Joseph Boyle, *Nuclear Deterrence: Morality and Realism* (Oxford: Clarendon Press, 1987).

3. It is true that some actions may be rightly chosen only by legitimate public authority (e.g., the decision to declare and carry on a war, capital punishment). But that does not imply a separate set of "public" moral principles, and there is none. There is in the tradition a usage, notably in *Dignitatis Humanae*, of "public morality." But there and elsewhere in the tradition, the reference is to the moral ecology of public spaces (schools, etc.). It presupposes rather than supplants morality as such. Again, there is no separate public morality in the sense of different, basic action guiding norms. Cf. *Dignitatis Humanae* (Washington, D.C.: National Catholic Welfare Board, n.d.), §8, p.7.

4. Pope John Paul II, *Veritatis Splendor* (Washington, D.C.: United States Catholic Conference, 1993), § 96.

5. "The same law of nature that governs the life and conduct of individuals must also regulate the relations of political communities with one another. . . . Political leaders are still bound by the natural law . . . and have no authority to depart from its slightest precepts": John XXIII, Encyclical *Pacem in Terris* (1963, part III, paras 80–81.

6. Lloyd Weinreb, "Natural Law and Rights," in *Natural Law Theory: Contemporary Essays,* ed. Robert George (Oxford: Clarendon Press, 1992), 279.

7. Ibid.

8. Ibid., 280.

9. Ibid., 289.

10. Ibid.

11. Ibid., 289–90.

12. Ibid.

13. Ibid., 291.

14. See Germain Grisez, Olaf Tollefsen, *Free Choice: A Self-Referential Argument* (Notre Dame: University of Notre Dame Press, 1976).

15. Ibid., 300–301.

16. Hadley Arkes, "That 'Nature Herself Has Placed in Our Ears a Power of Judging': Some Reflections on the 'Naturalism' of Cicero" in *Natural Law Theory: Contemporary Essays,* ed. Robert George.

17. Ibid., 246.

18. Ibid., 248.

19. Ibid., 251.

20. Ibid., 267.

21. Ibid., 272.

22. *Veritatis Splendor,* para. 80.

23. *Natural Law Theory: Contemporary Essays,* supra n.17, at 274.

24. Ibid.

25. L. Strauss, *Natural Right and History* (Chicago: University of Chicago Press, 1953), 159–60.

26. Ibid.

27. Joseph Boyle, "Natural Law and the Ethics of Traditions," in *Natural Law Theory: Contemporary Essays,* ed. Robert George.

28. Ibid., 18.

29. Ibid., 20.

30. Ibid., 18.

31. Ibid., 26.

32. *Dignitatis Humanae,* § 10, 9.

33. Ibid., § 1, 2.

34. Robert George, *Making Men Moral: Civil Liberties and Public Morality* (Oxford: Clarendon Press, 1993), 220.

35. *Michael H. v. Gerald D.,* 491 U.S. 110, 127 (1989).

36. That Blackmun so distinguishes the three does not inspire confidence in his grasp of practical reason.

37. *Callin v. Collins,* 114 S. Ct. 1127 (Scalia, J., concurring).

38. 498 U.S. 146 (1990).

39. *Barnes v. Glen Theatre,* 501 U.S. 560 (1991).

40. *Cruzan v. Director,* Missouri Dept. of Health, 497 U.S. 261 (1990).

41. Ibid., 275 (Stevens, J., dissenting).

8

Natural Law and International Order

Robert P. George

Introduction

Among the achievements of contemporary analytical jurisprudence is its virtual elimination of false oppositions between "natural law theory" and "legal positivism." Theorists of natural law, such as John Finnis,[1] and legal positivists, such as Neil MacCormick,[2] have developed refined understandings of the relationships between law and morality in the lights of which it no longer makes sense to suppose that a commitment to legal positivism logically excludes belief in natural law. Legal positivists, whatever their meta-ethical and normative commitments, recognize that nothing in the idea of legal positivism as such necessarily commits them to moral skepticism or cultural relativism; natural law theorists, acknowledging important respects in which law and morality are, indeed, "conceptually distinct," recognize concepts of law which, for perfectly valid theoretical purposes, systematically prescind from questions of the justice or injustice of particular laws of legal systems.[3]

The concern of the legal positivist is fundamentally with the accurate and theoretically interesting description of laws, legal institutions, and legal systems. His endeavor is to describe the social practices that constitute the phenomenon of law at various times and in various places. Thus, Herbert Hart begins the *Concept of Law* by advising the reader to regard his book "as an essay in descriptive sociology."[4] By contrast, the concern of the natural law theorist is fundamentally with *justification,* that is to say, *moral evaluation* or *prescription.* Insofar as laws, legal institutions, and legal systems are concerned, he is

133

interested in their moral goodness or badness, that is, their approximation to an ideal of natural justice. Thus, Finnis begins *Natural Law and Natural Rights* by declaring that

> [t]here are human goods that can be secured only through the institutions of human law, and requirements of practical reasonableness that only those institutions can satisfy. It is the object of this book to identify those goods, and those requirements of practical reasonableness, and thus to show how and on what conditions such institutions are *justified* and the ways in which they can be (and often are) defective.[5]

In this essay, I consider understandings of international order as they are, or could be, advanced by theorists operating within the tradition of natural law theorizing. I have, in other works, argued in support of the new classical natural law theory deployed by Finnis, though originally developed by Germain Grisez in collaboration with Finnis and Joseph M. Boyle, Jr.; however, I will make no efforts in this essay to defend that theory or the broader tradition of which it is a part. My goal, rather, is to provide a sound exposition of the natural law tradition, and of the new classical theory, and to relate some of what the tradition and the theory have to say about the constitution of international society. Along the way, I will refer to pronouncements on natural law and international order in papal encyclicals and other official documents of the Roman Catholic Church. I cite these pronouncements, not because the Church or her officials have any special authority that it is appropriate to invoke in philosophical discussion or debate, but rather because the Church is, I believe, the principal institutional bearer of the tradition of natural law theorizing in the modern world. And, of course, the Church is herself an international institution and a longstanding actor in international affairs.

Natural Law Theory

The natural moral law, if there is such a thing, is a body of practical principles comprising two types or sets of noninstrumental reasons for action: first, reasons provided by "basic human goods," which make available to human agents rationally grounded options for choice (i.e., practical possibilities); and second, reasons provided by moral norms, which exclude some practical possibilities as in one way or another unreasonable. Moral norms, where they are in force, provide conclusive "second order" reasons not to choose certain practical possibilities despite one's "first order" reasons (and/or other motives) to choose them.[6] Natural law theories are accounts of basic human goods, moral norms, and the reasons for action they provide.

Plainly, natural law theorists are cognitivists, or "realists," about morality. However, they are not accurately classified as either teleologists or deontologists. Unlike deontologists, they give basic human goods a crucial structural role in their accounts of practical reasoning and moral judgment; at the same time, they reject the consequentialist methods of moral judgments favored by contemporary teleologists.

Any comprehensive theory of human good(s) will say something about the common good, just as any comprehensive theory of morality will say something about political morality. It is hardly surprising, then, that natural law theorists have something to say about law (including international law), economics (including international economics), and politics (including international politics). It is generally unhelpful, however, to attempt to classify natural law theories or theorists as liberal or conservative, capitalist or socialist, individualist or communitarian, and so forth. The natural law tradition itself tends to be rather undogmatic about the proper solution to a great many of the political, social, and economic issues that divide people in such camps. For example, while modern popes have, in the name of natural law, defended certain capitalist principles, such as the market economy and the private ownership of property, they have at the same time allowed that a significant measure of economic regulation and governmental intervention in the economy can be permissible and may even be required as a matter of justice.[7] Furthermore, the popes have made no efforts to settle once and for all questions of the proper scope of economic regulation and governmental intervention; nor have they provided precise guidelines as to when public ownership of this or that property is in order. Rather, they treat questions of this sort as prudential ones on which people may (within limits established by the requirements of justice and other moral principles) legitimately differ, and whose proper solution will, in any event, vary with the circumstances of any particular society at a given time.

The natural law tradition's well-known commitment to the idea of moral absolutes, forcefully reiterated by Pope John Paul II in his encyclical letter *Veritatis Splendor,* should not obscure the degree to which the tradition recognizes that many important issues of social and economic policy do not admit of a single uniquely correct solution, which should, as a matter of natural moral law, govern in all places and at all times. In politics, just as in personal affairs, the natural law may exclude only some (or, indeed, none) of the interesting options, leaving the matter to be settled by prudential judgment or, indeed, sheer preference. In one set of circumstances (e.g., in a great depression) prudence might dictate a strongly interventionist economic policy, while in other circumstances a policy of nonintervention or governmental withdrawal from certain sectors of the economy may be indicated. Relativities of this sort in fact abound when one considers the implications of natural law theorizing for the constitution of international society.

The New Classical Theory

Before turning to the question of international order, however, let me fill out my sketch of natural law theorizing by describing in a little more detail the fundaments of the new classical theory.

According to this theory, the first principles of natural law are not themselves moral principles. Rather, they are principles that extend to and govern all intelligent practical deliberation, regardless of whether it issues in morally upright intelligible benefit (and not *merely* emotional satisfaction). Such principles refer to noninstrumental (and, in that sense, basic or ultimate) reasons for action. Reasons of this sort are provided by ends that can intelligently be wanted, not merely as means to other ends, but as ends-in-themselves (even when pursuit of some such end, in the particular circumstances in which one finds oneself, or by the only means available to one here and now, would be morally wrong).[8] Many philosophers refer to such ends as "intrinsic goods"; Grisez, Boyle, and Finnis call them "basic human goods."

Qua basic, such goods, and the reasons for acting they provide, cannot be deduced from still more fundamental practical principles or from theoretical truths (such as putative facts about human nature that are not themselves practical principles or derived from premises that include practical principles).[9] They are, rather, underived, and, in that sense, "self-evident."[10] They come to be known in noninferential acts of understanding wherein one grasps, in reflecting on the data of one's experience, the intelligible point of possible action (whether or not it is morally upright) directed toward the realization of (or participation in) the good in question by oneself or others (whether or not one happens to be interested in pursuing that good oneself here and now).

Following Aquinas,[11] proponents of the new classical theory hold that there are many basic human goods, including life and health, knowledge and aesthetic appreciation, excellence in work and play, and various forms of harmony within each person and among persons (and their communities) and between persons (and their communities) and any wider reaches of reality.[12] These basic goods can be realized and participated in by an unlimited number of persons, in an unlimited number of ways, on an unlimited number of occasions. This multiplicity of basic goods and of their possible instantiations in alternative interesting possible lines of action entails great complexity in intelligent motivation. The incommensurability (i.e., rational irreducibility) of motives, at least one of which bears on an anticipated benefit whose unique goodness can come to be only through following practical reason's direction (which is often a nonexclusive direction) toward it, requires free choice—that is, making up of one's indeterminate self to act on this motive rather than that one. Paradigmatically, one may have, and be aware of, a noninstrumental reason to do X, yet at the same time, have, and be aware of, a noninstrumental reason not to do X, or to do Y, the doing of which is incompatible here and now with doing X.[13] Whichever option one chooses, one chooses it for a noninstrumental reason; in that sense, the choosing of either option is *rational*.

Where it is the case that, of each of some set of incompatible options one has a reason to choose it, yet one has no conclusive reason to choose one option rather than the other(s), one chooses between options that each present an undefeated reason for action. Where one has, and is aware of, undefeated competing reasons for action, one's choice, though rationally grounded, is rationally underdetermined.[14] In such cases, reason does not narrow one's options to a single possibility. More than one practical possibility is not only rationally grounded, but fully reasonable. Sometimes, however, a moral norm (e.g., the Golden Rule of fairness) provides a conclusive reason not to choose one (or some) option(s), despite one's reason to choose it (or them). In such cases, at least one of one's first-order reasons (i.e., reasons provided by basic human goods) is defeated by a second-order reason (i.e., a reason provided by a moral norm), which provides a conclusive reason (and, thus, a moral obligation) to choose the undefeated option.

Still, one's first-order reason, albeit defeated, is not destroyed or eliminated; the morally excluded option retains intelligible appeal. For one to choose that option, while practically unreasonable (inasmuch as one's reason for choosing it has been defeated by a conclusive reason not to choose it), is not utterly irrational; this is because one's action in choosing it, however moral, is for the sake of some true good, and will, to the extent one is successful, instantiate some intelligible benefit for oneself or someone else. If, *per impossible,* a moral norm were to destroy or eliminate one's basic reason not to choose a certain option, then one's choosing that option would not merely be unreasonable, but irrational, and, as such, intelligible, if at all, only as action motivated purely by feeling or some other subrational factor.

According to the new classical theory, basic human goods are not "Platonic forms" that are somehow detached from human persons; rather, they are constitutive aspects of the well-being and fulfillment of flesh-and-blood individuals in their manifold dimensions, that is to say, as animate, as rational, and as agents through deliberation and choice.[15] Basic human goods provide reasons for action precisely, and only, insofar as they are constitutive aspects of human well-being or flourishing.[16]

Taken together, the first principles of practical reason that direct action toward these goods and reasons outline the (vast) range of possible rationally motivated actions, and point to an ideal of "integral human fulfillment," that is to say, the complete fulfillment of all human persons (and their communities) in all possible respects. Of course, no choice or series of choices can actually bring about integral human fulfillment; it is an ideal rather than an operational objective. Nevertheless, it is morally significant inasmuch as the first principle of morality (which, contrary to the representations of some expositors and critics of the new classical theory,[17] is no mere ideal) directs that choice and action for the sake of basic human goods can be compatible with a will toward this ideal.

Given its abstractness and generality, the first principle of morality must be specified if it is to be useful in actually guiding people's choosing. Its specifications take account of the (necessarily subrational) motives people may have for choosing and otherwise willing incompatibly with a will toward integral human fulfillment; to act on such motives (i.e., in defiance of moral norms) is to permit one's reason to be fettered by emotion and, typically, harnessed to it for the purpose of producing rationalizations for immoral conduct. The specifications of the first principle of morality guide action by excluding options that seem reasonable only if one's reason has been thus fettered.

These specifications are not, however, the most specific moral norms. They state propositions such as "do unto others as you would have them do unto to you," and "evil may not be done that good may come out of it," rather than more specific norms such as "thou shalt not steal," and "thou shalt not kill the innocent and just." They are, as it were, midway in generality between the first principle and fully specific norms. Finnis refers to these moral principles as "requirements of practical reasonableness"; Grisez and Boyle (and Finnis in his collaborative writings with them) refer to them as "modes of responsibility." Where controlling, these principles provide conclusive second-order reasons not to choose certain practical possibilities, despite one's first-order reasons (and one's more or less powerful emotional motives) to choose them.

Moral principles, according to the new classical theory, are norms for free choice. In freely choosing, that is to say, in choosing for (or against) reasons provided by basic human goods, one integrates the goods (or the damaging and consequent deprivations of the goods, i.e., the evils) one intends—whether as ends or as means to other ends—into one's will, thus effecting a sort of synthesis between oneself as an acting person and the objects of one's choices (i.e., the goods and evils one intends). Hence, one's free choices are self-constituting: they perdure as virtues or vices in one's character and personality as a choosing subject unless or until, for better or worse, one reverses one's previous choice by choosing incompatibly with it, or, at least, resolves to choose differently should one face the same or relevantly similar options in the future.[18]

Noting the different ways that different types of willing bear on human goods and evils, proponents of the new classical theory distinguish as distinct modes of voluntariness "intending" a good or evil (as end or means) from "accepting" (as a side effect) a good or evil that foresees as a consequence of one's action but does not intend (i.e., which serves as neither an instrumental or non-instrumental reason for one's choice and action). Although one is morally responsible for the bad side effects one knowingly brings about, one is not responsible for the evils one intends. And sometimes no moral norm excludes one's bringing about as a side effect of an action one has a reason (perhaps even a conclusive reason) to perform, some evil that one could legitimately intend. On the other hand, often one will have an obligation in justice or fairness to others (and thus a conclusive reason supplied by a moral norm) not to bring about a certain evil that one knows or believes would likely result, albeit as an unintended side effect from one's action.

"Common Good" and "Complete Community"

Aristotle treated the Greek polis as the paradigm of a complete community, that is, one capable of securing the overall well-being and fulfillment of its members. Later theorists of natural law retained the term "politics" for the affairs of a complete community, but treated the territorial state as the truly "complete community" and the politics of such states as "politics" in its focal sense. Similarly, they treated the nation-state as the paradigm of a legal system and the law of such states as "law" in its focal sense. Similarly, they treated the nation-state as the paradigmatic case and focal sense of the "common good." Of course, the tradition of natural law theorizing recognizes that any group or association can have a politics, a law, and a common good. To the extent, however, that a community is incomplete, that is to say, less than fully self-sufficient, it has a politics, law, and common good in a derivative or, in any event, nonfocal sense.

What does it mean, though, to speak of a common good in any sense? Finnis's primary definition has gained wide acceptance among contemporary natural law theorists: "a set of conditions which enables the members of a community to attain for themselves reasonable objectives, or to realize reasonable for themselves the value(s), for the sake of which they have reason to collaborate with each other (positively and/or negatively) in a community."[19] In light of this definition, we may ask: Is there a common good of the "international community?" Indeed, is there an international community at all?

A central feature of medieval and modern natural law theorizing is belief in a universal human nature. In the absence of such a belief, the tradition could not speak meaningfully of a *common* good of members of different tribes, clans, nations, or races, or, indeed, of an international community at all. Even with such a belief in place, however, the mainstream of the tradition has tended to treat the international community, and its politics, law, and common good, as nonparadigmatic. Increasingly, however, natural law theorists are coming to view the nation-state as crucially incomplete, that is to say, incapable of doing all that can and must be done to secure conditions for the all-round flourishing of its citizens. Finnis states the implications of this change in view for the natural law theory of the international order:

> If it now appears that the good of individuals can only be fully secured and realized in the context of international community, we must conclude that the claim of the national state to be a complete community is unwarranted and the postulate of the national legal order, that it is supreme and comprehensive and an exclusive source of legal obligation, is increasingly what lawyers call a "legal fiction."[20]

In other words, the nation-state can no longer (if it ever could) secure the conditions of its citizens' overall well-being (i.e., their common good) without more or less systematically coordinating its activities with other nation-states and, indeed, without the active assistance of supranational institutions, at least some of which must possess powers to enforce multilateral agreements and international law. Hence, it has become necessary to develop institutions that will enable the international community to function as a complete community and, thus, a community whose politics, law, and common good are paradigmatic and focal.[21]

One need not accept any of the distinctive claims of the natural law tradition in order to recognize the urgent need for international cooperation, and, indeed, for the (further) development of international institutions to deal with modern social, economic, and political problems. The distinctively modern problems of nuclear and other weapons of mass destruction, not to mention global environmental problems, such as ozone depletion, oceanic pollution, and mass deforestation, simply do not admit of effective solutions without substantial international cooperation. Moreover, international action is necessary to combat mass starvation and other evils, whether they are the intended or unintended consequences of human action or the result of earthquakes, hurricanes, and other natural catastrophes, to promote the economic development of poor nations and to protect human rights.

World Government

Does this mean that natural law theory, as applied to the problems of today, envisages the institution of a world government? The answer is, I think, "yes";

however, it is subject to certain clarifications and, perhaps, qualifications. Ideally, a central political authority would attend to the common good of mankind in, for example, avoiding (or at least limiting) war, protecting the physical environment, preventing starvation and other forms of misery, promoting economic development, and protecting human rights. However, the concentrating of power, and, particularly, the force of arms in a central government that is not subject to effective countervailing power is obviously risky. To be sure, some risks are entailed by the creation of any central authority; and risks of this sort are usually, or, in any event, often, worth bearing. At the same time, ways must be found to lessen the risks by, for example, constitutional schemes that divide, check, and limit governmental powers. Moreover, the risks of permitting individuals and communities subject to a world government to retain armaments must be weighed prudentially against the risks of disarming them. The concerns that prompted late-eighteenth-century Americans to entrench in their federal constitution a right of the people to keep and bear arms[22] may not be anachronistic. Perhaps those in power in a world government should not be left entirely secure against the possibility of armed resistance should their rule degenerate into tyranny.

"Determinatio" in the Constitution of International Society

According to natural law theory, just and good positive law, including constitutional law, is always in some sense derived from the natural law. As Aquinas observed, however, this derivation is accomplished in at least two quite different ways. In the case of certain principles, the legislator translates the natural law into positive law more or less directly. So, for example, a conscientious legislator will deal with grave injustices, such as murder, rape, and theft, by moving according to an intellectual process akin to deduction from the moral proposition that, say, the killing of innocent persons is unjust to the legal prohibition of such killing.[23] In a great many cases, however, the movement from the natural to the positive law in the practical thinking of the conscientious legislator or constitution maker cannot be so direct.

For example, it is easy to understand the basic practical principle that identifies health as a basic human good and the preservation of human health as an important goal. A modern legislator will therefore easily see, for example, the need for a scheme of coordination of vehicular traffic to protect the health and safety of drivers and pedestrians. The common good, which it is his responsibility to foster and serve in this respect, clearly requires such a scheme. Ordinarily, however, he will not be able to deduce from the natural law a uniquely correct scheme of traffic regulation. The natural law does not determine once and for all the perfect scheme of traffic regulation or establish one or another set of trade-offs (e.g., so much convenience or efficiency for so much safety) as uniquely or definitively right. A number of different schemes—attended by different and often incommensurable costs and benefits, risks and advantages—may be consistent with the requirements of natural law. So the legislator must exercise a certain creative freedom in authoritatively choosing from among competing reasonable schemes. He must move, not by deduction or any intellectual process akin to it, but rather by an activity of the practical intellect that Aquinas called *determinatio*.[24]

Unfortunately, no single word in English captures the meaning of *determinatio*. "Determination" has some of the flavor of it; but so too does "implementation," "specification," and "concretization." The key thing to understand is that in making *determinationes,* the legislator or constitution maker enjoys a type of creative freedom that Aquinas analogizes to that exercised by the architect. An architect must design a building that is sound and sensible for the purposes to which it will be put. Ordinarily, however, he cannot identify a form of the building that would be uniquely correct. A range of possible designs will likely satisfy the relevant criteria. Obviously, a design in which doors are no more than three feet high is unlikely to meet an important requirement for a functional building. No principle of architecture, however, sets the proper height of a door at $6'2''$ as opposed to $6'8''$. In designing a particular building, the conscientious architect will strive to make the height of the doors make sense in light of a variety of factors, some of which are themselves the fruit of *determinationes* (e.g., the height of the ceilings); but even here, he will typically face a variety of acceptable but incompatible design options.

Contemporary legal theory has brought to light the importance of authoritative legal enactments as norms for regulating and coordinating human action for the common good.[25] More often than not, such enactments are not direct deductions from the natural law; rather, they are *determinationes*. Whether they are products of legislation or multilateral agreements, the norms of international law that have been, or could be, put into force to regulate and coordinate the activities of states, corporations, and other actors in international affairs for sake of the common good, in the majority of cases, would be *determinationes*. For example, in the case of a particular international environmental problem, the natural law may well require that some action be taken, but not prescribe any particular scheme among the range of possible reasonable schemes for dealing with the problem. Nor, perhaps, will the natural law dictate a uniquely correct solution if, in the case, a choice must be made between tolerating a certain amount of environmental pollution and sacrificing a certain measure of economic development. Where trade-offs of this sort must be made, natural justice requires only that choices be made by fair procedures that take fully into account the rights and interests of all parties who will be affected.

Indeed, key questions pertaining to the proper constitution of the international order are themselves matters for *determinatio*. They do not admit of uniquely correct answers. Rather, choices must be made from among a range of reasonable possible constitutional schemes. Natural law requires that one of these schemes be selected for the sake of the human goods to be fostered and protected by international authority; however, there is no scheme of international authority that is uniquely required as a matter of natural law.

Is natural law theory relativistic, then, on the question of the proper constituting of the international order and on other questions pertaining to the common good of international society? The answer is no. The principles of natural law rule out certain possibilities, usually on the ground that they are unjust. For example, a constitutional scheme based on racist suppositions would be excluded as a matter of natural law. So too would any scheme that unfairly distributed the burdens and benefits of international cooperation in dealing, to stay with the example, with ecological problems. The relativism of the natural law theory of international order is limited: it follows from the belief that the principles of natural law that exclude certain possibilities as unjust or otherwise immoral will not necessarily narrow the possibilities for a just and upright ordering of international society, or a fair and effective solution to global environmental problems, to a single uniquely correct option.

I repeat, however, that a substantively acceptable scheme of constituting a society, or the international society, or solving other problems pertaining to the common good of national or international societies, might nevertheless be judged according to natural law theory to be morally unacceptable on the ground that the procedures employed to select that scheme from among the range of possible reasonable schemes were themselves unjust. For example, wealthy and powerful nations might arbitrarily or otherwise unjustly exclude poor and weak nations from participating effectively in decisions affecting the constitution of international society. Or the interests and preferences of developing nations might be left out of account in making tradeoffs between, say, environmental protection and economic development.

Subsidiarity and International Order

I have suggested that contemporary natural law theory envisages a world government that would function as the central authority in a complete community. Does this mean that natural law theory is statist? I think not. I have already noted that risks, as well as benefits, would attend the creation of any world government, and have spoken of the recognition by natural law theory of the need to lessen these risks, where possible, by checking and limiting the powers of that government. In addition to prudential considerations, however, natural law theory proposes principled grounds for decentralizing power wherever practicable.

Recall Finnis's definition of the common good as a "set of conditions which enables the members of a community to attain *for themselves* reasonable objectives, or to realize reasonably *for themselves* the value(s) for the sake of which they have reason to collaborate . . . in a community" (emphasis supplied). Under the natural law account of human good(s), it is important not only that basic human goods be realized, but that people and peoples realize these goods *for themselves,* as the fruits of their own deliberation, judgment, choice, and action. On the basis of this consideration, the tradition of natural law theorizing has developed the so-called principle of subsidiarity.[26] The meaning and implications of subsidiarity were nicely stated by Pope Pius XI in his 1931 encyclical letter *Quadragesimo Anno:*

> just as it is wrong to withdraw from the individual and commit to a group what private initiative and effort can accomplish, so too it is an injustice . . . for a larger and higher association to arrogate to itself functions which can be performed efficiently by smaller and lower associations. This is a fundamental principle. . . . Of its very nature the true aim of all social activity should be to help members of a social body, and never to destroy or absorb them.[27]

As applied to the question of international order and a possible world government, the principle of subsidiarity would restrict the authority of any world government to those problems that cannot be successfully dealt with by national governments, just as it restricts the authority of national governments to those problems that cannot be successfully dealt with by regional governments, of regional governments to those problems that cannot be dealt with successfully by local governments, of local governments to those problems that cannot be dealt with successfully by neighborhood groups and other private associations, of such groups and associations to problems that cannot be dealt with successfully by families, of families to those problems that cannot be dealt with successfully by individuals.

Toward the end of his 1963 encyclical letter *Pacem in Terris,* Pope John XXIII reflected on the implications of the principle of subsidiarity for the precise question of the constitution of international society. He unambiguously affirmed the idea of an international or "world-wide" public authority that would serve "the universal common good" by coming to grips with problems that "the public authorities of individual states are not in a position to tackle with any hope of a positive solution."[28] This universal public authority would, he said, "have as its fundamental objective the recognition, respect, safeguarding and promotion of the rights of the human person."[29] However, he insisted,

[t]he world-wide public authority is not intended to limit the sphere of action of the public authority of the individual state, much less to take its place. On the contrary, its purpose is to create, on a world basis, an environment in which the public authorities of each state, its citizens and intermediate associations, can carry out their tasks, fulfill their duties and exercise their rights with greater security.[30]

In the understanding of Pope John, and the tradition in which he speaks, world government is in principle limited government. Such government is, to be sure, envisaged as the central authority of a complete community; yet it is not meant to displace regional, national, or local authorities. Indeed, a world government may legitimately exercise power only where regional, national, or local authorities are not competent to solve the problems at hand.

Of course, the application of the principle of subsidiarity is more a matter of art than of science; and, in the modern world, the principle must be applied under constantly shifting conditions. In many cases, problems that are appropriately dealt with at one level in the conditions prevailing today may more appropriately be dealt with at another level (higher *or* lower) in the conditions prevailing tomorrow. And often enough it will prove impracticable to shift authority to deal with a certain problem from one level of government to another, or from governmental to private hands, or vice versa, at every point at which it would be ideal to do so. Natural law theorists are confident that the principle of subsidiarity can guide the practical thinking of conscientious statesmen, but they do not pretend that it can be applied mechanically or with anything approaching mathematical precision.

A Contractual Association of Nations?

If the tradition of natural law theorizing envisages world government as limited in the scope of its just authority by the principle of subsidiarity, and if it maintains that such government must refrain from displacing national governments (and, indeed, subnational governments) or interfering with the exercise of their authority in matters within their competence, does the tradition conceive of international society and its government as a contractual association of nations?

Certainly no nation is under an obligation in natural justice to submit to the jurisdiction of a world government that is in itself unjust or that was brought into being by procedures that excluded that or any other nation from fair participation in the *determinationes* embodied in the design of that government. The substantive or procedural injustice of an international authority can provide an undefeated reason (and, indeed, under some circumstances, a conclusive reason) for a nation to refuse to submit to the jurisdiction of that authority. The fact that the international common good demands the institution of (limited) world government does not impose on any nation the obligation to accept the first offer of world government that comes along.

At the same time, the tradition of natural law theorizing does not suppose that a nation may justly fail to submit to the jurisdiction of a just world government that has been, or is being, created in accordance with basically just procedures. The tradition does not view international cooperation to secure the worldwide common good as somehow optional for states or peoples. The reality of international problems demanding international responses imposes on every nation, as a matter of natural justice, a duty to cooperate with other nations to secure the international common good. Thus, submission to the jurisdiction of a just world government is not morally optional in the way that participating in a contract is ordinarily morally optional. The common goods to be achieved (and common evils to be avoided) by the institution of a central international authority provide conclusive reasons for nations to submit to the jurisdiction of a just world government. For any nation to resist the jurisdiction of such a government is contrary to the international common good, and, as such, constitutes the sort of practical unreasonableness in political affairs that the natural law tradition treats as a paradigmatic case of injustice.

None of this should be taken to imply, however, that there would be no place for bilateral or multilateral treaties and other contracts between nations in a properly constituted international order. Nor should it be taken to mean that the contractual *form* is somehow inappropriate for the establishment of a world government or other international political institutions.

Cultural Diversity

For the natural law tradition, the obligation of international authority to respect cultural autonomy and diversity is rooted in the principle of subsidiarity and in the diversity of basic human goods and of upright and reasonable ways of instantiating these goods in the lives of individuals and their communities. Contemporary natural law theory recognizes that dramatically different cultures provide people with the resources they need to live fulfilling and morally valuable lives. This recognition is perfectly compatible with the natural law tradition's historic rejection of cultural relativism. To say that some cultures are morally bad (or, more precisely, that certain practices deeply rooted in, or central to, some cultures are morally bad) is not to say that there is only one culture that is morally good.

In speaking of the obligation of international institutions to assist the economic and social development of impoverished nations, Pope Paul VI in his 1967 encyclical letter *Populorum Progressio* was careful to highlight both the principle of subsidiarity and belief in legitimate cultural autonomy and diversity: "We hope . . . that multilateral and international bodies . . . will discover ways which are still underdeveloped to break through the barriers which seem to enclose them and to discover for themselves, in full fidelity to their own proper genius, the means for their social and human progress."[31]

According to the pope and the natural law tradition, international cooperation and even the institution of international authority, for the sake of the universal common good, entails neither statism nor cultural uniformity. Indeed, it is important to protect the human values to be realized by people and peoples precisely in their acting "for themselves" and "in fidelity to their own proper genius."

Natural law theory rejects the idea that we must choose between cultural chauvinism and cultural relativism. Far from supposing that the natural moral law imposes a single cultural norm to which all peoples should aspire, contemporary natural law theorists maintain that respect for the integrity of diverse legitimate cultures is itself a requirement of natural justice. They hold that international law and government must, to the extent possible, not only permit diverse national and subnational communities to control their own affairs, but also respect (and, if necessary, help to protect) the right of such communities to preserve, by legitimate means, their distinctive languages, customs, traditions, and ways of life.

This in no way implies that international authority acts illegitimately in forbidding and repressing violations of human rights, even when they are sanctioned by cultural norms. The question here, of course, is what constitutes a violation of human rights. Natural law theorists are by no means in agreement among themselves on this question; and everyone recognizes certain hard cases. Natural law theorists generally do agree, however, in recognizing a wide-ranging legitimate cultural diversity, and in holding that the repression of cultural practices by public authority is justified only for the sake of preventing fundamental injustices or other grave evils.

Notes

1. See *Natural Law and Natural Rights* (Oxford: Clarendon Press, 1980), esp. chaps. 1 and 7; also see "The Truth in Legal Positivism," in Robert P. George (ed.), *The Autonomy of Law: Essays on Legal Positivism* (Oxford: Clarendon, 1995).

2. See "Natural Law and the Separation of Law and Morals," in Robert P. George (ed.), *Natural Law Theory: Contemporary Essays* (Oxford: Clarendon Press, 1992).

3. Hence, natural law theorists need not object to "positivism" in either of the two senses of meaning discussed by Terry Nardin in "Legal Positivism as a Theory of International Society," unpublished, 1993.

4. *The Concept of Law* (Oxford: Clarendon, 1961), vi.

5. *Natural Law and Natural Rights, supra,* n.1, 3 (emphasis supplied).

6. For a fuller explanation, see Robert P. George, "Does the Incommensurability Thesis Imperil Common Sense Moral Judgments?" *American Journal of Jurisprudence* 37 (1992): 185–95.

7. For example, Pope Paul VI, in harmony with the tradition of papal social teaching inaugurated in the late nineteenth century by Pope Leo XIII, taught that "without abolishing the competitive market, it should be kept within limits which make it just and moral, and therefore human" (*Populorum Progressio,* paragraph 61).

8. I explain the idea and significance of ultimate reasons for action in "Recent Criticisms of Natural Law Theory," *University of Chicago Law Review* 55 (1988): 1371–1492, 1390–94.

9. In this respect, the new classical theory differs markedly from familiar neo-scholastic accounts of natural law, such as the one propounded by Thomas Higgins in *Man as Man: The Science and Art of Ethics* (Milwaukee: Bruce Publishers, 1958).

10. For a careful explanation of the much misunderstood claim that the most basic practical principles are self-evident, see Joseph M. Boyle, Jr., "Natural Law and the Ethics of Traditions," in *Natural Law Theory,* supra, n. 2, 3–41, at 23–27.

11. *Summa theologiae,* I–II, q. 94, a. 2., on which see Germain Grisez's pathbreaking article, "The First Principle of Practical Reason: A Commentary on the *Summa theologiae,* I–II, q. 94, a. 2," *Natural Law Forum,* 10 (1965): 168–201.

12. See John Finnis, Joseph M. Boyle, Jr., and Germain Grisez, *Nuclear Deterrence, Morality, and Realism* (Oxford: Clarendon Press, 1987), 279–80; see also Germain Grisez, Joseph Boyle, and John Finnis, "Practical Principles, Moral Truth, and Ultimate Ends," *American Journal of Jurisprudence* 32 (1987): 99–151, at 107–8.

13. In the limiting case, one may make a free choice between options, one of which is rationally grounded and the other of which is purely emotional motive (e.g., repugnance).

14. See Joseph Raz, *The Morality of Freedom* (Oxford: Clarendon Press, 1986), 339.

15. I explain the point more fully in "Does the Incommensurability Thesis Imperil Common Sense Moral Judgments?" (*supra,* n. 6).

16. See "Practical Principles, Moral Truth, and Ultimate Ends" (*supra,* n. 12).

17. See, for example, Russell Hittinger's exposition and critique in *A Critique of the New Natural Law Theory* (Notre Dame, Ind.: University of Notre Dame Press, 1987), 50–51.

18. On the lastingness and character-forming consequences of free choices, see John Finnis, *Fundamentals of Ethics* (Oxford and Washington, DC: Oxford University Press and Georgetown University Press, 1983), 139–44.

19. Finnis, *Natural Law and Natural Rights* (*supra,* n. 1, 155).

20. Id. at 15.

21. See *Gaudium et Spes,* paragraph 84.

22. The Second Amendment to the Constitution of the United States: "A well regulated Militia, being necessary to the security of a free State, the right of the people to keep and bear arms, shall not be infringed."

23. See St. Thomas Aquinas, *Summa theologiae,* I–II, q. 95, a. 2.

24. Id.

25. See generally Edna Ullman-Margalit, *The Emergence of Norms* (Oxford: Clarendon Press, 1980).

26. From the Latin "subsidium," "to help."

27. Paragraph 79. According to Finnis, "an attempt, for the sake of the common good, to absorb the individual altogether into common enterprise would be disastrous for the common good, however much the common enterprises might prosper," *Natural Law and Natural Rights* (*supra,* n. 1, 168).

28. Paragraph 140.

29. Paragraph 139.

30. Paragraph 141.

31. Paragraph 64 (emphasis supplied). The phrase, "for themselves," reflects the pope's commitment to the principle of subsidiarity; the phrase "according to their own proper genius," reflects his belief in legitimate cultural diversity, not only as a matter of past practice, but something that rightly continues as peoples progress.

9

Jacques Maritain and the Rapprochement of Liberalism and Communitarianism

Michelle Watkins and Ralph McInerny

Introduction

Increasingly in recent years, the two major rival conceptual schemes in contemporary political debate have been liberalism and communitarianism. Among the major tenets of the former are the notion that what is most essential and morally significant about the self qua moral person is to be self-determining, and that this autonomy of the self is thoroughgoing, with the result that there is no such thing as *the* good, objectively true and universally applicable to all human beings as human, and hence discoverable by all. Rather, what counts as the good or the good life is left for each one to decide for himself. This means that liberalism's political community is not predicated on any privileged account of the good, but must be neutral with respect to rival conceptions of the good. A primary function of the political community, therefore, is to protect and actively promote *each* person's capacity to decide for himself what is indeed the good, to plan his life accordingly, with the proviso that one person's expression of autonomy does not infringe upon another's. This is the liberal thesis of the primacy of the right over the good. That is, the individual pursuit of the good has to be constrained by impartial principles of justice that everyone finds reasonable.

Communitarianism is a reaction against liberalism; and its conceptions of the self, the good, and community seem diametrically opposed to those of liberalism. It sees the identity of the self as essentially embedded in a particular community and views the self's moral agency as characterized by its *discovery* and pursuit of the good, thanks to the resources afforded by the community to which one belongs. This means that the political community is predicated on a conception of the good that it takes to be privileged, not neutral in the way liberalism requires.

This schematic description of liberalism and communitarianism raises the question of their conceptual compatibility. Are they simply incommensurable? Or can they be successfully synthesized in such a way that a philosophical defensible *via media* is attainable? This essay pursues the last question by invoking the political thought of Jacques Maritain. This may seem anachronistic, since the liberalism/communitarianism debate came after Maritain, who died in 1973. Obviously Maritain's ideas were not fashioned to adjudicate the debate between liberalism and communitarianism. Nonetheless, his ideas are highly relevant to the contemporary debate, as the present essay attempts to show.

The essay's aim can be described from the other end as well. During his lifetime, Maritain was criticized by those on the left for being conservative, even fascist and totalitarian, and by those on the right for selling out to individualistic liberalism. The basic criticism, which continues today, is that Maritain sought to synthesize two inherently incompatible political doctrines. Frederick Crosson, for example, chides him for making use of the liberal language of individual rights, thereby getting himself into a "conceptual muddle," and Alasdair MacIntrye points to Maritain's "uncharacteristic lapse" on the same ground.[1] Are these criticisms fair? An examination of Maritain's political philosophy in the light of distinctions afforded by the contemporary debate between liberalism and communitarianism helps to answer that question as well as provide a better understanding of the nature of Maritain's project.

In what follows, we presuppose the liberal and communitarian accounts of self, the good, and the community given in the introduction to this volume, and turn to a detailed discussion of Jacques Maritain's views of the self, the good, and community, showing in what ways he is a liberal and in what ways he is a communitarian. Four possible interpretations of Maritain's blend of communitarianism and liberalism are examined, after which the question of whether Maritain has succeeded is confronted. Success will be gauged in terms of internal consistency. This essay is not an effort to settle the communitarianism-liberalism debate as such, but has the more limited goal of exploring Maritain's contribution to an understanding of it. A result of this may well be to cast light on whether or not liberalism and communitarianism are conceptually compatible and on the prospect of an ongoing debate between liberals and communitarians.

Maritain on the Self, the Good, and Community

The Self

It is no exaggeration to say that Maritain's entire political thought rests on his understanding of the self. What is especially crucial is his distinction between "individual" and "person," a distinction between two irreducibly different aspects of the human being. Maritain in no way holds that what he calls person and individual are two separate realities or entities: the individual and person are wholly united in each human being. Furthermore, he insists that, since human society is made up of persons in relation to each other, a true understanding of society requires a prior understanding of the human person. Thus, he states that the distinction between person and individual is "the fundamental subject of all social and political philosophy."[2] Moreover, he consequently points out that the failure to note the distinction or the misunderstanding of it are the greatest causes of error in political philosophy. A misunderstanding of person opens the door to totalitarianism and a misunderstanding of individual results in individualism of one form or another.

What does Maritain mean by the assertion that, in one respect, the self is an individual? First of all, the assertion itself is based on his broader Thomistic metaphysical view that it is through the matter, the material constitution of a thing, that a given entity is individuated. The human being is no exception to the rule. Hence, the self qua individual is that aspect of the self whose drives, actions, and the like are rooted in the body which encloses a narrow ego separated from all other human beings, since individuality is that "In virtue of which every nature can posit itself in existence as distinct from other beings."[3] Hence, Maritain explains, "In each of us, individuality, being that which excludes from one's self all that other men are, could be described as the narrowness of ego, forever threatened and *forever eager to grasp for itself.*"[4] The emphasized phrase is suggestive of the liberal conception of the self as it is portrayed or, as some would argue, caricatured, by communitarians and the critics of liberalism. First, the self qua individual seeks gratification in the same way the liberal self does, as a *disinterested* maximizer of preference; the self is purely a chooser asserting its own will in pursuit of its own good. Second, the defining characteristic of the self qua individual is that it is independent and distinctly separate from other selves. A similar idea is expressed by the autonomy of the self. Third, the self qua individual is looked at purely for its individuality, that is, in virtue of itself and nothing else, thereby excluding, among other things, the individual's goals, psychological constitution, character traits, notion of the good, and plan of life. This point parallels Rawls's claim that the self-identity qua moral person cannot be linked to particular goals, traits, and the like that it may choose to have, since the latter are arbitrary or at best irrelevant from the moral point of view. In short, a communitarian would say that Maritain's notion of the self qua individual is analogous to Rawls's idea of the liberal self insofar as, among other things, they both constitute a conception of the self as "thin" and abstract.

However Rawls and other liberals might react to this analogy, Maritain's self qua individual has strong communitarian dimensions as well. In his view, the individual stands in relation to the community as a part to the whole, and thus the individual is subject to community. Maritain explains that "it is . . . in the nature of things that man should surrender his temporal goods and if necessary even his life for the welfare of the community; and that social life should impose on him *as an individual,* as part of the whole, many restraints and sacrifices."[5] This view of the individual as subordinate to the community seems to drive a certain wedge between the liberal self and the self qua individual, for the language of "subjecting" the individual to the community is more akin to the communitarian thesis of the self as being firmly embedded in the community than to liberalism's emphasis on the autonomy and inviolability of the individual vis-à-vis the policies of the community as a whole. This is rendered more evident in Maritain's assertion that each human being necessarily belongs in community, in part "because of the needs and indigence of human nature, by reason of which each one of us has need of others for his material, intellectual, and moral life."[6] Maritain is seemingly claiming that the natural needs of the self are such that the point of its involvement in the community is not so much to engage in a "cooperative venture of *mutual advantage,*" as liberals might argue, as to recognize the fact that the good of the individual is inseparable from participation in the life of the community. That is to say, the community is not *simply* a means for promoting what is advantageous to me and others, but rather is valued for its own sake precisely because interaction with others in the context of the community is *constitutive* of the good of the individual. Maritain's references to "intellectual" and "moral" needs of the self qua individual seem to support this interpretation.

The strong communitarian streak in Maritain's conception of the self qua individual seems to carry over to his account of the self qua person. This is primarily due to the fact that he understands the latter as "a reality which subsists *spiritually,*" insofar as "man is a person who holds himself in hand by his intelligence and his will, he exists not merely in a physical fashion; he has spiritual super-existence through knowledge and love . . . by virtue of the existence itself of his soul, which dominates time and death; spirit is the root of personality."[7] Note the stress on the person's interactions with others, with his community, and with the world, as fundamental to what it means to be a person. Maritain insists time and again that the self qua person "requires the communications of knowledge and love." For knowledge and love are the person's abilities to go outside of himself, to extend himself beyond the physical boundaries of his individuality, to be in deep contact with the world and with others: "By love, he can give himself completely to beings who are to him, as it were, other selves . . . through knowledge . . . he is, in a way, a microcosmos in which the great universe in its entirety can be encompassed through knowledge."[8]

Such a characterization of the person obviously goes well beyond the liberal construal of the self. It is "thick" inasmuch as it is predicated on a variety of human goals, traits, and capacities such as intelligence, knowledge, love, and spirituality. It considers the person's ends, activities, and traits to be constitutive of the self. Recall that the communitarian self is defined in terms of its social roles and its participation in social practices and the life of a community; in this respect, it resembles Maritain's person whose very identity is bound up with his dependence upon and interaction with others and with the world. Moreover, generally speaking, the overt metaphysical underpinning of Maritain's account of person renders it more palatable to communitarians than to liberals, whose aversion to metaphysical speculation is manifested in more than one way—for instance, in Rawls's rejection of teleology and insistence on the priority of the right over the good.

Yet, one must not overestimate the communitarian dimension of Maritain's account of person; as one delves into it, strong liberal themes emerge, just as they did in the case of the individual.

> The notion of personality thus involves that of totality and independence . . . he is a whole and as a person, subsistent in an independent manner . . . he is more of a whole than a part and more independent than servile . . . the value of the person, his dignity and rights belong to the order of things naturally sacred.[9]

Maritain clearly echoes here the characteristically liberal concern with freedom and autonomy. He clearly conceives of the person as an independent "whole," suggesting that the person's fulfillment is independent of others and of the community. His account thereby deviates from the communitarian idea of the self as embedded through and through in the community, such that its identity, goal, good, and the like are inseparable from those of the community. Despite Maritain's claim that the self qua individual is related to the community as a part to the whole, it must not be forgotten that the individual is simply one aspect of the self or human being; from the other aspect, namely, the person, the self is conceived as a "whole" in and of itself. That is to say, even though Maritain believes in true human flourishing only within the context of a community, he nonetheless has a fuller conception of the precommunity self, of what the self is solely in virtue of itself, than the communitarians. Hence, the self qua person has a certain autonomy vis-à-vis the community to which it belongs, an autonomy that does not seem to have application in the conceptual scheme of the communitarians. This is why Maritain maintains that a political community is "a whole composed of 'wholes' " and that the community owes the person freedom and autonomy due to the person's higher spiritual telos, and thus, the community is, in a sense, subordinated to the individual person. That is, Maritain shares in the liberal notion of the community's responsibility, as it were, to act for the good of each individual and to protect his freedom, sometimes even at the expense of the welfare of the whole community. Hence, he says, "the community is not its [the multitude's] final end. It is ordered to something better i.e., the supra-temporal ends of the human person. . . . It has its own proper goodness on condition that it recognizes this subordination [to the individual persons of the community]."[10]

In sum, then, Maritain's position with respect to the self's relation to the community might be stated as follows: (1) every member of the community qua individual is subject to the community as a whole, and (2) the community is subject to every member qua person. Alternatively, one could say that on the physical level Maritain has communitarian tendencies, whereas on the spiritual level, liberal tendencies. This is in many ways a misleading oversimplification, for, among other things, it ignores the fact that Maritain does not see a dichotomy between the physical and spiritual. He holds that the self qua individual and the self qua person are not in opposition to each other, nor are they two separate entities within the self. They are, rather, as mentioned already, two aspects of being human. Whether or to what extent the communitarian dimensions of his account of the self, on the one hand, and the liberal dimensions, on the other, can be held together without internal incoherence is an issue to be explored later. For now, suffice it to note that Maritain himself was aware of the tension within his account.

> On the one hand, life in society is natural to the human person, and, on the other hand—because the person as such is a root of independence—there will always exist a certain tension between the person and society. This paradox, this tension, this conflict, are themselves both natural and inevitable.[11]

The Good

Now it will be evident in what follows that Maritain's account of the common good is conceptually inseparable from his distinction between the self as individual and the self as person. This is clear when Maritain maintains, for example, that the common good of the community is "neither the mere collection of private goods, nor the proper good of the whole . . . which sacrifices the parts to itself; it is, therefore, common to both the whole and the parts in which it flows back and which, in turn, must benefit from it."[12]

The notion of a good common to both the community and the self is crucial for Maritain, for things that are perfective of the self will benefit the community as a whole, and things that are perfective of the community will benefit the self precisely because these goods are shared. Maritain's scheme of the *individual* serving the community and the common good, in turn, serving the person is rendered more intelligible in this context. The individual is subordinated to the common good, for such service is due to the community of which the individual is a part and of which he has a fair share of goods and privileges and that makes it possible for him to live a truly *human* life in the first place.

Although the *individual* is subject to the common good as just described, it is clear that this common good to which he contributes "flows back" to the *person* in the form of goods that are more valuable that those he originally contributed. Hence, Maritain states that the good of the person and the common good are related "in terms of reciprocal subordination and mutual implication."[13] The individual goods that constitute the common good and that flow back and forth between it and the self, according to Maritain, include, among others, "roads, schools, stable financial condition of the state, formal laws, institutions, military power, traditions, cultural treasures," and a sort of moral good described as "the civic conscience, political virtues and sense of right and liberty, spiritual riches, unconsciously operative hereditary wisdom, moral rectitude, justice, friendship, happiness, and virtue."[14] Clearly, these goods are necessary for the good life of a person. They are, in fact, what makes that person fully human, and, thus, Maritain asserts that "society is *required* to accomplish human dignity."[15]

Maritain explains that the foregoing is true because he adheres to the Thomistic–Aristotelian view that man is an essentially political and social animal and thus that human nature is fulfilled only within political society and that the good of a community is common to all of its members: "Man is a political animal because he is a rational animal, because reason requires development through character training, education, and the cooperation of other men."[16] It follows from all of this that the common good and the political life are a genuine good of the person, a good perfective of himself, and a fulfillment of part of the natural telos of human being, for "its [politics'] end is the good human life."[17] Maritain explains this as follows: "The social polity is essentially directed, by reason for its own temporal end . . . to lead the generality to a level of material, moral, and intellectual life . . . such as will positively assist each person in the progressive conquest of the fullness of personal life."[18]

This is not the whole of Maritain's conception of the good, however, for he asserts that a human being has an even greater good, to aspire to, namely, his *ultimate* end or good, which is perfective of his spiritual capacity and as such transcends the political sphere. It is important to note that even though the ultimate human end is beyond political society, the good human life provided by the common good and political society is still a good and an end in itself, a "temporal end," and it is thereby constitutive of the human *telos*. It is, however, only *partially* constitutive of the human *telos* because of the transcendent end to which man is ordered. In relation to this transpolitical end, the common good can be seen as a constitutive means to this higher good, for it prepares the person inasmuch as it provides him with what is necessary for pursuing this higher end, such as education, "moral rectitude," the virtues, and the ability to transcend his individuality through the shared ends of the community and through the opportunity for knowledge and love within society. This is why Maritain says that "politics' end is a system of life worthy of what is of most importance to man, that is to say, the spirit"[19] and that

> the common good is at once material and moral. But it is not its [the multitude's] final end. It is ordered to something better, the supratemporal ends of the human person . . . the temporal common good is its intermediate or infravalent end. . . . It has its own proper goodness [that is, it is an end of its own] on condition that it recognizes this.[20]

The common good, therefore, serves both as a temporal human good — and in this manner, as an end in and of itself — and as an intermediate end to the higher transcendent human good. Furthermore, it is in virtue of the human being's transcendent end that Maritain asserts that "the person, his dignity and his rights belong to the order of things naturally sacred."[21] Although the "material, moral and intellectual goods" are incorporated into the community and into the functioning and goals of the state, that is, they are instituted in the political domain, the spiritual good of the transcendent end is divorced from the political sphere and consequently is beyond the domain of the common good. Therefore, it follows that the person is "free to choose his religious path at his own risk; his freedom of conscience is a natural inviolable right."[22] With respect to material, moral, and intellectual goods, the person finds them in community and attains them by virtue of being a member of this community. The spiritual good, however, is not provided in the political community, but rather it is the community's function to (1) respect the dignity of each man in virtue of his ultimate, spiritual end, and leave each man free to choose and pursue this end according to his own "conscience" and (2) provide the means for the pursuit of this end and the goods necessary for personal spiritual development. Therefore, Maritain states, "in light of the eternal value and absolute dignity of the soul, society exists for each person and is subordinate thereto."[23]

Given the foregoing explication of Maritain's general conception of the good, we can now examine its relevance to the communitarian and libertarian conceptions of good. As far as Maritain's account of the *common* good is concerned, what he has in mind is very much akin to the communitarian account. This affinity can be seen in at least four points: (1) the common good is common to the community as a whole and to each member; (2) the common good and the community are constitutive of the good of each member; (3) the good of the human being as such is realizable *only* within the context of a community, since man is by nature a "political animal"; (4) the common good functions, among other things, as an objective standard by which the preferences, goals, and the like of each member are evaluated and molded.

However, with respect to the spiritual *telos*, to that which transcends the common good, Maritain begins to sound more liberal. When he is concerned with the distinctly *spiritual* good, he no longer calls for the good to be communally embodied but grants the person certain autonomy in pursuing the good. Maritain, thus, holds the freedom to choose one's spiritual good to be sacred and inviolable. It is very important to keep in mind that the person is granted this freedom *not* by virtue of the fact that doing so is for the sake of the common good, but rather, by virtue of the person's own spiritual good; and thus the rights of the human person "are rights rooted in the vocation of the person."[24] That is, it is not granted to the person qua community member but qua person. Moreover, his emphasis on the "inviolability" of the person's freedom renders him sounding more like a liberal.

The Community

As should be evident by now, the notions of the community and of the good are intertwined and mutually interdependent for Maritain. But more must be said about his notion of community.

For one thing, Maritain says, unsurprisingly, that "living together does not mean occupying the same place in space; living together means sharing as men in a certain common task."[25] Living in a community does not merely mean a group of people gathered together and contingently related to one another; it implies an interactive and cooperative whole comprised of persons who are all working toward the common good and who are all dependent upon each other for their personal development or perfection. As Maritain says, "man is a political animal . . . because reason requires development through character training, education, and the cooperating of other men, and because society is thus indispensable to human dignity."[26] The community's aim is to provide for human development in a very broad sense, that is, to provide for a good human life in general. This includes providing for "man's need of others for his material, intellectual, and moral life," needs due to "the indigence of human nature."[27] This is reminiscent of the communitarian idea of the self as embedded within a community and needing the community to find itself and to define its ends, roles, and activities.

Second, it is obvious that for Maritain there is no dichotomy between politics and morality, nor between public and private morality. The common good that the community seeks is moral through and through. The community seeks the moral good as its end and guides its members to a proper moral life and to moral rectitude through moral education. Maritain concludes that "the common good requires the development of the virtues in the mass of citizens."[28] He even goes so far as to state that "a general Christian education for the nation, a general development of Christian habits and Christian instincts is in fact a condition for the political success of democracy."[29]

Third—and this is perhaps the most important point in the light of what is to come in the next part of this essay—the assumption to this point has been that, for Maritain, the very concept of community is more or less straightforward and unproblematic. For example, we have assumed for the sake of theoretical simplicity that for him "political community," "community," "society," and "state" are more or less extensively equivalent. It is now necessary to say something about why this is not the case. The community or society is a cooperative framework that is natural to human beings as such insofar as its very existence and function is to actualize or perfect their distinctive potentialities. It is the community or society that the self as individual serves and to which he is "subject, and the community or society, in term, serves the self qua person. The state, however, is a *part* of the community; it is the community's 'topmost machine.' "[30] It is "concerned with the maintenance of law, the promotion of the common welfare and public order, and public affairs," and this institutional superstructure is "an instrument in the service of man."[31] Maritain brings out the significance of the distinction when he goes on to say that "the human person as an individual is for the body politic (or society) and the body politic (or society) is for the human person as a person; but man is by no means for the State and the State is for man."[32] Is this not to say that the state is a mere means for imposing the order of the common good and for establishing the principles of the common good as public principles? Then it is not a good in and of itself, but good only qualifiedly, that is, insofar as it aids the community in actualizing the common good. The community or society, however, is a natural manifestation of what is characteristically human and as such it is intrinsically good.

Interpretation and Evaluation

Having delineated Maritain's views on the self, the good, and community, let us explore in greater detail how his views relate to communitarianism and liberalism. Here are four plausible and philosophically interesting ways to interpret Maritain, only one of which turns out to be adequate.

1. Maritain could be taken for a true liberal, someone firmly and theoretically committed to the conceptual framework of liberalism. How then make sense of his pervasive communitarian rhetoric? By calling it rhetoric; and suggesting that, while he often talks of community and the common good, he is not really theoretically committed to what he then says.

2. Maritain could be taken as genuinely and theoretically committed to the conceptual schemes of both communitarianism and liberalism in one way or another. Whether he is talking like a liberal or like a communitarian, he does so sincerely and with assent. It is not, pace the proponent of (1), mere rhetoric.

3. Another plausible interpretation would be the reverse of (1). Maritain could be taken as a true communitarian who sometimes uses the rhetoric of liberalism in order more effectively to communicate his ideas to a modern and largely liberal audience.

4. Finally, Maritain could be taken as theoretically committed to communitarianism. Thus far (4) is no different from (3). The difference is the absence of the rhetoric defense when confronted with liberal language in Maritain. Maritain is seen as somewhat committed to liberalism at the practical level. Alternatively, one might express it this way: Maritain is a thoroughgoing communitarian with respect to *ideal* political order, but he is a liberal with respect to *practical* politics. When it comes to putting his ideas into practice, that is, he makes certain genuine concessions to liberalism.

The prima facie plausibility of (1) rests on statements of Maritain indicating his serious concern with human dignity, freedom, rights, and fair distribution of goods due to each individual. For example: "The primary reason for which men, united in a political society, need the State, is the order of justice."[33] A proponent of (1) would interpret Maritain's notion of the common good as a "thin" theory of the good, referring to those primary social goods that every individual considers desirable and worthy of pursuit, regardless of his conception of the good or plan of life. Accordingly, one could argue that Maritain's emphasis on community as indispensable to human persons merely refers to the fact that it is only within a community that the individual's freedom can be guaranteed.

Nonetheless, (1) is patently implausible: there are too many obstacles in the way of sustaining it. First, when Maritain says that the self as individual is subordinate to the common good, he clearly could not be referring to a "thin" theory of the good, let alone defending the inviolability and autonomy of the individual. Second, he often asserts that the aim of the political community is intrinsically moral — moral in the "thick" sense of the word, as it were — and this is quite incompatible with liberalism's politics of neutrality. Third, his emphasis on the need of human beings to pursue the good in community and the need of the common good to include the intellectual, moral, and "quasi-spiritual" aspects of the good, as well as material goods, clearly demonstrates that he holds objective standards for the good rather than promoting the individual's autonomy in choosing his conception of the good as he sees fit.

The second possibility is more plausible than the first, insofar as it recognizes that Maritain is genuinely committed to communitarianism. And the impetus for (2) finds its origin in certain statements made by Maritain, such as the following:

> The true conception of political life is neither exclusively personalist nor exclusively communal . . . [political society] is both personal and communal in such a way that these two terms call for and imply one another. Hence, there is nothing more illusory than to pose the problem of the person and the common good in terms of opposition. In reality, it is posed in terms of reciprocal subordination and mutual implication.[34]

But what would it really mean, with respect to (2), to say that Maritain is theoretically committed to both liberalism and communitarianism? On the one hand, as communitarian, Maritain would have to endorse, inter alia, a thick, substantive notion of the good that guides the community as a whole and its members. On the other hand, as a liberal, he would have to say that a person's pursuit of this thick, substantive good would be in accordance with his dignity if and only if the person freely or autonomously chooses to do so. This would mean that on the one hand the community is so structured that certain substantive values — be they moral, intellectual or aesthetic — are promoted as the constitutive means for attaining the good. On the other hand, the community, insofar as it is a liberal community, must not only permit its members freely to choose or accept the community's conception of the good and its attendant standard of evaluation, but it must also actively promote the intrinsic value of the autonomy of each person to make the choice for himself. The proponent of (2) could argue that the community truly recognizes and respects the spiritual dignity and worth of each person.

Whatever merits it may have, (2) is highly implausible for several reasons. First, if Maritain were truly committed to the conceptual frameworks of both communitarianism and liberalism, most of his writings in political thought would be reduced to mere wishful thinking. He would be endorsing the communitarian good and values but he would not endorse promoting or enforcing these values unless all the members of a community freely choose to pursue them and to work together for the common good. Since such an ideal situation is unlikely, to say the least, his writings would not be about how a community or state ought to operate but merely about how they *would* operate if the ideal state of affairs were actualized; that is, if everyone ended up freely choosing the true good. His political thought would then have no possible practical application. His thought would not be, in the phrase, "action guiding."

Second, (2) leads to insurmountable internal inconsistencies. The two most obvious are these. It entails two incompatible views of human nature: the liberal view of human nature, according to which the identity and essence of the moral agent is given prior to and independently of the community and is manifested most fully in the exercise of autonomy or freedom, *and* the communitarian view of human nature, according to which human beings can flourish only in the context of a community and in the pursuit of and attainment of the good that is not so much chosen as discovered. Furthermore, it entails two incompatible views of the role of the political community. According to liberalism, the political community as a whole is to remain neutral with respect to any substantive conception of the good, whereas communitarianism requires it to be committed to a particular conception of the good.

The third reason for the implausibility of (2) lies in the fact that even Maritain's alleged liberal values are not really liberal in the ordinary sense of the adjective. When he endorses certain liberal ideas, such as freedom and rights, it is not at all clear that he is promoting them in the same way that an ordinary liberal does or even that he is speaking of the same things. That is to say, it is quite evident from his writings that his account of liberal values and theses are highly revisionary. Take, for example, the concept of rights. He emphasizes the rights of smaller communities, the rights of the Catholic Church, and especially rights of the family, which he calls the "primordial society . . . prior to the state."[35] This is a far cry from the standard liberal thesis that only individuals are legitimate bearers of rights, insofar as rights are, among other things, an individual's entitlements as an autonomous being. Moreover, according to Maritain, rights are not absolute or inviolable: "these rights, being human, are, like everything human, subject to conditioning and limitation . . . the rights of man as a person involved in the life of the community cannot be given room in human history without restricting, to some extent, the freedoms and rights of man as an individual person." That is, considerations of community may often override the individual's rights.[36] The same applies to freedom. Once one examines closely what Maritain means by it, it is evident that he and liberals scarcely mean the same thing by the word. These matters come up again in discussing (3) and (4).

The merit of (3) is that, unlike (1) and (2), it does justice to Maritain and recognizes that the *basic* orientation of his thought is communitarian. According to this interpretation, his emphasis on human freedom in no way implies that members of the community are free to choose whatever conception of the good they see fit. Instead, to understand the emphasis on freedom, the argument goes, we need to understand exactly what Maritain means by "freedom," for it is not at all similar to liberal freedom.

That this is true is made evident by the fact that, for Maritain, the condition of freedom is not satisfied simply by acting autonomously without any external or internal constraints. The additional criterion that must be satisfied is that one must do the "right" thing; otherwise, one is not truly free. And the standard for doing the "right" thing is none other than the good that is discovered, not merely chosen. For Maritain, one is granted freedom in order to pursue the objective good in the deepest and most *human* manner, that is, to pursue the good *freely.* Only free actions are fully human, because the very "vocation of the human person" is to be "a spiritual and free agent."[37] The aim of the political community in fostering freedom is to allow its members to be fully human in pursuing the objective good, their spiritual *telos.*

Maritain differs from the liberals not only in his theoretical understanding of freedom but also on a more practical level. For the liberal, freedom requires the state to remain neutral with respect to exercising freedom in any particular way; it lessens the practical role and responsibility of the state because the state is required only to protect individual freedom but not to dictate how or in what way freedom is to be exercised. If it did, liberals argue, the very point of having freedom in the first place would be undermined. Maritain's conception of freedom, however, gives the community and the state additional responsibility, for it requires them to aid the person in exercising his freedom *properly,* as well as to protect this freedom. The aim of society is to "positively assist each person in the progressive conquest of the fullness of personal life and spiritual liberty."[38] Maritain often refers to the "conquest" of freedom, implying that freedom needs to be tamed or conquered by being ordered to its proper ends. He explains that to pursue one's spiritual *telos* requires knowledge and love, which allow the person to transcend physical individuality. Maritain states that "the openness to the communications of intelligence and love is the nature of the spirit . . . and demands an entrance into relationship with other persons."[39] Clearly, since a person can attain such relationships and truly develop his abilities to know and to love only in community, the community takes on a quasi-spiritual role, so to speak. Therefore, Maritain's "liberal tendencies," manifest in granting persons freedom in virtue of their spiritual calling, are scarcely liberal because, one, the belief in this spiritual and transcendent end clearly constitutes a specific, thick, substantive, conception of the good, and, two, the community's function is to help persons pursue their spiritual end, which requires the partial incorporation of the spiritual good into the communal realm. In a word, "the conquest of freedom in the social and political, as well as in the spiritual order . . . is the aim of true *democracies*."[40] The clincher comes when Maritain asserts that "to thus obey him [who is rightfully in the position of authority] who really fulfills the duty to direct the common work toward the common good is to act as a *free* man."[41]

The merit of (3) is that it pierces through the surface of Maritain's liberal language to the communitarian values beneath. Its demerit lies in its not doing justice to the liberal elements of his thought by dismissing them as rhetorical. What Maritain means by "freedom" is indeed different from what a typical liberal means by it. Yet it is equally true that freedom is not a fundamental concept in the communitarian framework. Communitarians are not so much opposed to freedom as that the concept has no significant application in their scheme. Hence (3) fails to do full justice to Maritain's belief in the centrality of the concept of freedom for political philosophy. Liberal elements may not be as pervasive as communitarian ones in Maritain's thought, but they are there. For Maritain, the self as person, though not as individual, transcends the political community, and this suggests a pre-communal or pre-political status for persons. The value of persons is ontologically prior to the value of the community, residing as it does in the person qua human being, not qua member of a community.

And so we come to (4). Like (3), it has the merit of recognizing that the fundamental orientation of Maritain's thought is communitarian, but it is free of (3)'s reductionism, for it also acknowledges that the liberal tendencies in Maritain's thought cannot be simply brushed away as mere rhetoric but must be fitted into his overall communitarian scheme. Maritain is taken to be a communitarian at the theoretical level, but a liberal at the practical level. Consider Maritain's reflection on how it was possible for him to sign the United Nations Universal Declaration of Human Rights along with those who adhered to conceptual schemes radically opposed to his own. He saw this as definite proof that "men mutually opposed in their theoretical conceptions can come to a merely practical agreement regarding a list of human rights."[42] But what exactly is the distinction Maritain has in mind?

At the theoretical level, Maritain is primarily a communitarian. This is abundantly clear from the fundamental importance he attaches to the notions of the common good, the community, and the inherently moral character of the political life. In addition to being primarily communitarian, however, he may also be called a revised liberal — call it liberal — at the theoretical level. He attaches importance to the characteristically liberal themes of freedom and rights, but his understanding of them is transformed by his communitarian outlook, inasmuch as he maintains that freedom is linked to doing the right thing in the light of an understanding of the true good. Not only are individuals bearers of rights; rights are sometimes overridden for the sake of the common good. This transformation notwithstanding, Maritain draws inspiration from the liberal framework. Thus it is that he is a liberal.

At the practical level, Maritain is mostly communitarian. This is quite clear from the fact that Maritain believes that his communitarian vision should be practically and concretely implemented. However, as was the case at the theoretical level, he is also liberal at the practical level. This practical liberalism — call it liberalism — is closer to what is ordinarily meant by liberals than theoretical liberalism. To understand why this is the case, take the notion of rights. According to Maritain, human rights are derived from the human *telos* and, among other things, promote the good of family life and of smaller communities, and are theoretically subject to being limited "to some extent" and some time "within human history."[43] In practice, however, the theoretical derivation is often left behind and the fact that rights are not in principle unconditional and absolute is easily forgotten since they are limited so rarely and so slightly. Therefore, in practice, they amount basically to liberal rights. As stated earlier, Maritain himself recognized this in signing the UN declaration. Simply put, Maritain's revisionary liberal rights involve a certain lofty vision of what they are meant to be in and of themselves, and since this lofty vision is not fully realized or acknowledged at the practical level for various reasons, the way they are exercised in reality is not altogether easy to distinguish from the way liberal rights in the ordinary sense are exercised.

The second reason that Maritain is more liberal in practice than in theory concerns the reality of modern politics. Although Maritain believes in and aims for communitarian ideals for the most part, he grants certain concessions to liberalism — concessions he deems necessary because of the exigency of pluralism and of the tendency of political power to be misused. Maritain makes it clear that he is concerned with the dangers of states becoming totalitarian. This had to be an urgent issue for him, living when he did and witnessing the rise of many totalitarian regimes. Maritain asserts emphatically that "the people are above the State . . . the State is for the people . . . the people have the will, and the means, to assert their own control over the State."[44] It is this fear of the abuse of state power that seems to explain Maritain's preoccupation with freedom.

Evaluation

If it is granted that (4) offers the most plausible way to interpret Maritain's political thought, a question still remains as to whether or not his liberal tendencies—what we have called liberal and communitarian—are internally consistent with his predominantly communitarian scheme. Before turning to this, a caveat must be issued. With respect to Maritain's practical considerations, he may be justified in fearing state power and endorsing freedom and rights in the light of this fear. This practical consideration is beyond the scope of this paper, however, which will confine itself to the theoretical basis of his thought.

It should be clear that Maritain firmly and uncompromisingly upholds the common good, and that he would adhere to the communitarian thesis of the priority of the good over the right since he believes that the common good has primacy. Justice must be understood in the light of the common good, therefore, for the conception of the good embodied in the life of the community is the standard for determining what is due to each person. This is also clear from the fact that the function of the common good, as it were, is to "flow back" to persons in the form of goods. The good that the common good and the community provide the person is a fully human good; consequently, it includes material, moral, and intellectual goods, as well as the "quasi-spiritual" goods the person needs to pursue his spiritual *telos*. Furthermore, the state as the primary instrument of the common good is itself subordinate to the common good and to the aim of the community in general. Thus, the state is also concerned with justice, with the distribution of goods, and, although more indirectly, with granting the person what he is due in virtue of the common good.

It follows directly from the foregoing explanation that in any community that embodies Maritain's conception of the common good and of the state, the person's goods and what would correspond to the person's "rights," that is, his entitlements qua member of the community, are intrinsic to the considerations of the common good and consequently are naturally and necessarily granted by the state acting for the sake of the common good. Therefore, it is not clear why Maritain finds it necessary to emphasize the importance of the person's freedom, and rights, whose very function is to protect the good of the person from the encroachment of the community and the state, when it is precisely the role and the nature of this community and state to provide for the good of the person in the first place. The good and the freedom of the person are being protected from that which provides the person with the good. That is to say, the language of freedom and rights presupposes a certain adversarial relationship, a relationship characterized by a certain degree of distrust, between the community and the state on the one hand and the individual members on the other.

Maritain states that "society is required to accomplish human dignity"[45] and, as explained earlier, it is the community that enables a person to live a fully human life. So why does Maritain find it necessary to guarantee the person freedom and rights that protect the person's dignity from the very community that originally granted the person his dignity in the first place and also from the very state that has promoted this dignity indirectly? No doubt Maritain is worried about the power of state, but if the state is subordinated to the common good, as it is according to his view, then the person, at least in theory, need not arm himself against the state.

Furthermore, one could argue that which is being guaranteed by rights and freedom is that which is beyond the scope of the common good, and this does need protection after all. For example, freedom of worship is beyond the scope of the common good in the sense that the common good does not specify or promote any specific religious belief. The right to worship, then, is simply a given. However, the common good is ordered to the good of the person in general, to what comprises the human good for each person, and it is ordered to the good of the community as a whole. Thus, it should recognize what will be beneficial to the person, including recognizing the need for freedom of worship if the community is pluralistic. Therefore, the community will respect this freedom and will do what is helpful to the proper fulfillment of the person's spiritual good, as is made clear by Maritain. In sum, there is no need for a person to assert his right to free worship over and against the community, which, in working toward the good of persons, will recognize what is good and what is "right" for that person and will therefore grant the person this freedom on its own and not as a response to its members clamoring for freedom of worship.

If and when the person's goods and rights are somewhat limited and overridden by the community, this will only occur when such limitation is necessary to preserve the common good or the good of the community as a whole. On such an occasion, the person accepts making a sacrifice for this common good, which provides him with so much, insofar as it allows him to lead a fully human life. Furthermore, he should realize that this sacrifice benefits him insofar as it is benefiting the common good and the community from which he receive his good.

Maritain states that freedom and rights are granted to persons by virtue of their human *telos,* that is, by virtue of the transcendent end of human nature. In essence, this is equivalent to granting rights to a person qua human being or in virtue of that person's humanity. Maritain indicates that this is in fact the case by sometimes referring to "primordial rights," rights of the prepolitical or precommunal person.[46] In essence, this means that the person is granted rights simply for being a human being. However, as Maritain explains it, it is the community and the political life that enable the person to be human and to fulfill or perfect this human nature. Why then the necessity of demanding from the community and the state the rights of a person qua human being when it is the community and the state that enable this person to become human in the first place? The goods and freedom are granted to the person through the common good because the common good embodies the good of all persons in the good of the community, and vice versa. Thus, a person receives goods in virtue of the common good and in virtue of the whole community. It would be more appropriate, therefore, to think of the person as being granted goods and "rights" qua member of a community than simply qua human being.

The foregoing argument is further buttressed by the fact that the human prepolitical or precommunal status by which Maritain grants persons freedom and rights is not consistent with the view that human nature is fulfilled in community where the opportunity is given to know and love, to develop morally and intellectually. If all these are necessary for the person, in what does the person's prepolitical or precommunal status lie? Maritain accepts the claim that humans are political and social animals. If human beings are defined by their political and communal interactions, one wonders if they truly have a prepolitical status.[47]

That Maritain's political thought seems to be fundamentally communitarian with liberal elements is due to his distinction between individual and person. But is this distinction tenable? Among the difficulties one can have about it is that it involves a dualism of the self, with body and its needs grounding the self as individual, and soul with its transcendent goal grounding personhood. The self as an individual is a part of the whole that society is, but as a person is a whole, not a part, and transcends it. Maritain explicitly denies this dualism, of course, but is the denial consistent with the distinction?

The suggestion some saw in the person/individual distinction as explained above was that the common good is subservient to the good of the individual person. This followed from Maritain's opposing of the political and the spiritual, and making the political common good subservient to the latter. To say that the common good is subservient to the good of the person who has a transcendent spiritual ultimate end is interpretable as making the private good of the person primary.

The 1943 controversy pushed Maritain in the direction of recognizing the primacy of the common good. The political common good, and the state that is its instrument, do not exhaust the good for man. Does this mean that some other, noncommon good takes precedence over the political common good? Or is it not rather the case that a more comprehensive common good, God himself, man's ultimate end, is primary? The person would not then be an autonomous whole but part of a whole larger than the political. Critics saw the liberalism of the autonomous self in Maritain's early discussion of the relation of person to the common good. When the dust settled, in *The Person and the Common Good,* it is clear that he does not wish to say that.[48] What does this do to the distinction between individual and person?

As John Paul II has emphasized in *Veritatis Splendor,* the human person is a unity of body and soul, acting as a single unit. The person is a member of, a part of, the domestic and political societies as a person and not simply because he has a body. Perhaps the reason that Maritain's talk of self as individual sometimes evokes the liberal self and sometimes does not is that he cannot really accept the liberal account of self. But this rejection renders otiose the distinction between the self as individual and as person. Is it only a dubious distinction in Maritain that suggests that his political theory can broker the differences between liberalism and communitarianism?

Conclusion

This essay started with two aims: first, to examine how the contemporary debate between liberals and communitarians could contribute to an understanding of the political thought of Jacques Maritain, and, second, to investigate the extent to which his political thought, insofar as it is a blend of communitarianism and liberalism, is internally consistent.

On the first point, it has been established that the most plausible way of characterizing his political philosophy is as fundamentally communitarian but including some liberal elements at both the theoretical and practical levels.

On the second point, it has been shown that the liberal elements at the theoretical level are in serious tension, if not inconsistency, with his overall communitarian framework. At the least, it has been shown that if he were truly committed to his communitarian framework, he would have no theoretical need for making room for such liberal concepts as freedom and human rights. If there is a need for such concepts at all in Maritain's political thought, it may be at the practical level.

Notes

1. Fred Crosson, "Maritain on Natural Rights," *Review of Metaphysics* (1983): 895–912; Alasdair MacIntyre, *Three Rival Versions of Moral Inquiry* (Notre Dame, Ind.: University of Notre Dame Press, 1990), 76.

2. Jacques Maritain, *Scholasticism and Politics,* trans. Mortimer Adler (New York: Macmillan, 1940), 56.

3. Jacques Maritain, *The Person and the Common Good* (New York: Charles Scribner's Sons, 1947), 24.

4. Ibid., 27. Emphasis added.

5. Jacques Maritain, "The Conquest of Freedom," *Freedom: Its Meaning,* ed. Ruth Ashen (New York: Harcourt Brace, 1940), 50.

6. Jacques Maritain, *The Rights of Man and Natural Law*, trans. Doris Anson (New York: Scribner's, 1943), 5.

7. Maritain, "Conquest," 635.

8. Ibid.

9. Maritain, "Conquest," 636.

10. Jacques Maritain, *True Humanism*, trans. Margot Adamson (New York: Scribner's, 1938), 127.

11. Maritain, *Rights*, 18.

12. Maritain, *The Person and the Common Good*, 40–41.

13. Ibid., 55.

14. Ibid., 42.

15. Maritain, *Scholasticism*, 69.

16. Maritain, *The Person and the Common Good*, 38.

17. Maritain, "Religion and Culture," *Essays in Order*, ed. Christopher Dawson and J. F. Burns (New York: Macmillan, 1931).

18. Maritain, *True Humanism*, 128.

19. Maritain, "Religion and Culture," 125.

20. Maritain, *True Humanism*, 127.

21. Maritain, "Conquest," 636.

22. Maritain, *True Humanism*, 128. See also *Rights*, 82.

23. Maritain, *Rights*, 13.

24. Maritain, *Man and the State*, 80.

25. Ibid., 207.

26. Maritain, *The Person and the Common Good*, 38.

27. Maritain, *Rights*, 5.

28. Ibid., 10.

29. Maritain, *Scholasticism*, 69.

30. Maritain, *Man and the State*, 12.

31. Ibid.

32. Ibid.

33. Maritain, *Man and the State*, 20.

34. Maritain, *The Person and the Common Good*, 55.

35. Maritain, *Man and the State*, 104.

36. Ibid., 106.

37. Maritain, *Man and the State*, 80.

38. Maritain, *True Humanism*, 128.

39. Maritain, *Rights*, 5.

40. Maritain, *Scholasticism*, 85.

41. Ibid., 101.

42. Maritain, *Man and the State*, 76. See Ralph McInerny, *Art and Prudence: Studies in the Thought of Jacques Maritain* (Notre Dame: Notre Dame University Press, 1988), "Maritain and Natural Rights," 123–36.

43. Maritain, "Conquest," 106.

44. Maritain, *Man and the State*, 26.

45. Maritain, *Scholasticism*, 69.

46. Maritain, *Scholasticism,* 61.

47. See Frederick Crosson, "Maritain and Natural Rights," *Review of Metaphysics* (1983): 895–912.

48. On all this, see Ralph McInerny, "The Primacy of the Common Good," in *Art and Prudence,* 77–91.

10

Personal Dignity and the Common Good: A Twentieth-Century Thomistic Dialogue

Mary M. Keys

Even the devils philosophize, at least if we are to take C.S. Lewis's word for it. In his *Screwtape Letters,* "ravenously affectionate uncle Screwtape" writes the following words of wisdom to his nephew Wormwood, whom he is instructing in the art of tempting: "The whole philosophy of Hell rests on recognition of the axiom that one thing is not another thing, and, especially, that one self is not another self. *My good is my good, and your good is your good.* What one gains another loses."[1]

Now thoughtful citizens of many a modern Western democracy will be likely to find "hell's axiom" regarding the self and the good hitting uncomfortably close to home. While Kant may have been correct in arguing that a civil society of enlightened devils is possible, it is becoming more and more doubtful whether such a society is desirable, to say nothing of durable. There prevails in our polities a growing sense of dissatisfaction with at least some of the "blessings" of individualistic liberalism, not least of which is the weakening, at times bordering on disintegration, of nearly every level of social bond. As Tocqueville predicted, individual persons are increasingly left with a sense of isolation, insignificance, and lack of fulfillment. They exalt liberty, but have all but forgotten responsibility.

To such persons the very notion of a "common good" may well seem utterly unintelligible, regardless of the longing or nostalgia it might yet evoke. Infinitely more common terms in our political discourse include the "GNP" and the "standard of living"—essentially referring, of course, to little more than the sum total or average amount of cash in individuals' wallets and bank accounts. *My income is my income and your income is your income; my choice of how to spend my income is mine and your choice is yours.* Ultimately, *"my good is my good and your good is yours."*

For many if not most North American intellectuals, this situation is interpreted as a sign of a real if bittersweet advance, a certain moral and intellectual coming of age. Witness, for example, the 1989 American Council of Learned Societies Report "Speaking for the Humanities." Oozing dogmatism and condescension, the report proudly proclaims that "what matters most in modern thought challenges claims to universality." Moreover, only hopelessly naive, simple souls continue to hold "the belief that members of a society can act against their own self-interest, recognizing a larger social good."[2]

Against this dismal backdrop, however, a small but serious group of scholars has sounded a warning call. Leaders of this new intellectual "counterculture" include Alasdair MacIntyre, who has forcefully argued that this radical "privatization of the good" is symptomatic of a serious societal and spiritual sickness[3], and Thomas L. Pangle. In his recent work *The Ennobling of Democracy,* Pangle makes the following case:

> [T]here is a discernible link between the weakened condition of our intellectual integrity and the relative laxness of our civic spirit: the two have an important source in common. Some widespread, if vague, awareness of this deeper truth has emerged from our discovery of the link between intellectual and civic virtue in Eastern Europe. . . .
>
> What most threatens us, I would suggest, is the deadening conformism to a bloodless and philistine relativism that saps the will and the capacity to defend any principled basis of life. This threat endangers civic and philosophic life equally.[4]

Pangle further suggests that we in the universities commence our liberation from this stifling situation by a frank and truly open-minded encounter with some of the great minds of the past, the thinkers who passionately searched for objective, universal truth on both the theoretical and moral planes. It is in this spirit that I propose to turn now to the thought of Thomas Aquinas, just such a philosopher–theologian who, moreover, held that for citizens, philosophers, and believers there exists a real "common good."

To recover a truly Thomistic conception of this "common good" and its relation to the good of individual persons, however, we ought first to note that some fifty years ago two well-respected interpreters of Thomas's thought engaged in a highly publicized debate on this very subject. These were professors Jacques Maritain and Charles De Koninck. In recent years several scholars have brought this exchange back out of dusty library corners into the light of day, with renewed interest perhaps attributable to the intensification of the crisis of individualism in both scholarly and civic life.[5] Yet to my knowledge none has attempted a comprehensive analysis of the respective arguments of these two philosophers. The principal reason for this neglect would appear to be twofold: on the one hand, the common good as such was not the focus of most of the studies in question; on the other, the terms of the debate appeared too difficult, abstract, and unfamiliar for the modern reader to be bothered.[6]

Before beginning our effort to fill this scholarly gap, we should note still one further possible cause for its existence. Unfortunately, the original exchange between Maritain and De Koninck became a little too heated and, many perceived, nasty. Personal loyalties to one or the other professor therefore threatened to preclude the dispassionate assessment of their arguments. De Koninck's principal work on this subject, originally written in French, was never translated into English and its author, unlike Maritain, is all but unknown to my generation of students. But now, with the advantage of hindsight and personal disinterest, the time is ripe for a reexamination.

Historical Background

To begin with, some historical background is in order. In 1943, the young dean of Laval University's faculty of philosophy, Charles De Koninck, published a little book bearing the inoffensive title *On the Primacy of the Common Good*. The problem was that he added a subtitle: *Against the Personalists*.[7] Now, De Koninck always maintained that his work was directed against what he regarded as erroneous *positions*, that he never intended an attack on specific *persons*. His message to all considering themselves "personalists" could be summarized with a piece of popular wisdom: "If the shoe fits, wear it."

But, if you will pardon the pun, some of those "personalists" took the whole thing personally. They read the book as an attack on Jacques Maritain, a major figure in the movement known as "personalist Thomism," and they leapt to his defense.

Things got still more interesting when two self-appointed witnesses for the defense—both distinguished professors, friends, and colleagues of Maritain—took the stand and proceeded to offer contradictory testimony. In a 1944 review of De Koninck's book, Yves Simon argued, in a generally civil and fairminded manner, that De Koninck's interpretation of Thomas and the positions he upheld were indeed correct; that these conclusions were shared by Maritain and that the positions De Koninck refuted were in no way those of Maritain; that De Koninck had probably not intended it, but that the net effect of allowing the public to believe that Maritain held such opinions resembled that of outright calumny.[8] But then, in 1945, I. Th. Eschmann published an essay entitled "In Defense of Jacques Maritain." He assured his readers that the positions assailed by De Koninck were indeed those of Maritain, *and* those of St. Thomas and of "all the Christian Fathers and theologians and philosophers"! Absolutely speaking, Eschmann maintained, the personal good holds primacy over the common, except within the well-defined confines of the practical or political sphere.[9] If nothing else, this confusion indicated that Maritain's views on this issue had not been set forth with sufficient clarity in early works such as *Three Reformers* (1927), *Integral Humanism* (1936), and *Scholasticism and Politics* (1939).

So the philosophic public awaited Maritain's own response. In the meantime, De Koninck wrote an extremely long response to Eschmann's attack entitled "In Defense of St. Thomas."[10] As had been the case with Eschmann's piece, the tone of this rebuttal left much to be desired. Polemics aside, it seems "fair to say that De Koninck demolished Eschmann," as Ralph McInerny has noted.[11] But it still remained to be seen whether Eschmann's argument that the good of the individual person takes precedence over the common good was in fact shared by Maritain.

At last, in 1947, the real Jacques Maritain stood up. He published a little book of his own, *The Person and the Common Good,* explicitly intended to answer what he also regarded as an "anonymous attack" and to clarify his views.[12] Since this is the work that Maritain himself regarded as the most precise and thorough presentation of his position, I will focus my analysis on a comparison of its argument with De Koninck's original presentation of his case in *On the Primacy of the Common Good,* although I will refer when necessary to other writings of our two authors.

Maritain and De Koninck Compared

The works of both Charles De Koninck and Jacques Maritain respond admirably to the twofold vocation of the political philosopher. Each recognizes his responsibility to the times and society in which it has been given him to live, and hence seeks to combat the manifest evils of fascism and Marxist totalitarianism, while at the same time pointing out the serious inadequacies of a politics founded upon the principles of acquisitive individualism. Furthermore, as philosophers they do not content themselves with providing a specific situational analysis and prescription: the concrete predicament of the modern West is treated within the context of an endeavor to bring to light the perennial truths concerning the human person, his place within society, and the ultimate end or purpose of his existence. Indeed, it is this latter aspect of their work that constitutes their primary concern: if we are to reach a true understanding of those things that are "first for us," we must never lose sight of those things that are "first simply," or "first in themselves."

Despite their shared purpose and equally professed Thomism, however, we have already indicated that De Koninck and Maritain do not arrive at precisely the same conclusions regarding the relation of the personal good and the common good. This fact can be gleaned from just a cursory glance at the first few pages of the two books on which this essay is based: Maritain's *The Person and the Common Good*, in which he professes proudly and early on his adherence to "Thomistic personalism," and De Koninck's not-so-subtly-titled *On the Primacy of the Common Good: Against the Personalists.*

How does a "personalist" interpretation of St. Thomas's thought differ from one that focuses on the "primacy" of the common good? In our endeavor to grasp this distinction, we may do well to choose as our starting point the concept of human dignity, or personal dignity. What is the real or ontological basis of this dignity? At the risk of oversimplification, we may say that for De Koninck it is the person's *rational nature*, foundation of the capacity to participate in and to adhere to freely, through knowledge and through love, an order (or better, as we shall see later, orders) that is greater than the individual; whereas for Maritain it is above all personal *freedom*, understood as the spiritual capacity to act independently of and to transcend any given order (with one crucial exception, as we shall also see).[13] De Koninck's approach to the problem is thoroughly and unabashedly classical, here taking this term to include medieval Christian or scholastic thought. Maritain's spirit is much more in tune with the times.

Nevertheless, modern as the thrust of Maritain's argument often seems, far from basing it upon, say, the thought of the German philosophers of freedom, he claims to ground it in the principles of the Angelic Doctor himself. How does Maritain proceed to substantiate this claim? His central piece of evidence drawn from the corpus of St. Thomas's writings appears to be the following line: "*Ratio partis contrariatur personae*"—"The concept of part is opposed to that of person." Whence Maritain maintains that "[i]t is a fundamental thesis of Thomism that *the person as such is a whole*,"[14] and therefore not primarily a part of a greater whole.

In the footnote to the above-mentioned citation, however, Maritain himself at least tacitly admits that this quotation, so crucial to his argument (especially insofar as he conceives it as building on the work of Aquinas), is used out of context. Thomas is not there considering human persons in their relation to society, or ordination or lack thereof to the common good; rather, he is discussing the separated human soul in relation to the whole or complete human person, a substantial unity of body and soul. Yet Maritain seems surprisingly undaunted by the scarcity and problematic nature of the textual support for his personalist position, despite the fact that most of his other citations from Thomas seem clearly to point the way to full agreement with De Koninck. In this same note Maritain contrasts the "sufficiently profound understanding" of Thomism possessed by himself and his associates with the mere "text-book Thomism" of at least one of his critics (our translator omits this passage, perhaps to smooth over the polemical aspect of the work). Maritain is surely correct in indicating that a deep understanding of a great philosopher's thought normally requires a thorough, careful, and penetrating study of the texts he has left us. But for this very reason we cannot but expect a correct understanding of Thomas's position and "principles" regarding so fundamental a question to find support in a far richer textual context than Maritain seems able to offer. A more careful examination of De Koninck's thesis and the interpretation on which it rests would then seem to be in order.

Against those who assert "that created persons are . . . absolute wholes and that their 'being-part' is secondary," De Koninck maintains, as his view and that of Thomas, that "we are, primarily and principally, *parts*" — parts of the family, of political society, of the created universe, of the City of God.[15] Now this is an awfully hard pill for children of modernity to swallow. We do not generally like the idea of being "parts." Kant has already written: we regard such a status as beneath our dignity. These circumstances serve to render De Koninck's book all the more helpful, for its author is that rare individual in modern times capable of making the counterargument in a manner that is both coherent and, remarkably, palatable. To be a part of a greater, more perfect whole; to use one's intelligence to recognize that fact; to freely choose to assume one's place in the order that constitutes the whole; and to work generously for the common good of that whole: all this serves to ennoble rather than to degrade a human being, to make him more of a person rather than less. The substantial integrity of his being remains untouched. Moreover, the human person's rational nature is essentially open to the whole and finds its fulfillment or perfection therein. What is of greatest value in our human constitution (the spiritual faculties of intellect and will) tends naturally toward the greater-than-self, toward those goods that are most *common* in the sense of being intrinsically communicable or sharable. "For this reason, we love naturally and preferentially the good of the whole."[16] Through participating in the common good, and indeed building it together with others on the practical planes of family, intermediate association and politics, the person achieves his end, i.e., attains perfection and finds happiness. Paradoxical as it may seem, it is by strictly subordinating our private goods to serve and partake of the common good that we achieve our truest and most complete *personal* good.

Here we must pause to emphasize that this understanding of common good is very far from modern collectivist or totalitarian notions of the nation-state as organic or substantial whole. One student of De Koninck has explicated this point as follows: Civil society is not itself a person, even though it is often compared to one. Its unity is only a "unity of order" (*unitas ordinis*), as distinguished from the substantial unity of the individual person. Its function is to enable its citizens to attain their full development, and it deserves its name only to the extent to which it promotes the ends to which human nature is ordered. The human beings who compose it are not destroyed by it, as they would be if they were parts of a substantial whole. The perfection that they reach remains intrinsic to them. Differently stated, the common good is not an alien good but the "proper good" (*bonum proprium*) of those who share in it. If the common good were not distributed among the members of the community, it would not be truly common. Only on this condition can it be an object of desire. The good sought by any being is necessarily its own good (*bonum suum*), whether it be a particular good or the common good, for which it has an even greater natural love. The need for justice and civic virtue is rooted in the potential conflict between these two types of good, or the tendency of the part to set itself up as the whole.[17]

In other words, the human being is a "part" of society in the sense that his or her fulfillment requires participating in or partaking of goods that transcend the purely private sphere of individuality. The person is not "part" of the community as the hand is part of the body, nor even, as some contemporary communitarian theorists suggest, as discovering his or her identity in a collective subjectivity, the only true repository of moral agency. To state the fundamental question in terms of "self (or even "person")-community," argues De Koninck, is to miss the heart of the matter. He proposes instead the following paradigm learned from Thomas:

> Instead of discussing the problem in terms of "person" and "society," I approach it in the fundamental terms of "proper good" and "common good". Ultimately, person and society are not to be judged by what they are absolutely, but by what is their perfection, i.e., by what is their good; that is the only way in which Aristotle and St. Thomas ever discussed this problem. To look upon the absolute comparison of person and society as the most basic consideration is distinctly modern. It is also distinctly modern to accord absolute priority to the subject. . . . From such a point of view, the problem of person and society quite naturally becomes the question: is the person better than society? instead of: is the proper good of the person better than his common good? When the problem has been so distorted, what can be expected in the solution?

The totalitarian solution is that the individual person is ordered and subjected to society. We are inclined, in rejecting this doctrine, to swing to the opposite extreme; but if we prescind from the common good of the persons which is the final, therefore first cause of society, we are left with a mere aggregate of individuals. . . . [18]

De Koninck thus indicates the way in which Thomas upholds the primacy of the common good while careful distinguishing it from the community per se. This is possible because for him the fundamental problem is not one of ontology simply, nor of epistemology, but rather of final causality. In other words, Aquinas takes the good seriously in its own right, focusing his concern on the good of persons and of the communities they comprise. For Aquinas, human persons—creatures possessed of reason and hence of free will—do have intrinsic moral worth. Their communities are not "organic" or substantial wholes with a quasi-independent status, but are rather "unities of order," "accidental unities." This sort of theoretical foundation appears well suited to support a moderate and balanced approach to political life.

To grasp the significance of De Koninck's argument, it will help to review the way which in such context Thomas characteristically employs the term "the good": not in the sense in which the good is formally identical with being as such, but rather in what is for him its most precise meaning, denoting final causality, the good as an end, the attainment of which constituted a being's proper perfection. "The essence of good consists in this, that something perfect another as an end, [and therefore] whatever is found to have the character of an end also has that of good. Now two things are essential to an end: It must be sought or desired by things which have not attained the end, and it must be loved by things which share the end. . . ."[19] Hence what Thomas most precisely means by a "common good": a final cause common to many, a single end which is capable of constituting the perfection of many. Moreover, he takes the good in this strict sense to be "*diffusivum secundum sui rationem,*" "diffusive of itself." It therefore follows that the better a good, the greater will be its intrinsic communicability. It is in this sense that De Koninck takes Aquinas to posit a "primacy of the common good" in human life.

To all of this Maritain responds with a "yes; but. . . . " The essential content of this "but" is summarized in the opening paragraph of his second chapter, "The Positions of St. Thomas on the Ordination of the Person to Its Ultimate End":

The human person is ordained directly to God as to its absolute ultimate end. Its direct ordination to God transcends every created common good—the common good of the political society and the intrinsic common good of the universe. Here is the fundamental truth governing the entire discussion—the truth in which nothing less than the very message of Christian wisdom in its triumph over Hellenic thought and every other pagan wisdom, henceforth toppled from their dominion, is involved.[20]

Maritain thus stresses the need to focus on the person's final, supernatural end, the intimately personal and incommunicable act that is "the beatific vision" (the unitive participation in the Trinitarian life, the core of that state of perfect bliss for humans more commonly known as "heaven"). He reminds us of St. Thomas's daring assertion that "*bonum gratiae unius majus est quam bonum naturae totius universi*"—"the good of grace of one [single person] is greater than the good of nature of the whole universe."[21] And this personal good of grace culminates in the state of being in which, according to Maritain, through "the intentional identification of each soul with the divine essence, the law of the primacy of the common good over the personal good comes to an end in a certain sense," for the two goods are at last one and the same.[22]

At this point in the debate De Koninck steps in to suggest that it is not wise to skip so freely from rung to rung on the ladder of goods when comparing the common and the private:

[I]t is necessary to emphasize that St. Thomas does not oppose the good of grace of a single person to the good of grace of the community, but rather to the natural good of the universe. And if the spiritual [supernatural] good of the person is superior to the entire created common good, and if, in accordance with this spiritual good, the person ought to be loved with preference, in no way does it follow that the created common good should as such be subordinated to the singular person. . . . [Furthermore,] the supernatural good of the singular person is essentially ordered to the supernatural common good.[23]

Human persons are ordained to participate in various common goods, according to the various "formalities" that they comprise and that are ordered according to the relative perfection of the good to which each corresponds. At the top of the scale of goods is God, supreme and infinitely communicable "separated [i.e., fully transcendent] common good," in which the human person participates by virtue of being a child of God and citizen of the Heavenly City. All inferior common goods are both subordinate to and ordained (directly or indirectly) toward this supreme common good.[24] The rational nature of the human being is, to repeat, essentially open to the whole, to the universal, to what is most communicable. Therefore, as De Koninck emphasizes elsewhere in his book

if the rational creature cannot limit himself entirely to a subordinate good—that of the family, for example, or that of political society—it is not because his singular good is as such greater, but rather because of his ordination to a superior common good to which he is *principally* ordered. In such a case the common good is sacrificed not to that of the individual *qua* individual, but rather to the good of the individual insofar as he is ordained to a more universal common good.[25]

Now, given the often-heated character of the polemic that ensued between these two Thomistic camps—the personalist people and the partisans of the common good—one might well be quite surprised to discover that Maritain and De Koninck are in essential agreement on most fundamental aspects of the matter at hand. And yet such is in fact the case. The only difficulty is that to grasp the full extent of the agreement one is compelled to do at least two things, the first of which is to read very carefully all the fine print in Maritain's book, that is, the footnotes, especially numbers 7 and 48. It would seem that what makes Maritain's text so murky at times is that its author wants to effect too close a union between a classical outlook and a decisively modern spirit. The end result is a work that upholds the primacy of the common good within each genus, while at the same time so focusing on the liberty and transcendence of the individual person that the centrality of the common good often fades from view. Maritain thus risks appearing to subscribe to a contemporary trend which in an earlier work he himself depicted as fatal to philosophy: that of "discard[ing] the object in order to seek itself in the folds of subjectivity—a subjectivity entrenched within the individuality of the ego, instead of being spiritualized and universalized by its communication with objective being. . . . "[26]

In more properly Thomistic terms, Maritain chooses to direct his attention above all to the subjective and uniquely personal act of ascent to and participation in an end (e.g., in the intrinsic common good of the universe, which the philosopher seeks to apprehend, or in God as separated common good), rather than to the objective, intrinsically communicable (therefore, "common") character of that end in itself, the ultimate goal common to all human persons. In short, he appears to be moved much more by the incommunicable than by the communicable aspects of personhood and its ends.

Yet Maritain's focus on the subjective is not in fact intended to displace— much less to deny—the objective. This is especially evident when *The Person and the Common Good* is read in context of a wider selection of Maritain's works. His theory and his interpretation of Aquinas can be read as endeavors to develop a truly Thomistic account of subjectivity, both as a task philosophically worth doing for its own sake, and as particularly urgent given the political context within which he writes. (We will return to this matter later). And this brings us to the second prerequisite needed to grasp the deep agreement between our two Thomists: namely, more of an appreciation than De Koninck evinces for the sense in which Maritain's focus is compatible with and indeed complementary to the preferred "objective" emphasis of traditional Thomistic theory.

We can begin to see how this is the case by turning to the "Treatise on Happiness," which opens the *Prima Secundae*. Thomas here presents our proper end or good as twofold: first, "the thing itself which we desire to attain" (the "end for which"); second, "the attainment or possession, the use or enjoyment of the thing desired" (the "end by which"). The "end for which" is what "constitutes" our happiness, as its "cause or object." But the "end by which" is what we generally mean when we speak of happiness, for to attain or to enjoy the good is "the very essence of happiness"[27] Moreover, in the *Secunda Secundae* Thomas argues that while "the right ends of human life are fixed," "[t]he means to the end, in human concerns, *far from being fixed,* are of manifold variety according to the variety of persons and affairs."[28] Hence Maritain's work, with its emphasis on the personal, the subjective, the incommunicable, may be understood as elucidating the character of Thomas's "end by which" and highlighting the unique path by which each individual human may attain our common final end or common good.

And yet, in response to the central place occupied by "freedom of autonomy" and related concepts in personalist literature, De Koninck suggests that "the personalists" have unwittingly fallen prey to the very individualism they seek to combat: "What the personalists understand as 'person' is in fact what we understand as mere individual, a material and substantial whole enclosed in itself; they reduce the rational nature to the sensible nature which has as its object the private good."[29] But here as elsewhere, some distinction among personalists of different stripes is called for.[30] This accusation simply is not justifiable with regard to Jacques Maritain's brand of personalism. Maritain's colleagues Mortimer Adler and Walter Farrell do indeed explicitly argue that the human person is, on the natural level, an essentially selfish being seeking first and foremost its own private or individual good.[31] But not so Maritain: after all, he stresses repeatedly the openness and generosity of the person. For him, as for De Koninck, the human person is, in the most fundamental aspect of his or her being, a "being-for-self-for-God"—and therefore "for-others."[32] And so Maritain defines the "freedom of autonomy" for which human persons strive not as absolute autarchy, but rather as "independence with regard to creatures and dependence with regard to God."[33] Nonetheless, this definition occurs far too infrequently to prevent the reader from mistaking Maritain's meaning for more common—and quite different—usages.

We ought further to note that De Koninck's strongly voiced concern that a personalist approach (or rather, individualism cloaked in personalist garb) is apt to give rise to totalitarian politics seems exaggerated, to say the least, when applied to the sort of "Thomistic personalism" advocated by Maritain. And yet in this case, interestingly enough, there does seem to be some foundation for this criticism in Maritain's argument.

In his eagerness to cast the person as an independent whole, Maritain finds himself led de facto to effect on the conceptual level a radical divide within the human being in order to explain the person's place within political society and consequent duty to obey legitimate political authority. On the one hand, we have the "material individual," wholly indebted to the political community and hence fully subordinate to the state. This individual relates to the community as a pure part of a greater and sovereign whole. On the other hand, we have the "spiritual person," whose ends by far transcend political life and who therefore deserves to be treated by the temporal community as a whole to which it is subordinated.[34]

Now in theory such a perspective clearly ought to protect against totalitarianism: all those noble things that belong to the realm of human spirituality are untouchable; the highest aspects of human existence lie safely outside the sphere of political authority. The only problem here is that politics outside of Socrates' "city of sows" (Plato's *Republic* 369a–372d) simply cannot avoid being concerned with some "spiritual"—moral and intellectual—aspects of human life. The *polis* is comprised of human beings, who are according to Thomas substantial unities of body and soul, of matter and spirit. As Maritain himself readily acknowledges, there are not two races of human beings, the material individuals and the spiritual persons. There are just plain persons, and these need to be governed. So, in practice, according to Maritain's criteria, where is the government of a given political community to draw the line between what lies within its competence to direct and what is off-limits? In this crucial context at least, the material individual-spiritual person formula seems to obfuscate more than it clarifies.[35]

Insofar as there is an important theoretical disagreement to speak of between the personalist Thomism of Maritain and De Koninck's focus on the common good, it hinges upon their respective understandings of just what constitutes a "common good" in the most precise sense of the term. Maritain's formulations suggest that a common good "in the strict sense" must belong to the practical order; more generally, it must obtain only within the context of an actual society, political or other:

> . . . In the natural order there is a community of minds in as much as minds communicate in the love of truth and beauty, in the life and work of knowledge, art and poetry, and in the highest values of culture. However, *this community does not succeed in constituting itself as a society in the proper sense of the word,* the kingdom of minds, as Leibnitz put it. We could speak of its common good only in an analogical sense. In fact, the common good of the intellects can be understood in two ways: in the first way, it is truth and beauty themselves, through the enjoyment of which minds receive a certain natural irradiation or participation of the Uncreated Truth and Beauty or of the separated common good. This common good of the in-

tellects is obviously superior to the personal act by which each intellect conquers a fragment of it; but *it is not a social good, a common good in the strict sense.*[36]

Maritain's criteria accord well with common sense: rare as it may be to hear of the common good in our contemporary discourse, when it is mentioned it is virtually always with reference to the well-being of (usually civil or political) society and its members. And yet De Koninck wants to argue, following Thomas's teleological understanding of the good, that "in the strict sense" the common goods of the theoretical order are in fact more deserving of the name. In scholastic terminology, "the good of the speculative intellect is as such *more common* because it is formally more abstract, more separated from the singularity of the operable which involves potentiality, and hence more communicable."[37] Take, for example, the case of truth, the attainment of which perfects reason, the highest human faculty. Truth of itself (leaving aside for the moment the sometimes formidable obstacles to its attainment) may be possessed by innumerable persons without being thereby diminished in value.[38] Moreover, on both the natural and supernatural planes, the speculative good is *divinius* as well as *communius,* for its possession constitutes the chief ingredient of *beatitudo* ("blessedness"), Aquinas's term for the happiness proper to rational creatures.

Given his understanding of the common good "in the strict sense," it is easy to see why Maritain avoids positing a generalized "primacy of the common good." In his eyes, such a maxim would inevitably tend towards the sort of blanket "subordination of the person to the state" which we have seen De Koninck at pains to reject as a valid interpretation of this Thomistic principle. Maritain does agree that this is not the drift of Aquinas's theory, but he fears that without some modification or development the classic philosophy of the common good is incapable of safeguarding the dignity of the human person:

> The adage of the superiority of the common good is understood in its true sense only in the measure that the common good itself implies a reference to the human person. . . . [T]he worst errors concerning society are born of the confusion between the substantial whole of the biological organism and the collective whole, itself composed of persons, of society. *But to understand these things more profoundly, we must uncover the metaphysical roots of the question and engage in more subtle considerations about the individual and the person.*[39]

Maritain thus develops his "material individual-spiritual person" distinction for much the same reason he focuses on freedom and indeed adopts a personalist stance to begin with: to make abundantly clear that the sacrificing of countless human beings to the idol of ideologically concocted "collective entities" and their supposed well-being is both inhumane and intolerable, that it has nothing whatsoever to do with the Thomistic doctrine of the primacy of the common good. While De Koninck's reading and presentation are more faithful to Aquinas's position on this issue, Maritain departs from the letter of Thomas's work in order to uphold the spirit which informs it. Theoretical differences aside, the European experiences of communism and fascism made such a "personalist" approach seem the only conscionable one.[40]

John Finnis and the Thomistic Debate

I would like to go on to consider briefly a more recent contribution to the (broadly speaking) Thomistic debate regarding the nature and status of personal and common goods. I refer to the work of "new natural law theorist," John Finnis.

In his *Natural Law and Natural Rights,* Finnis defines the common good of the political community as the "point of continuing cooperation" among individuals, families, and groups in political association: namely, the securing of "the whole ensemble of material and other conditions, including forms of collaboration, that tend to favor, facilitate and foster the realization by each individual of his or her personal development."[41] Moreover, as Finnis states with greatest rigor in a recent conference paper, this common good is to be regarded as "inherently instrumental," and thus not a "basic, intrinsic, or constitutive" good or "value" for human beings.[42] Its proper aim and function must be solely to establish and foster a healthy social environment in which citizens can pursue with greatest freedom whichever of Finnis's "basic" or "fundamental" goods they so choose: life or health; knowledge; play or "skillful performance"; aesthetic experience; friendship; marriage; "inner integrity" and "authenticity"; "practical reasonableness"; "religion" broadly conceived.[43] These basic goods may be identified as such for the simple, practical reason that it is immediately evident to us that a person in pursuit of any one of them is acting intelligibly, that his or her activity "has a point" or makes sense.

Finnis thus declines to adopt the properly teleological (perfective) notion of "the good" characteristic of traditional Thomistic theory and presupposing a particular understanding of nature, especially human nature. His fundamental goods are not to be conceived of as hierarchically ordered among themselves. Rather, Finnis explicitly postulates among the basic goods an "incommensurability," which law directed toward the attainment of the political common good must recognize and respect:

[The foundation of civil law in the need to coordinate the various activities of individuals, families and intermediate associations] itself derives partly from the requirements of impartiality between *persons, and of impartiality as between the basic values and openness to all of them,* given certain facts about the ensemble of empirical conditions under which basic goods such as health, education, science, and art can be realized and realized in the lives of each person according to the measure of his own inclinations and capacities.[44]

In his notes, Finnis mentions that his definition of the political common good is "close to that worked out by French commentators on Aquinas in the early mid-twentieth century."[45] While Jacques Maritain is not mentioned by name, Finnis's treatment of the common good calls to mind some key characteristics of Maritain's theory, not least of which is a certain subordination of the common good to the personal (although not in the same sense, as we shall see). Moreover, Finnis calls our attention to the close similarity between his definition of "the common good" and that put forth by the Second Vatican Council in its *Pastoral Constitution on the Church in the Modern World (Gaudium et Spes)*, a document widely regarded as heavily influenced by Maritain's social and political philosophy. And Finnis explicitly argues that the council also holds that the common good is of purely instrumental value, *bonum utile* through and through, with not a trace of *bonum honestum*.[46]

Since I consider that Ernest Fortin and Louis Dupré have already brought to light the principle strengths and weaknesses of Finnis's position on the common good from the general standpoint of political philosophy, I would like here to focus my attention on his reading of Catholic social teaching as upholding an inherently instrumental common good. Finnis's interpretation and position on this issue fit nicely with the noblest, most decent liberal theories of person and society; yet I would suggest that in the last analysis his approach remains too individualistic to do justice to conciliar and postconciliar Catholic teaching.

Catholic social teaching begins from the premise, rooted in both reason and revelation, and stated explicitly at considerable length in major documents such as *Gaudium et Spes*[47], that human beings—substantial unities of body and soul, hence possessed of reason and will—are by their very nature social creatures. To achieve their specific perfection and reach happiness, human persons must under normal circumstances participate in common goods that transcend in some way their purely individual well-being and that are only made possible by life in society, from the family up through the political community and the universal *cosmopolis*. This natural social end of the human being suggests that the common good is a superior proper good of the persons in that society, rather than a mere assortment and coordination of individual goods and liberties. By building from a teleological foundation of this sort, Catholic social doctrine prepares the way for a richer presentation of the common good than

Finnis's practical reasonableness allows, asking as it does no more of our aims and actions than that they have an intelligible point to them.

It is then in this context, significantly different from that of Finnis's work, that we must understand the description of the common good in *Gaudium et Spes* (para. 26) as "the sum total of social conditions which allow people, either as groups or as individuals, to reach their fulfillment more fully and more easily."[48] Pope John Paul II, in his 1991 encyclical *Centesimus Annus,* during a discussion of the increasing inability of modern democracies to make policies aimed at the common good, refers to our *Gaudium et Spes* definition and explicates it as follows:

> [T]here is a growing inability to situate particular interests within the framework of a coherent vision of the common good. *The latter is not simply the sum total of particular interests; rather it involves an assessment and integration of those interests on the basis of a balanced hierarchy of values;* ultimately, it demands a correct understanding of the dignity and rights of the person.[49]

While much of what John Paul has to say here is to be found in Finnis's presentation (concretely, emphasis on rights and personal dignity), the Pope's insistence on a hierarchal ordering of goods as necessary to achieve a viable common good would seem incompatible with the "incommensurability of fundamental values" posited by Finnis in the same context. In this critical respect among others, modern Catholic social teaching appears closer to Maritain's neo-Thomistic understanding of personal and common good than to Finnis's account.

John Paul next considers the "principle of subsidiarity," which forms the cornerstone of Finnis's argument for the pure instrumentality of the political common good.[50] He summarizes this principle, which has been used extensively in magisterial social teaching since Pius XI, as follows: "[A] community of a higher order should not interfere in the internal life of a community of a lower order, depriving the latter of its functions, but rather should support it in case of need and help to coordinate its activity with the activities of the rest of society, always with a view to the common good."[51] Once again, it seems to me that John Paul's explication of Catholic teaching does greater justice to the common good: he does not speak of the common good as a mere means to personal choice of reasonable ends. Rather, he still speaks in terms of the proper *order* of communities and their ends, and of the [political, and ultimately the universal] common good as the highest temporal end of individuals and "communities of a lower order." Individuals, families, and associations are to be given the necessary freedom and direction to make their own proper contributions to the common good.

Perhaps this approach also accounts, at least in part, for the more prominent role that both the council and John Paul assign to moral virtue and duty in bringing about the good of persons and societies.[52] Legal and institutional reforms will not suffice without the corresponding personal cultivation of the "virtue" of "solidarity," "*a firm and persevering determination to commit oneself to the common good;* that is to say to *the good of all and of each individual,* because we are *all* really responsible *for all.*"[53] As Louis Dupré has observed, only when individuals view their own personal responsibilities to family, nation, and world community as more fundamental than their right to maximum self-fulfillment and autonomous choice can we reasonably expect a society in which human rights and the dignity of persons are upheld.[54]

But if this reading of Catholic social teaching regarding personal and common goods is really on the right track, how then are we to account for the many explicit statements in recent documents to the effect that the social order must be conceived of as subordinate "to the person," or to the good of the person?[55] This undeniable emphasis in modern magisterial teaching would seem the strongest evidence in favor of an "inherently instrumental" interpretation of the common good, close to if not identical with that advanced by Finnis. Yet once again we must take these statements in their actual context, a teleological account of human nature. In Maritain's terms, they are meant to remind us that human persons are ordered to an ultimate good that transcends the political and even the entire natural order and gives to each one of them an immense dignity. This absolute, common end is of course God himself.[56] And while Maritain, as we have seen, prefers to refer to God as the deepest personal good of each of the blessed, he acknowledges nonetheless the fittingness of speaking, as Thomas Aquinas did, of God as our greatest common good. As Maritain explicitly states, "[t]he common good of the political society is an 'honest good.' But it is a practical good, and not the absolute good.[57] Any subordinate good must be expected to be to some extent a "useful good," desirable as a means to other goods. But if one were to relegate the political common good to a purely instrumental status, it would seem difficult to account for the sentiments most recently voiced by many newly enfranchised South Africans, to whom the good of citizenship and full participation in political life seems eminently desirable in and of itself.

The personalistic thrust of such statements from Vatican II and Pope John Paul therefore seem intended especially to remind political leaders and citizens of two crucial truths: first, that as the political common good is not the good of some abstract, organic entity, it must be the proper good of the human beings comprising the political order. To truly be such, the common good must not be reduced to the GNP of our introduction: the spiritual aspect of human nature needs much more than "things" or untrammeled power to achieve perfection in social context. True social development must transcend economics. And the moral dimension of the common good cries out against the many outrageous assaults on innocent human life that our century has witnessed, despite unprecedented talk of "human rights" and "dignity."

Second, this teaching underlines the limited, subordinate character—not thereby wholly instrumental—of the political common good, which, as both Finnis and Dupré illustrate, must be open to and foster the universal common good.[58] Moreover, even the most noble civic activity is insufficient to satiate the longings for perfect happiness that flow from human nature and its supernatural elevation: the Augustinian restless heart and the Thomistic restless intellect can be satisfied with nothing less than God. Participation in the political common good ought to elevate a person's existence, "help[ing] him greatly ... in fulfilling his calling (even his religious calling)." But given the sad state of actual affairs, "it cannot be denied that he is often turned away from the good and urged to evil by the social environment in which he lives."[59] The achievement of a genuine political common good is not to be found in regimes that forcefully propagate atheism, or which do so, practically speaking, by holding up material acquisition, comfort, and the minimally limited exercise of choice as the goals of human life. Once again, the practical urgency of such a teaching in contemporary context could not be more evident.

In conclusion, then, it seems to me that we owe a great deal to John Finnis for returning "the common good" to a central place in legal and political theory. Moreover, he has done so in a manner coherent with liberal political realities and suited to constructive dialogue with persons of the most varied philosophic persuasions. His lack of dependence on a properly teleological understanding of human nature and society renders him immune to some of the most powerful objections leveled against traditional Aristotelian-Thomistic theories of the common good. Yet, as I have tried to suggest, his presentation of the common good as a mere instrument for securing individual access to personal choice among any of the incommensurable human goods or values is in an important sense detrimental to sound civic life, and does not accurately reflect the central message of Catholic social teaching.

The powerful influence of life in liberal societies such as our own makes it extremely difficult to conceive of anything other than individual well-being as the ultimate aim to which other ends and duties may rightly be sacrificed. In this context a letter to the editor that I once read in one of the student papers of Boston College, my alma mater, comes to mind. The writer, responding to an article on a topic very different from our own, argued that Christianity gives the individual good primacy over the common; Christ clearly taught this by directing those he had chosen to leave their families and follow him. This interpretation seems a coherently liberal distortion of the spirit of the Gospels, where duties to parents are given heavy weight, and where the call to discipleship is "*propter regnum coelorum.*" The well-being of the family is subordinate, not to the imperative of self-fulfillment, but to the service of God and the universal human community under his care. And, for those called to a more immediate service to these superior common goods, to take up such tasks is in the last analysis a duty, if a joyful one, which must be taken up willingly, not a purely personal choice to pursue the value of "religion" over that of, say, play or health. According to the Second Vatican Council, such a duty is also incumbent upon "those with a talent for the difficult yet noble art of politics":

[T]hey should prepare themselves for [political leadership], and, forgetting their own convenience and material interests, they should engage in political activity. They must combat injustice and oppression, arbitrary domination and intolerance by individuals or political parties, and they must do so with integrity and wisdom. They must dedicate themselves to the welfare of all in a spirit of sincerity and fairness, of love and of the courage demanded by political life.[60]

This is the spirit to be found at the heart of modern Catholic social teaching, and I fear that Finnis's interpretation of Vatican II fails to do it justice. For a theory more capable of helping us transcend our individualistic environment and recover a profound appreciation of the common good, of the demands it makes of us even while ennobling our personal existence, we must allow Jacques Maritain and especially Charles De Koninck to lead us back to the thought of Thomas Aquinas.

Notes

This essay grew out of a paper entitled "The Dignity of the Person and the Primacy of the Common Good: The Maritain-De Koninck Debate," presented at the 64th annual meeting of the Southern Political Science Association, November 1992, in Atlanta, Georgia.

I would like to thank Ernest L. Fortin, Ralph McInerny, Brian Midgeley, Clifford Orwin, and John Roos for kindly taking time to read drafts of this essay and to offer some very helpful suggestions. I am particularly indebted to Edward A. Goerner for his probing, extensive, and instructive critique, to which at this point I have yet to respond adequately. Thanks are also due to the Connaught Foundation, the University of Toronto, and the Earhart Foundation for the financial support that made work on this essay possible.

1. C. S. Lewis, *The Screwtape Letters* (New York: The Macmillan Company, 1943), 92.

2. Quoted in Thomas L. Pangle, *The Ennobling of Democracy: The Challenge of the Postmodern Age* (Baltimore: Johns Hopkins University Press, 1993), 76, 78.

3. See, for example, Alasdair MacIntyre, "The Privatization of the Good: An Inaugural Lecture," *Review of Politics* 52 (1990): 344–77.

4. Pangle, *Ennobling of Democracy,* 212–13.

5. For the most helpful recent discussions of the Maritain-De Koninck exchange, see J. Brian Benestad, "Rights, Virtue and the Common Good," *Catholicism in Crisis: A Journal of Lay Catholic Opinion* 2, no.1 (December 1983): 28–32; Louis Dupré, "The Common Good and the Open Society," *Review of Politics* 55 (1994): 690–92; Ernest L. Fortin, "The New Rights Theory and the Natural Law," *Review of Politics* 44 (1982): 598–601; and Ralph McInerny, *Art and Prudence: Studies in the Thought of Jacques Maritain* (Notre Dame, Ind.: University of Notre Dame Press, 1988), 77–91.

6. For an example of this rationale, see M. Novak, *Free Persons and the Common Good* (Lanham, Md.: Madison Books, 1989), 4: "In one sense, the fine points of this debate among Thomists need not detain us; much of it was ontological, even theological, in substance, rather than political or institutional."

7. Charles De Koninck, *De la primauté du bien commun, contre les personnalistes* (Québec: Éditions de L'Université Laval, 1943).

8. Yves R. Simon, "On the Common Good," *Review of Politics* 6 (1944): 530–33.

9. I. Th. Eschmann, "In Defense of Jacques Maritain," *Modern Schoolman* 22 (1945): 183–208.

10. De Koninck, "In Defense of Saint Thomas: A Reply to Fr. Eschmann's Attack on the Primacy of the Common Good," *Laval Théologique et Philosophique* 1, no.2 (1945): 9–109.

11. McInerny, *Art and Prudence,* 85.

12. Jacques Maritain, *La personne et le bien commun* (Paris: Desclée De Brouwer, 1947); except where indicated, citations are from John J. Fitzgerald's translation, *The Person and the Common Good* (Notre Dame, Ind.: University of Notre Dame Press, [1947] 1985).

13. See Thomas Aquinas, *Summa Theologiae* (*ST*) III 4,1: The cause of human "dignity" is that "human nature, as rational and intellectual, was made for attaining to the Word to some extent by its operation, viz, by knowing and loving him"; cf. also I 29,1 and 29,3,ad 2. For an extremely clear presentation of the Thomistic ontological grounding of human freedom in our rational nature, see Antonio Milan Puelles, *La síntesis humana de naturaleza y libertad* (Madrid: Editorial Nacional, 1961).

14. Maritain, *The Person and the Common Good,* 56; cf. Aquinas, In III Sent. d. 5, 3, 2, cited by Maritain, and *ST* I 29,1, ad 5.

15. De Koninck, *De la primauté,* 57–58; cf. *inter alia* the references to Aquinas in Fortin, "The New Rights Theory and the Natural Law," 598, n.14.

16. Ibid.; cf. *ST* I, 60, 5.

17. Fortin, "The New Rights Theory and the Natural Law," 600–601, n.22.

18. De Koninck, "In Defense of St. Thomas," 93–94; cf. 18–20.

19. Aquinas, *Quaestiones Disputatae De Veritate,* 21,2; cf. 1.

20. Maritain, *The Person and the Common Good,* 15.

21. Ibid., 18, n.7; *ST* I–II 113,9, ad 2.

22. Ibid., 88–89; but cf. ibid., n.48, and De Koninck, *De la primauté,* 62–63. In this context, consider also Maritain, *The Person and the Common Good,* 62–63, especially

n. 33, where he makes a parallel argument for the primacy, in a certain sense, of the "personal good" over the common good within the *natural* order. He makes reference to Aristotle's teaching of the superiority of the philosopher's contemplative good to the common good of his *polis*. And yet, later in the same note, Maritain explains, in agreement with De Koninck, that this personal good proper to the contemplative life is of a higher dignity than that of the practical political life precisely because it constitutes a greater participation in and service to a superior *common* good: the truly cosmopolitan, spiritual common good of the universe.

23. De Koninck, *De la primauté,* 62–63 (emphasis added).

24. Ibid., *inter alia* 66–67.

25. Ibid., 14–15 (emphasis added).

26. Maritain, *The Range of Reason* (New York: Charles Scribner's Sons, 1952), 47.

27. Aquinas, *ST* I–II 1,8; 2,7; 3,1.

28. *ST* II-II 47,15 (emphasis added).

29. De Koninck, *De la primauté,* 66–67.

30. See Simon, "On the Common Good," 532.

31. Mortimer Adler and Walter Farrell, "The Theory of Democracy," *The Thomist* 4 (1942): 323–24, 329–30. Cited in De Koninck, *De la primauté,* 129–130.

32. Cf., *inter alia,* De Koninck, *De la primauté,* 41, with Maritain, *The Person and the Common Good,* 15, 39–41.

33. Maritain, *Range of Reason,* 215.

34. Maritain, *Person and Common Good, inter alia* 70–76.

35. The political thrust of this distinction appears in some tension with other elements of Maritain's own thought. In *Things That Are Not Caesar's,* for example, he insists that the "temporal good" at which politics properly aims is a good "not only of the *material* order, but also and preeminently of the *moral and spiritual order . . .*" (Appendix II, 125; emphasis in original). Again, in his *Range of Reason,* Maritain maintains that the political common good [a "communicable good"] is "at once material, intellectual, and moral, and principally moral, as man himself is; it is a common good of human persons . . ." (142).

This tension may be resolved by maintaining that while the political association and its legitimate authority ought to foster the moral and intellectual development of its citizens, the modern democratic state may direct or interfere with properly spiritual aspects of human life (religious, intellectual/scientific, etc.) only when compelling moral or practical necessity so dictates, for the common good (cf. *inter alia The Social and Political Philosophy of Jacques Maritain,* eds. J. Evans and L. Ward [New York: Charles Scribner's Sons, 1955], "The Democratic Charter," 141–44, and Maritain, *The Person and the Common Good,* 73–74). Still, the suggestion that only the "material individual" is a full part of the political community cannot but cause some confusion within Maritain's broader understanding of the political association's nature and purpose.

36. Maritain, *The Person and the Common Good,* 82–83 (emphasis added).

37. De Koninck, "In Defence of St. Thomas," 88 (emphasis added).

38. Cf. Augustine's treatment of truth as common good in *On the Free Choice of the Will* II, 12–14.

39. Maritain, *The Person and the Common Good,* 29–30 (emphasis added).

40. Father Eschmann suffered prolonged imprisonment in Germany at the hands of the Gestapo; Maritain's France was of course shamed by Vichy collaboration. For an account of the Nazi use and abuse of the slogan "the common good before the good of the individual," see Josef Pieper, *No One Could Have Known: An Autobiography: the Early Years, 1904–1945. [San Francisco: Ignatius Press, 1987] 95 and 175; cited in Michael Sherwin, O.P., "St. Thomas and the Common Good: The Theological Perspective: an Invitation to Dialogue,"* Angelicum 70 (1993): 307–28. From the opposite side of the iron curtain, the remembrances of a survivor of the "terror-famine" (the term is Robert Conquest's) illustrate well the nightmare misinterpretation of "the primacy of the common good" which Maritain sought to avoid at all costs:

[In context of a visit to a Ukrainian village by "solemn, grim" Party officials who were "travelling throughout the county arresting people for no apparent reason":] Comrade Representative spoke first. The gist of his speech is as follows: a stray ant is of no account; it can become lost in its search for food; it may be mercilessly crushed by someone . . . or destroyed by other means. Who cares about a stray single ant? What really counts is the anthill, for in it the ant's life is protected and perpetuated. The ants manage to survive only because they live in a close-knit and well-organized ant society. An ant is inconceivable without that society. So it is with human beings: alone, they are helpless; they can be exploited, persecuted, forgotten, or destroyed. Only in the Communist society can an individual find happiness, prosperity, and freedom. The collective farm is everything; the individual is nothing! The collective farm is the first step toward this Communist society; therefore, we all must join it. The Party so orders, and the Party knows what is best for farmers. There is no choice. (Miron Dolot, *Execution by Hunger: The Forgotten Holocaust* [New York: Norton, 1987] 70–71)

41. John Finnis, *Natural Law and Natural Rights* (Oxford: Clarendon Press, 1980) 153, 148; cf. "Is Natural Law Theory Compatible with Limited Government?" (presented at the 1993 meeting of the American Public Philosophy Association in Washington, D.C.; publication forthcoming), 9.

42. Finnis, "Is Natural Law Theory Compatible," 1, 7.

43. Cf. Finnis, "Is Natural Law Theory Compatible," 7–8, with *Natural Law and Natural Rights,* 92–95.

44. Finnis, *Natural Law and Natural Rights,* 149 (emphasis added).

45. Finnis, *Natural Law and Natural Rights,* 160; Finnis, "Is Natural Law Theory Compatible," 9.

46. Finnis, "Is Natural Law Theory Compatible," 10–12.

47. Cf. *Gaudium et Spes,* in *Vatican Council II: The Conciliar and Post Conciliar Documents,* ed. Austin Flannery, O.P. (Grand Rapids, MI, 1992) paras. 12, 14–18, 24–25.

48. Ibid., para. 26 (emphasis added).

49. John Paul II, *Centesimus Annus,* Vatican English translation (Sherbrooke, QC: Editions Paulines, 1991) para. 47 (emphasis added).

50. Cf. Finnis, "Is Natural Law Theory Compatible," 10–12.

51. John Paul II, *Centesimus Annus,* para. 48.

52. Cf. *Gaudium et Spes,* para. 30–31 with John Paul II, *The Lay Members of Christ's Faithful People* (Boston: Daughters of St. Paul, 1989), para. 17, 40, and 42. For a timely reminder of the centrality of conversion and personal virtue to the common good, see J. Brian Benestad, "Virtue in Catholic Social Teaching," in *Private Virtues and Public Policy,* ed. James Finn (New Brunswick, N.J.: Transaction Publishers, 1990), 29–47.

53. John Paul II, *Concern for the Social Order* (Sherbrooke, QC: Editions Paulines, 1988), para. 38 (emphasis in original).

54. See Dupré, "The Common Good," 707–11.

55. See, for example, *Gaudium et Spes,* para. 26.

56. Cf. *Gaudium et Spes,* para. 24.

57. Maritain, *The Person and the Common Good,* 63. Cf. *The Range of Reason,* 142: " . . . [the political common good] is not only something useful, an ensemble of advantages and profits, it is essentially something good in itself—what the Ancients termed *bonum honestum.* Justice and civic friendship are its cement."

58. Cf. Finnis, *Natural Law and Natural Rights,* 148, 160, with Dupré, "The Common Good," 705–12.

59. *Gaudium et Spes,* para. 25.

60. Ibid., para. 75.

11

The Quest for the Historical Murray

Robert P. Hunt

Murray and the Murray Project

Over forty years ago, John H. Hallowell of Duke University delivered a series of lectures at the University of Chicago that was to become a book entitled *The Moral Foundation of Democracy*. Hallowell's professed goal was to develop a sounder, more full-bodied defense of constitutional democracy than that supplied by most versions of philosophical or political liberalism, inclined as they were to some variant of positivism. He eschewed the fashionable credo of his day, which held that constitutional democracy was preferable to totalitarianism precisely because it took no view of human nature and the goods appropriate to that nature, thus allowing all groups, equally legitimate, to have their say in the rough-and-tumble of the governmental process. Hallowell maintained that the American experiment in self-government could be sustained only if it were grounded in a moral realist view of human nature. In opposition to those proponents of ethical proceduralism who refused to push the envelope and opted, therefore, for some sort of pseudoneutrality on the question of the good life, Hallowell argued that "underlying every system of government there is some predominant conception of the nature of man and the meaning of human existence. More often than not, this idea of man is implicit rather than explicit. But if not always explicit, it is always fundamental."[1] In other words, every society defined itself by how it answered certain basic questions about human nature and the goods appropriate to it. The decision not to answer these questions at all was, paradoxically, just as much of an answer as any other, and the consequences of such a decision for our constitutional way of life would be profound. Hallowell argued that the envelope needed to be pushed.

At the same time that Hallowell was arguing for a moral realist understanding of the foundations of American constitutional democracy, the Reverend John Courtney Murray, S.J., was engaged in much the same effort in Catholic theological circles. In a series of groundbreaking articles for the journal *Theological Studies* in the late 1940s and early 1950s, Murray attempted to lay out an explicitly moral realist (and recognizably Roman Catholic) defense of constitutional democracy, particularly as it had been actualized in America.[2] His primary polemical opponents, however, were not the legal positivists or proceduralists confronted by Hallowell. Rather, they were those of Murray's brethren who argued that any defense of constitutional democracy in general, and of the principles of limited government embodied in the religion clauses of the First Amendment in particular, must be made upon prudential rather than principled grounds," as a practical concession, *in hypothesi,* to the fact of religious diversity rather than as a statement, *in thesi,* of the proper ordering of society and state, of religion and politics. If Hallowell's goal was to convince the proceduralist that America needed a substantive moral and political consensus, Murray's was to convince his fellow Roman Catholics that such a substantive consensus need not extend, in principle, to matters of religious doctrine. And the statesman whose role it was to support that consensus was neither "*episcopus externus* nor amoral policeman. His function is high indeed but not messianic."[3]

In 1960, Murray's most famous book—in fact, a revised compilation of earlier articles—*We Hold These Truths: Catholic Reflections on the American Proposition* was published. Times had changed and so had Murray's audience. No longer was he trying primarily to convince his fellow Roman Catholics that they had nothing to fear from constitutional democracy if it were grounded in a proper understanding of human nature. Now he was trying to convince his fellow Americans that they ought not to abandon the body of substantive truths that underlie the American experiment in self-government, and he argued in tones reminiscent of Hallowell's:

> Granted that the unity of the commonwealth can be achieved in the absence of a consensus with regard to the theological truths that govern the total life and destiny of man, it does not follow that this necessary civic unity can endure in the absence of a consensus more narrow in its scope, operative on the level of political life, with regard to the rational truths and moral precepts that govern the structure of the constitutional state, specify the substance of the common weal, and determine the ends of public policy.[4]

If Murray's objective in his *Theological Studies* articles was to convince his coreligionists that they could learn something from the American experiment in ordered liberty, his objective in *We Hold These Truths* was to convince his fellow Americans that they could learn something from the great tradition of Catholic social thought, and that this education might well save them from the spiritual, moral, and political abyss into which they seemed to be falling. And Murray was just as explicit as Hallowell in rejecting any specious efforts to avoid asking basic questions about human beings, their nature, and their destiny. "Every moralist has his concept of the moral order. All practical moral inquiry has theoretical presuppositions. Each moral theory has its own categories of statement and its own style of argument, *and in the end every structure of moral doctrine and decision rests on a concept of the nature of man*" (284, emphasis mine). Pseudoneutrality will not suffice. It will not suffice at the practical level, for every society has some ensemble of truths to which it adheres, that gives it a sense of purpose for action in history. It will not suffice at the theoretical level because our practical health depends on a deeper metaphysical commitment. Or, as Murray puts it, "the Basic Issues today [i.e. 1960] can only be conceived in metaphysical and theological terms. They are issues of truth" (199). If we continue to give the wrong theoretical answers to certain basic questions about human nature, it is only by accident that we give the correct practical answers to questions of public policy. Beyond this, it is only by sheer accident that we are capable of sustaining what Murray describes as "the fundamental structure of a free society" (198).

Over the course of the past thirty-odd years since Murray wrote *We Hold These Truths*, such questions about the fundamental structure of a free society have been raised again, and the renewed contemporary interest in the ineluctable relationship between religion and politics is but one aspect of the question. This renewed interest has sparked what might be termed "the John Courtney Murray Project," an effort to reinvigorate a truly American public philosophy of democratic self-government that avoids the Scylla of totalitarian monisms and the Charybdis of contentless proceduralism. Robert McElroy has noted that many of the leading public theologians of the past decade have, "despite their sectarian and ideological diversity, . . . almost uniformly drawn their central insights from the works of John Courtney Murray."[5] Keith Pavlischek contends that this diverse community of scholars has drawn its insights from Murray precisely because Murray integrated religion, freedom, order, and justice in a "penetrating, non-superficial manner."[6]

Pavlischek also points out, however, that the depth and breadth of Murray's life work has its downside, that is, "that someone intent on highlighting one aspect of his thought can easily do so at the expense of others."[7] This danger is heightened by the fact that Murray was not a systematic writer, and it is easy, in order to prove his pedigree, to extract various quotations and aphorisms from what are for the most part a collection of articles written within distinctive polemical contexts and directed at distinctively different philosophical opponents. In addition, Murray often employed a terminology, and made dichotomies, that did not fully serve to explicate the principles that he was attempting to validate.[8]

In the face of these difficulties, a cynical interpreter might be tempted to throw up his hands and brand Murray as hopelessly ambiguous on major questions of religious and philosophical importance. The resolution of interpretative difficulties lies, however, not in cynicism but in the application of Murray's own critical methodology (as employed in his analyses of figures such as John of Paris, Robert Bellarmine, and Pope Leo XIII) to Murray himself.[9] Murray argued that the task of the theologian was to formulate "principles in such terms that they may be asserted as constantly valid, and [organize them] into a coherent system that will cover all contingencies because it is dependent on none."[10] Murray thought that he was doing precisely this: distilling permanently valid theological, moral, and political truths from manners of statement (upon the part of Bellarmine, for example) that were only valid within particular historical contexts. "In this new context the old principles were still valid, but the newness of the context required their renewal, their purification from a manner of statement and application that was only valid in the old context."[11]

But Murray himself was just as prone as Bellarmine, as has been noted, to assert those truths in a particular contextualized manner against particular philosophical opponents. The goal then for any interpreter of Murray must be to discern "the bedrock of [theological, moral, and political] principle itself [for which Murray argued], on which the truths of transtemporal significance are found." In other words, the effort to discover the real import of Murray's project must take cognizance of the historically situated Murray, of the tensions that might exist between his underlying principles and the historically contingent manner in which he was forced to elaborate those principles. This critical methodology of discernment will surely not answer every question about Murray's pedigree, but it might rebut some of the more egregious misinterpretations of his thought and misapplications of his project.

The Quest for Murray: Murray
as Americanist Liberal Democrat

David Novak, in an essay entitled "John Courtney Murray: A Jewish Appraisal," notes that his own theological "transitional summer" of 1961—a summer marked by the then-recent publication of *We Hold These Truths*—was characterized by an unfortunate tendency on the part of many intelligent Catholics and Jews to choose one of two undesirable options in the realm of civil discourse. The first of these options was to withdraw from the larger community of civil discourse and narrowly affirm the integrity of one's own faith tradition to the exclusion of others. The second option, chosen by many whom Novak describes as "the best and the brightest," was "to opt for the present realm and thus bracket [one's] faith tradition if not leave it altogether."[12]

Those Catholics who chose the first path believed that any effort to reconcile their faith tradition with the precepts of constitutional democracy required an abandonment of their faith, and so they opted to maintain the integrity of their faith. Those Catholics who chose the second path could well be described as full-fledged Americanists who wanted to resolve the tension between their faith tradition and the precepts of liberal democracy by adopting a church model and view of ecumenical ethics that was fashioned upon a distinctively modernist (and, ultimately, historicist) view of human nature and social institutions. These Catholics went so far as to raise the question of whether Catholicism was truly compatible with democracy, conceived in voluntarist terms. Given a choice between what they perceived as an authoritarian church and a voluntarist social ethic, the Americanists, unlike their more traditional brethren, opted for the latter and sought to make the Catholic Church over in their own image of what a "church/society" should be.

Novak argues, rightly, that John Courtney Murray framed for himself the project of developing a third option that did not ensnare itself on the horns of a false dichotomy that forced devout Roman Catholics either to withdraw from the larger civil conversation or to accept the conversation itself as the procedural and substantive embodiment of Catholic social ethics. Unlike those who opted for withdrawal and insularity, Murray believed that Roman Catholics in America could bring the full weight of their tradition to bear upon the American experiment in self-government. The American experiment—a nation dedicated to certain truths about human beings—needed to be reexamined and reappropriated by each generation of Americans, and Roman Catholic Americans were particularly well-suited to contribute to this reappropriation because they were able to set the truths of democratic self-government in their proper setting—the natural moral law.[13] In other words, Murray defended the American Constitution not solely because it set up technical processes for resolving divisive issues but because it was grounded, as Murray himself put it, "in the dictates of practical political sense, themselves guided by a concern for justice and liberty and illumined in their highest underlying intuitions by a belief in God and an order of natural law."[14]

If Murray was a critic of those Catholics who opted for insularity, he was an even harsher critic of those Americanists who wanted to judge Catholicism in light of a particularly voluntarist view of American democracy:

the principles of Catholic faith and morality stand superior to, and in control of, the whole order of civil life. The question is sometimes raised, whether Catholicism is compatible with American democracy. The question is invalid as well as impertinent; for the manner of its position inverts the order of values, whether American democracy is compatible with Catholicism. (ix–x)

Murray attempted to give an affirmative answer to this question, an answer that in no way bracketed his faith tradition or forced him to leave his faith tradition in pursuit of some more modernist god.

What is remarkable, therefore, is the contemporary effort to turn Murray into a "new hat," and fully Americanist, liberal theologian for whom "civil conversation" becomes not only the best principled means for resolving the issues that divide us but also the *terminus ad quem* to which the substantive truths of Catholicism must be subordinated. The most notable and comprehensive effort on behalf of this "new and improved" Murray is J. Leon Hooper's *The Ethics of Discourse: The Social Philosophy of John Courtney Murray.*[15]

Hooper presents a Murray whose thought "evolved" over a period of about twenty-five years between 1943 and 1967 (the year of his death). The word "evolution" is critical, since Hooper is not content with pointing out possible refinements in Murray's arguments over that period of time. Rather, he distinguishes between the earlier, immature Murray and the later "historically conscious" Murray. In doing so, he establishes a dichotomy between "natural law reasoning" and "historical consciousness" that is foreign to Murray's understanding of his own project.

The immature and ideologically biased Murray, we are told, was a proponent of "the timeless, socially naive natural law theory."[16] As such, Murray was disposed to argue for the existence of immutable first principles of justice and the need for prudential reasoning in applying those principles to historically contingent circumstances. At the theological level, this Murray defended a hierarchically ordered church as the repository and expositor of revelational truth. What saved Murray from being forever entrapped by these historically contingent judgments, and by the naive natural law theory upon which such judgments are based, was his commitment to ethical dialogue, a *method* of civic conversation that opened his mind to new, emergent truths generated within the historical process.

At the end of his life, Hooper argues, Murray's transformation into an improved, "historically conscious" ethician and theologian was almost complete. He refused to grant a priori validity to "any political philosophy or rights theory, or, for that matter, of any ethical theory regarding social reality, familial structuring, common moral affirmations, or even the principles of justice themselves." Moreover, he had begun to question the process whereby the Catholic Church itself made known the truths of Christian revelation. By committing themselves to an "ethics of discourse," contemporary ethicians and theologians would be recognizing "the need to adjust to the new configurations of values that might arise [within history], and the need for each age to appropriate in a mature human manner the values which ought to survive from one age to the next." The final foundational theme for the mature Murray, according to Hooper, is an experiential openness, a recognition of new and emergent values in the spiritual, cultural, and political realms. Thus, Murray finally commits himself to an ethical methodology that democratizes and relativizes all human truth-claims and pretensions of all human actors, and he calls for dialogic conversation among free, moral agents.[17]

Hooper's interpretation of the "evolution" of Murray from what he describes as naive natural law theorist to historically conscious (and, in fact, historicist) theologian rests heavily on the proposition that Murray was influenced tremendously by the works of Bernard Lonergan. The evidence that he adduces to support this claim, however, is, at best, elusive. For example, Hooper claims that "it was only about 1966 that Murray began to catch on to Lonergan's notion of 'historical consciousness' as a distinct differentiation on human understanding, a new perspective on the contingent and social nature of all human truth claims." Yet Hooper admits that "even in 1967 . . . [Murray] was still hesitant to view the development of 'theological truth' within the church as itself submerged within the historical process of emerging understanding and judgment."[18]

If Hooper's interpretation of Murray is correct, what was maintained earlier about Murray's effort to provide a foundation for American constitutionalism in moral realist, natural-law principles must be incorrect. Hooper would argue that Murray's rejection of classical consciousness (i.e., the positing of principles and structures of justice in a historical vacuum, usually associated with some form of unmodified Platonism) entailed an acceptance of historicism (i.e., the historicity of all human truth-claims). But Murray himself did not believe that these were the only philosophical alternatives. In fact, he argued for a historically conscious theory of natural law: "the natural law philosopher does speak of a 'natural law with changing and progressive applications,' as the evolution of human life brings to light new necessities in human nature that are struggling for expression and form. Natural law is a force conservative of all acquired human values; it is also a dynamic of progress toward fuller human realization, personal and social" (331).[19] Murray never believed that the only philosophical alternatives were an arid rationalism that posits principles of justice in an historical vacuum or a historicism that rejects any possibility of discerning transcendent substantive moral and political standards. His growing sense of "historical consciousness" did not entail an embrace of historicism and rejection of natural law. Similarly, his embrace of natural law in no way implied a failure to understand that even the most principled arguments are made within distinctive historical contexts that influence their manner of statement and application. Murray proposed a distinctively Christian understanding of the relation between nature and history that rejected the limiting options of classicism *and* modernism. It is only by imposing upon Murray dichotomous categories foreign to his own tradition that we can turn him into a "new hat" theologian.

It is only within the context of this historically conscious, but nonhistoricist, *support* for natural law that Murray's principled arguments about constitutional democracy and religious liberty, and his interpretations of Bellarmine and Pope Leo XIII, make sense. Murray did not argue for the historicity of all human truth claims. Rather, he argued that the theologian and the moralist must be able to distinguish "where the process of history ends and the moral order begins (surely there must be such a point)" (p. 283). The ability to distinguish the lineaments of this moral order, and of the conception of human nature associated with it, provides the contemporary Catholic moralist with an armature of substantive political principles, principles whose implications were not developed fully by Bellarmine or Leo. And these substantive principles, grounded in the natural moral law, are the surest foundation for the formal institutions of constitutional democracy. Murray lays out his substantive view of political democracy in *We Hold These Truths:*

> I take it that the political substance of democracy consists in the admission of an order of rights antecedent to the state, the political form of society. These are the rights of the person, the family, the church, the associations men freely form for economic, cultural, social and religious ends. In the admission of this prior order of rights—inviolable as well by democratic majorities as by absolute monarchs— consists the most distinctive assertion of the service character of the democratic state. And this service-character is still further enforced by the affirmation, implicit in the admission of the order of human rights, of another order of right also antecedent to the state and regulative of its public action as a state; I mean the order of justice. In other words, the democratic state serves the ends of the human person (in itself and in its natural forms of social life) and also the ends of justice. As the servant of these ends, it has only a relative value. (326)

If we were to accept Hooper's interpretation of Murray's project, we would be forced to conclude that Murray's own principled commitment, as he saw it, to a particular substantive view of constitutional democracy and religious liberty is nothing more than a contingent human truth-claim—a claim that could be superseded by some further awakening of historical consciousness.

Yet Hooper is unwilling to push Murray quite this far, and his "historically conscious," sophisticated Murray does indeed endorse a particular kind of political regime. But in place of the real Murray's effort to answer basic questions about what substantive view of human nature can best sustain an experiment in democratic self-government, Hooper posits Murray's commitment to ethical proceduralism:

> it is in the public commitment to human attentiveness, intelligence, and judgment that finally, for Murray, the core and timeless moral reality of human society resides. Without personal and collective commitments to the processes of human social reasoning, the discussion of any moral, justice, or religious issue quickly resolves into a factionalistic play of blind force.[20]

Murray would undoubtedly agree with Hooper that a democratic society ought to commit itself to critical public dialogue, but he would also maintain that this *procedural* commitment is impossible unless there is an underlying *substantive* commitment to the possibility of achieving a multifaceted view of the human good and the various social institutions (i.e., the family, churches, voluntary associations) that promote the dignity of the human person. The most basic and fundamental questions for Murray were not legal, procedural, or even juridical. For Murray, "few of the real problems [concerning the fundamental structure of a free society] are susceptible of solution, or even statement, in legal language. I mean rather the ontological structure of society, of which the constitutional order should be only the reflection" (198–99).[21]

Vanishing in the sea of Hooper's historical consciousness, amid the purported contingencies of all human truth-claims and principles of justice, is any substantive view of what constitutes the truly human good. Murray himself seems to be reduced to a twentieth-century proponent of a societal debating club in which all questions remain open and for which all answers are possible as long as all participants respect the process. He becomes a theologian who is more concerned about how public arguments are conducted than about the substantive outcomes of those debates.

This type of Americanist liberal theologian might be quite at home in an academe populated by antiperfectionist liberals such as John Rawls or Ronald Dworkin, but it is a far cry from the Murray who raised basic questions about the ontological structure of a free society. Unless one unpackages Murray's *substantive*, as opposed to proceduralist, commitments, it is impossible to understand, and extend, the Murray project.

A deeper appreciation of the religious, moral, and political bedrock (that is, the conception of human nature) lying at the heart of Murray's acknowledgedly contextualized style of argument precludes his being categorized as "liberal" in little other than a formal sense. He is liberal in the sense that he defends "constitutionalism, the rule of law, the notion of sovereignty as purely political and therefore limited by law, the concept of government as an empire of laws and not of men" (32). In other words, he defends the political institutions that are generally associated with the Western liberal tradition of politics.[22] But this formal "liberalism" is tempered within Murray, just as it is tempered within John Hallowell, by the sober recognition that constitutional democracy rests, fundamentally, upon a commitment to moral and political principles that are non-Lockean and nonhistoricist in nature. Moreover, any effort to make American constitutional democracy more thoroughly Lockean or historicist would constitute a "retheoretization" of America along undesirable monist lines.

Unpackaging the Real John Courtney Murray

Murray, as has been noted, attempted to develop a moral realist, and distinctively Catholic, defense of constitutional democracy and religious freedom. In doing so, he took issue, at various times and in different polemical contexts, with political Augustinians, Hobbesian and Lockean secularists, Protestant individualists, and contemporary Aristotelians. In rejecting the Protestant individualist account of religious freedom, however, Murray made a practical distinction that threatens to unravel his own project, a distinction between seeing the religion clauses of the First Amendment as "articles of peace" for a religiously fragmented society and seeing them as "articles of faith" with specific religious content.

Murray argued that the Framers of the American Constitution, speaking in deist and Protestant terms (i.e., the language of individual natural rights and social contract theory), gave a distinctively Catholic answer to the problem of religious liberty. They displayed a "prejudice in favor of the method of freedom in society and therefore the prejudice in favor of a government of limited powers, whose limitations are determined by the consent of the people" (47).[23] This commitment to the method of freedom led them to adopt the First Amendment's religion clauses, and these clauses, Murray argues, were seen by the Framers as "articles of peace" for a dogmatically divided nation. The clauses, in short, are good law and reflect a sound appreciation of the principled need for limited, constitutional government. But they say nothing about the nature of religion itself; they are not "articles of faith" with a particular religious (i.e., liberal Protestant) content. The genius of the American constitutional system was that civic rulers were henceforth "constitutionally inhibited from passing judgment in matters of religious faith."[24]

Murray's practical distinction, intended as it was to refute any liberal effort to turn religion into a purely private matter between each man and his own God, is ill-used when it is hardened into a principled dichotomy. What might have been an effective rhetorical device directed against a particular substantive orthodoxy (i.e., liberal Protestantism or secularism) within a particular historical context becomes, in the hands of an able Hobbesian or historicist interpreter of Murray, a pronouncement against all orthodoxies and a preoccupation with toleration as the only enforceable norm in a liberal regime. And this toleration must be extended from religious matters to all fractious moral issues that threaten to divide the nation. In short, the Murray Project is turned into a defense of antiperfectionist liberalism, and Murray's articles of peace are hardened into a new social monism.

Nowhere is this effort more evident than in a *Los Angeles Times* editorial in June 1989, in which the editors took Archbishop Roger Mahony to task for upbraiding those Catholic public officials who failed to take a principled stand against abortion. The editors commended:

the great Jesuit theologian and exponent of religious liberty, John Courtney Murray, [who] once argued that "The law, mindful of its nature, is required to be tolerant of many evils that morality condemns."

In our pluralistic society, as Father Murray's discerning remark suggests, the boundary between church and state is not always a clear line one can walk with sure-footed confidence. Moreover, it is a kind of social precipice approached across treacherous, shifting soil that may give way at any moment. Prudent people stay well back from the edge.[25]

The implications of the editorial are clear: In a pluralist society, a public official must often tolerate what he personally believes to be morally wrong, especially when we are discussing a particularly neuralgic issue about which there is little moral concord. The prudent public official must not push his claims too far in the public square, for when he does so, he upsets the pluralist nature of American society, attempts to "impose" his own views on those who do not share them, and violates the cherished American "articles of peace" — the wall of separation between church and state.

The *Times* editors have thus popularized J. Leon Hooper's scholarly interpretation of Murray. They have turned Murray's reading of the religion clauses, and his principled awareness of the inherent limitations of positive law, into an article of faith with a specific content—the content of secular, rights-oriented liberalism. Whereas Murray believed that it was possible to lay out a conception of constitutional democracy that was based on, and hospitable to, the Catholic social tradition purified of its "thesis-hypothesis" claims, these appropriators of Murray would adopt a view of Catholicism that does not pose a threat to the regnant orthodoxy of political liberalism. Moreover, they adopt a "Catholic" position that comes remarkably close to the secularist and Protestant individualism against which Murray directed his distinction in the first

place. In other words, this Hobbesianized Murray is precisely the sort of theologian and constitutionalist against whom Murray directed his polemical attacks in *We Hold These Truths.*

Under the dispensation of this new pluralism (which is, as we shall see, actually a very old monism), the religion clauses of the First Amendment become
"dogmas, norms of orthodoxy, to which one must conform on pain of excom-
munication. They are true articles of faith." These articles would, as Murray
said in another context, "consider the church to be true in proportion as its organization is commanded by the norms of secular democratic society, and
bring about a coincidence of religious and secular-liberal concepts of freedom"
(49). Secular neutralist liberalism becomes the foundational norm for a proper
understanding of the relationship between religion, morality, and law. The
pseudoneutrality of antiperfectionist liberalism becomes a potent monism of
its own.

By hardening Murray's practical distinction into a principled dichotomy,
and then extending the dichotomy into moral as well as religious issues, we run
the risk of turning Murray into another variety of proceduralist. But Murray
himself recognized that government can never be morally neutral. Just as all
action is directed to some end, so the public action engaged in by government
must, by its nature, be directed to some end; it must move in some moral direction. To deny the moral function of government would be to "imply a concept of government that is altogether unhistorical."[26] And what is true of government in the moral realm must also be true in the religious sphere.
Government must adopt some view of the role of religion in public life, even
while it professes to adopt no particular sectarian doctrine regarding ecclesial
structures. In short, its role is limited, not neutral. On the other hand, if we refuse to turn Murray's practical distinction into a principled dichotomy, we are
brought back to the same set of basic questions, asked in a different manner:
What is the distinctive worldview (i.e., the article of faith) upon which substantive political democracy and religious freedom depend for sustenance?
And conversely, what distinctive worldviews are destructive of an experiment
in ordered liberty? Murray does not answer these questions by distinguishing
between classical and historical consciousness (or between "ancients" and
"moderns"), and then embracing one or the other. Rather, he defends social and
juridical dualism (or "dyarchy") against all monisms, ancient and modern.

Murray maintains that the permanent goal of the Church in its relation to the
state is to argue for a "juridical and social dualism under the primacy of the
spiritual, against the tendency to juridical and social monism under the primacy
of the political which is inherent in the state to a greater or less degree, whether
the state be pagan, Christian, or secularized in the modern manner." The
Church itself must be free "to teach, rule and sanctify." In addition, the dignity

and fundamental integrity of the human person (as a child of God who seeks both spiritual and temporal satisfaction) can be secured only when there is no disharmony between ecclesiastical and civil law.[27] In other words, while the state has an autonomy commensurate with its fundamental purpose — securing public order as an aspect of the temporal common good — it must respect the primacy of man's spiritual end. It must not impose upon society an alien ideology that threatens to subordinate the truths of religion (i.e., the *res sacra*) to the perceived requirements of statecraft (i.e., the *res politica*).

The juridical and social dualism of which Murray speaks was, and can again become, the foundation for the Western liberal tradition. Continental Liberalism (or laicism), on the other hand, "was a deformation of the liberal tradition . . . another form of state monism, to which the liberal tradition stands in opposition."[28] The present task of Roman Catholics, particularly of those who are participants in the American experiment, is to "purify" the Western tradition of its potential deformities "by restoring both the idea and the institutions of democracy to their proper Christian foundations."[29] Not only must the Roman Catholic in America unashamedly enter the public square as an equal partner in the American civil conversation, he must also unabashedly affirm the distinctively Christian dualist view of man that provides the best sustenance against the perennial monist tendency of all states, be they pagan, Christian, or secularist.

And what precisely is this monist tendency, this deformation of the Western constitutional tradition that ultimately issues in some variant of totalitarianism? For the monist

> there is only one Sovereign, one society, one law, one faith. And the cardinal denial is of the Christian dualism of powers, societies, and laws — spiritual and temporal, divine and human. Upon this denial follows the absorption of the Church in the community, the absorption of the community in the state, the absorption of the state in the party, and the assertion that the party-state is the supreme spiritual and moral, as well as political authority and reality. It has its own absolutely autonomous ideological substance and its own absolutely independent purpose: it is the ultimate bearer of human destiny. Outside of this One Sovereign there is nothing. Or rather, what presumes to stand outside is "the enemy."[30]

The monist concept of the indivisibility of political, social, religious, or individual sovereignty has hung over the whole of modern politics, threatening to undermine the freedom of the Church, the dignity of the human person and the natural institutions that sustain him, and the true purposes of any legitimate constitutional order. The fragile experiment that is constitutional democracy cannot be sustained unless this monist temptation is combatted. The Catholic social tradition, as developed historically from Aquinas and Bellarmine through Leo XIII and *Dignitatis Humanae,* possesses the armature for such combat, but it must clearly and unequivocally distinguish its conception of politics from pagan and Liberal conceptions.

Murray clearly believes that the Catholic social and political tradition is not some form of baptized Aristotelianism. Rather, "the essential political effect of Christianity was to destroy the classical view of society as a single homogenous structure, within which the political power stood forth as the representative of society in its religious and in its political aspects" (202). Classical political philosophers saw man as a *polis* creature who realizes his social nature only insofar as he participates in the organized activity of politics, that activity that distinguishes man from God and beast. They argued that the fundamental purpose of politics was to direct human beings to the life of virtuous activity as discerned by human reason. But this reason, Murray held, had not been tempered and modified by the truths of Christian revelation and the only limits it would place upon the practical art of politics were those limits imposed by the canons of prudence—a prudence that, in turn, was governed not by fixed and immutable principles of natural law but by the wise man's superior perception of natural right.

The problem with an Aristotelian view of politics is not its substantive moral realism but its commitment to the primacy of the political. To the question "Are there two or one?", the classical philosopher (and, for that matter, disciples of medieval Averroism) must answer "There is one." And because he gives this answer, he is willing to subordinate the truths of religion to the practical exigencies of statecraft, thereby making him willing to endorse some form of civil religion that stands in judgment over other truth-claims. Religion itself is endorsed not because of its superior and transtemporal worth, but rather for its ability to instill certain virtues that are essential for the sound ordering of the body politic. Moreover, any contemporary effort to reinvigorate untempered political Aristotelianism must by its nature reject Christian dyarchy. It would entail a conscious effort to transform the *res sacra* (the freedom of the Church to teach and to administer the sacraments) and the *res sacra in temporalibus* (the spiritual truths of personal, family, and communal life) into a purely *res politica*. The product: a profanation of the sacred.

Murray argues that Christianity has done more than merely construct a second tier of supernatural ends over the foundational tier accessible to unaided human reason. Christianity has "freed man from nature by teaching him that he has an immortal soul, which is related to matter but not immersed in it or enslaved to its laws. . . . It taught him his own uniqueness, his own individual worth, the dignity of his own person, the equality of all men, the unity of the human race" (192). This conception of man's spiritual and personal dignity does not merely sit atop the Aristotelian conception of man as a political animal. Rather, it transforms that conception with the light of its radiance. A loving God has created each person in His image and has ordered each to a life that transcends the natural. The political order itself must recognize the superior intrinsic dignity of the human person and the natural institutions (i.e., families, churches, neighborhoods, voluntary associations) that allow the person to develop fully. Or, as Murray put it as early as 1948, the state's political duty to the human person is to create, or to assist in creating, those political, social, economic, and cultural conditions that "favor the ends of human personality, the peaceful enjoyment of all its rights, the unobstructed performance of all its duties, the full development of all its powers."[31] This task, while limited in nature, is both material and *moral*.

So much then for any effort to portray Murray as a closet Hobbesian. The state, while limited to pursuing the requirements of public order, cannot adopt a truncated view of civil peace if it is to create conditions under which personal development is possible. The concept of "public order" must be subordinated to a more comprehensive conception of the temporal common good if true public order is to be achieved: "The political order of the state is not the total order of human life; the citizens recognize other orders and higher loyalties, expressed in institutions, forms of sociality, that the state does not create and must not destroy."[32] The natural institutions of civil society, defined by Murray as "the multitude of men, things, institutions, associations with their various 'ideas' and ends, their independencies and inter-relationships," are primarily responsible for attaining the common temporal good.[33] The state itself must abide by the first principle of political life: it must do no harm to those institutions in its pursuit of public order. Rather, it must provide conditions under which human personhood can truly flourish, and it cannot do so if it sees itself as either *episcopus externus* or amoral policeman.

Murray's principled commitment to the dignity of the human person and the natural institutions that contribute to human flourishing is clearly demonstrated in his interpretation of the religion clauses of the First Amendment. The meaning of the religion clauses, says Murray, cannot be discerned on the basis of a narrow view of original legislative intent. "While the historical canon of original legislative intent is important, . . . it is hardly decisive [in the practical matter of government aid to religion]. What will be decisive is the full American tradition itself." The tradition reveals that the primary concern of the Framers was "the right to the free exercise of religion, . . . the more lofty provision, to which separation of church and state is instrumental" (150). The Framers' effort to prevent an establishment of religion should be read not as a defense of the privatization of religion, nor as a desire to prevent the baneful effects of religiosity from intruding into the public square. Rather, the Framers prohibited "an establishment of religion" as an ancillary means of protecting worshippers and worshipping communities (of both individualist and nonindividualist bent).

Freedom of religion in the American form of constitutional democracy rests then on a political theory — not a Hobbesianized article of peace — that juridically limits governmental power. This political theory in no way implies "any 'atheism of the state,' any false 'separation' of religion and society (or education), any restriction of the freedom of the Church within society, any pseudo-neutrality of government toward the interests of religion, any monistic, 'closed' concept of the political order, any destructive secularization of the political process."[34] The purified theory of constitutional democracy to which Murray adheres, and the dualist view of human nature upon which it is based, opposes any of these tendencies. It opposes, therefore, the Continental Liberalism of Locke and his intellectual descendants, in whom all of these tendencies are either implicit or explicit. Under the banner of a concern for individual rights and limited government, these Liberals would weave a new monism into the fabric of constitutional democracy that is, ultimately, more destructive of human dignity than the monism woven by contemporary disciples of classical political philosophy.

The organizing principle of Continental Liberalism (or laicism), according to Murray, is "the absolute autonomy of the individual human reason," wherein "each man is a law unto himself; and there is no higher law than that which he individually gives to himself."[35] The theory of freedom to which this liberal adheres is that of the "outlaw conscience" (*conscientia exlex*) — a conscience that makes itself the arbiter of truth and error, of right and wrong, with no reference to anything higher than its own sense of justice. In contrast to the traditional maxim of Thomist (and Murray's) moral realism that the truth sets the mind free, the maxim of Continental Liberalism is that the free mind makes the truth.

Thus, Liberalism grounds a defense of human freedom in a form of rationalism that ultimately must deny man's ability to discern the elements of a natural moral law that is not of his own making. Nowhere is this more evident than in the philosophy of John Locke, whose "rationalism, individualism, [and] nominalism" sowed the seeds for a particularly virulent brand of political monism against which the Catholic Church battled through the nineteenth century (305).[36]

While Locke's subjectivist epistemology would seem to result in a defense of nothing in particular, this did not stop him from attempting to employ it to defend natural rights and limited constitutional government. But Locke's radical individualism resulted in what Murray describes as "a complete evacuation of the notion of the 'rights of man.' " Locke's state of nature reveals nothing more than a set of power relationships—"the absolute lordship of one individual balanced against the equally absolute lordship of others" (307). These absolute lords (or, to use a more contemporary phrase, sovereign selves) become the constituent parts of civil society, and the only limitation on their sovereign lordship over themselves and their possessions is an obligation to recognize the sovereign lordship of others. Absent from Locke's theory is any concept of *ordo iuris* and it is only by piggybacking on the Western constitutional tradition (and its medieval underpinnings) that he is able to supply one.[37]

Locke's brand of voluntaristic rationalism, and those political regimes that base their "public philosophies" upon it, might at first glance appear to be providing a more defensible argument for a pluralist society because it claims to adopt a less comprehensive view of the human good than that of classical Aristotelianism. In addition, Continental Liberalism in general advances what it believes to be a principled, rather than prudential, defense of limited constitutional government. Why then does Murray believe that it is more dangerous than classical Aristotelianism?

According to Murray, the danger of modernity (and of one of its philosophical strands—Continental Liberalism) lies in its unwillingness to accept any concept of "true order" as discernible in the nature of things. It reduces all connections between and among individuals and groups to "power" relationships—relationships grounded in will, not reason. Power is seen as the imposition of will alone, and the modernist regime, left to its own devices, swings wildly from an abstract defense of the rights of the isolated individual or sovereign self (á la Locke, Rawls, or Dworkin) to an abstract defense of the will of the *demos* (á la Rousseau). Or, as Murray puts it, "society, trapped in the false antithesis of unlimited freedom vs. unlimited power, will swing helplessly between the extremes of individualistic anarchy and totalitarian tyranny."[38] In fact, the Continental Liberals of the nineteenth century—the French laicists—made a somewhat paradoxical effort to latch on to both poles at the same time, endorsing a statist individualism whose primary objective was the total emancipation of all individuals from the arbitrariness of any social and political institutions to which they have not voluntarily chosen to be tied.

Thus, any variant of laicist democracy is a form of pseudoreligiosity that dares not speak its name, a monism that would comprehensively reorder our spiritual and political lives under the guise of maintaining civil peace in a religiously and morally fractured community. This monism, like all monisms, threatens to undermine the fragile institutions of constitutional democracy:

1. It would restore the notion of man as *polis* animal alone, although this *polis* animal would be radically different from the Platonic or Aristotelian seeker of an objectively definable good life. It would emphasize the primacy

of the political over the spiritual precisely because it is through the "despiritu-alized" (i.e., laicized) institutions of political life that man is to be freed from the chains of those arbitrary spiritual authorities whose "truths" contradict its own orthodoxy. (This new *polis* animal also differs from the *polis* animal of classical Greece because the latter lived in ignorance of revelation. This sov-ereign self explicitly rejects any law higher than that of his own choosing.)

2. This new orthodoxy rejects Christian personalism, and its careful effort to balance a concern for human rights with legitimate social responsibilities. Instead, it espouses a monist conception of sovereignty, be it the sovereignty of the autonomous self, the *demos,* the political process, or the state.

3. The laicized state has the right and duty to spread *"les lumieres"* to those unenlightened individuals who refuse to accept the newly regnant political or-thodoxy. Prejudice must be rooted out, and any traditional form of religiosity must be transformed into a *res privata*. Persons are free to be orthodox Chris-tians or Jews, or fundamentalist Christians, as long as their beliefs are subor-dinated to the political truth that every individual (or state or *demos*) must be the autonomous determiner of his own goals and purposes.

Murray himself opposed this kind of Liberalism and he expressed the fear, as early as 1950, that American constitutionalism was undergoing a retheo-retization along more radical laicized lines. While it is beyond the scope of this essay to determine whether Murray's fears have been fully realized, it is inter-esting to note that many of the critics of contemporary American Liberal con-stitutionalism speak in decidedly Murrayan terms about the problems that con-front us. For example, Gerard V. Bradley has argued that the antiperfectionist liberalism of Rawls and Dworkin (and of those Supreme Court justices who follow their cue) provides a playground for the autonomous self, a self that de-fines its own moral norms consistent with a similar right of "self-definition" on the part of others.[39] Under this dispensation, freedom of religion—and, indeed, freedom from religion—must be protected because many individuals *choose* to follow religious precepts (or ignore them). And the establishment of reli-gion, or even support for religion generally, is deemed unconstitutional pre-cisely because religion is a *res privata*. Whereas Murray argued for the subor-dination of the establishment clause to the free exercise clause in order to protect the *res sacra* at the hands of the *res politica,* the antiperfectionist Lib-eral constructs a new *res sacra* and encharges the political and legal branches of government to enforce it.

Stanley Hauerwas has argued that this kind of retheoretizing of the political order has an effect not only upon what we think of religion but also upon what we think about all the institutions of civil society:

> the very language of "intermediate associations" [i.e., the language employed by Liberals] already betrays liberal presuppositions which distort the moral reality of

such institutions as the family. Whatever else the family is, it is not but another voluntary association. The very means used to insure that the democratic state be a limited state — namely, the rights of the individual — turn out to be no less destructive for intermediate institutions than the monistic state of Marxism. For it is the strategy of liberalism to insure the existence of the "autonomy of cultural and economic life" by insuring the freedom of the individual. Ironically, that strategy results in the undermining of intermediate associations because they are now understood only as those arbitrary institutions sustained by the private desires of individuals.[40]

Murray would undoubtedly agree that the liberal preoccupation with individual rights (conceived, of course, in a rationalist rather than Christian personalist sense) is destructive of the natural social institutions that make for a truly good life. He might even maintain that this development is inevitable given the worldview upon which antiperfectionist liberals attempt to construct a defense of constitutional democracy.

Conclusion

It might be argued that Murray's principled defense of Christian personalist dualism as the best moral foundation for an experiment in democratic self-government is "modernist" and "liberal" in emphasis and tone. In fact, his argument for a juridical state that protects God-given personal rights from encroachment is personalist, not liberal. One can describe Murray as a "liberal" public philosopher only if one imposes upon his thought dichotomies that were foreign to Murray himself. Murray was neither a classical nor modernist political theorist. Rather, he attempted to lay out a defense of substantive political democracy that avoided the monisms implicit in classical and Liberal political thought, concerned as they were with asserting the superiority of the *res politica* over the *res sacra* and thereby transforming the *res sacra in temporalibus* into a purely political matter.

Murray's appreciation of the principled grounds for limited constitutional government is grounded in a distinctively Christian differentiation on political things, an article of faith that would reject the statist communitarianism of classical political thought and the statist individualism of modern liberal political thought. Murray defends a constitutional tradition that finds its roots in the moral realism of Thomas Aquinas. The "Basic Questions" confronting modernity must be answered, and they can be answered intelligibly, according to Murray, only if we recover a tradition of moral argument and civil conversation that finds its roots in the natural moral law. Those who would maintain that this recovery is impossible do not undermine the validity of Murray's ba-

sic argument. They point out, however, the fragility of Murray's project, per-
ilous times in which we live, and the precarious condition in which we find
American constitutional democracy.

Notes

1. John Hallowell, *The Moral Foundation of Democracy* (Chicago: University of
Chicago Press, Midway reprint, 1973), 89.

2. The following articles by Murray are indicative of Murray's effort during this
time period to lay out a principled Catholic defense of religious freedom and constitutional democracy: "St. Robert Bellarmine on the Indirect Power," *Theological Studies*
9, no. 4 (December 1948): 491–535; "Contemporary Orientations of Catholic Thought
on Church and State in the Light of History," *Theological Studies* 10, no. 2 (June 1949):
177–234; "On Religious Freedom," *Theological Studies* 10, no. 3 (September 1949):
409–32; "The Problem of State Religion," *Theological Studies* 12, no. 2 (June 1951):
155–78; "The Church and Totalitarian Democracy," *Theological Studies* 13, no. 4 (December 1952): 525–63.

3. Murray, "Governmental Repression of Heresy," *Proceedings of the Third Annual Meeting of the Catholic Theological Society of America,* Chicago, 1948, 56.

4. Murray, *We Hold These Truths: Catholic Reflections on the American Proposition* (New York: Sheed and Ward, 1960), 72–73. (All further references in the body of
the text are to this edition.)

5. Robert McElroy, cited in Keith Pavlischek, "The Real John Courtney Murray,"
First Things 6 (October 1990): 48.

6. Pavlischek, 49.

7. Ibid.

8. For an excellent discussion of precisely this point in regard to Murray's analy-
sis of the religion clauses of the First Amendment, see Gerard V. Bradley, "Beyond
Murray's Articles of Peace and Faith," in *John Courtney Murray and the American
Civil Conversation,* ed. Robert P. Hunt and Kenneth L. Grasso (Grand Rapids, Mich.:
Eerdmans, 1992), 181–204.

9. In addition to those works cited in note 2, supra, see: "Leo XIII on Church and
State: The General Structure of the Controversy," *Theological Studies* 14, no. 1 (March
1953): 1–30; "Leo XIII: Separation of Church and State," *Theological Studies* 14, no.
2 (June 1953): 145–214; "Leo XIII: Two Concepts of Government," *Theological Studies* 14, no. 4 (December 1953): 551–67; "Leo XIII: Government and the Order of Culture," *Theological Studies* 15, no. 1 (March 1954): 1–33. In each of these four articles,
Murray engages in a masterful exegesis of Leo's political thought, attempting to discern the bedrock of Catholic political principles from the contingent manner in which
Leo expressed them.

10. Murray, "Governmental Repression of Heresy," 34.

11. Murray, "Bellarmine on the Indirect Power," 513.

12. David Novak, "John Courtney Murray: A Jewish Appraisal," in *John Courtney Murray and the American Civil Conversation,* 45.

13. See Richard John Neuhaus, "Democracy, Desperately Dry," in *John Courtney Murray and the American Civil Conversation,* 3–18, for further development of this theme.

14. Murray, "Contemporary Orientations," 188.

15. J. Leon Hooper, *The Ethics of Discourse: The Social Philosophy of John Courtney Murray* (Washington, D.C.: Georgetown University Press, 1986). My treatment of Hooper's thesis, upon which this section of my essay relies, can be found in *The Journal of Law and Religion* 7, nos. 1 and 2 (1990): 485–90.

16. Hooper, 7.

17. Ibid., 202ff. It should be noted here that Hooper's interpretation of Lonergan is also open to question, but that questioning lies outside the scope of this essay.

18. Ibid., 176, 142.

19. As late as 1965, Murray was still affirming "the rational imperatives that rise from the depths of the concrete human person, the dictates of reason that claim affirmation as natural law" (Murray, "Religious Freedom," in *Freedom and Man,* ed. Murray [New York: P.J. Kenedy and Sons, 1965], 138). Thus, the later historically conscious Murray hardly rejected the idea of natural law. Rather, the natural moral law served as a foundation for a defense of the substantive dignity of the human person.

20. Hooper, 203.

21. For further elaboration of this effort on Murray's part to push the ontological envelope, see Kenneth L. Grasso, "We Held These Truths: The Transformation of American Pluralism and the Future of American Democracy," in *Murray and the American Civil Conversation,* 89–115.

22. See Neuhaus, *supra,* for the argument that Murray was "most determinedly, a liberal" (4). Neuhaus's "liberal" Murray, however, is a determinedly different kind of liberal from the Americanist Murray depicted by Hooper.

23. See also Murray, "The Problem of State Religion," 164.

24. Murray, "For the Freedom and Transcendence of the Church," *American Ecclesiastical Review* 126, no. 1 (January 1952): 34.

25. "A Response to Mahony: Zeal and Politics," *Los Angeles Times,* 6 June 1989. For a more extended development of this interpretation of Murray's jurisprudential worldview, particularly regarding the issue of abortion, see Mary C. Segers, "Murray, American Pluralism, and the Abortion Controversy," in *Murray and the American Civil Conversation,* 228–48.

26. Murray, "Government and the Order of Culture," 12.

27. Murray, "The Problem of State Religion," 155.

28. Ibid., 162, 166. See also Murray, "Contemporary Orientations," 187–89.

29. Murray, "The Problem of State Religion," 163.

30. Murray, "The Church and Totalitarian Democracy," 531.

31. Murray, "Governmental Repression of Heresy," 72–73.

32. Ibid., 79.

33. Ibid., 31

34. Murray, "On the Structure of the Church-State Problem," in *The Catholic*

Church in World Affairs, ed. Waldemar Gurian and M. A. Fizsimons (Notre Dame, Ind.: University of Notre Dame Press, 1954), 29–30.

35. Murray, "The Church and Totalitarian Democracy." 553.

36. Murray maintained that Locke's own common sense, caution, and feeling for a constitutional tradition that was not of his own making prevented him from carrying his own metaphysical principles to their logical conclusion. The French Revolutionists, and their progeny, had no such inhibitions (*We Hold These Truths,* 306–7 ff.).

37. Here Murray's reading of Locke is similar to Hallowell's; cf., *The Moral Foundation of Democracy,* 68–88.

38. Murray, "Government and the Order of Culture." 5.

39. See, for example, Bradley's "The Constitution and the Erotic Self," *First Things* 16 (October 1991): 28–34. See also my own "Moral Orthodoxy and the Procedural Republic," in *Murray and the American Civil Conversation,* 249–70.

40. Stanley Hauerwas, "Christianity and Democracy: A Response," *Center Journal* 1 (Summer 1982): 44–45.

12

The Importance of Being Catholic: Unsolicited Advice from a Protestant Bystander

Stanley Hauerwas

Personal Reflections

"I was a Communist for the FBI" was the way the fifties television show began. In a similar manner, for fourteen years, "I was a moral theologian, if not for the Roman Catholic Church, at least for some Catholics around the University of Notre Dame." Of course, there is a great deal of hubris in that claim, since many Catholics, both at Notre Dame and elsewhere, would be quick to point out that few ever counted me among those who held the high office of moral theologian for the Church of Rome. No doubt they are right. At best, I was a Christian ethicist who was graciously given the opportunity to live, work, discuss, argue, and most importantly, worship with Roman Catholics. Moreover, my stay with Roman Catholics left its mark on me, for which I shall ever be grateful. I have been given more than I ever gave.

I am, therefore, grateful that I have been given the opportunity to make some contribution to the ongoing discussion of Roman Catholic moral theology and/or how to think and live as Catholics in the American context.[1] I hope that what I have to say will not be received as from an outsider, but at least from one who was, and hopefully still is, a little Catholic. I am a bystander because I want Catholics to be better Catholics than I can be, or am perhaps prepared to be.

I suspect Catholics should be a bit suspicious of Protestants who are enthusiastic about the current possibilities of the Church of Rome. For example, Richard Neuhaus in his wonderfully intriguing book *The Catholic Moment: The Paradox of the Church in the Post-Modern World*, could not say enough in support of John Paul II and Cardinal Ratzinger. He castigated Catholic liberals for following Protestants whose theology has become a form of anthropology.[2] In this regard, I must admit I am deeply sympathetic with Neuhaus. Despairing of the incoherence of theological discourse in mainstream Protestantism, we cannot help but have thought that Catholicism still possessed enough substance to mount a good argument. As Neuhaus said, prior to Vatican II:

> The problems of Roman Catholicism were "their" problems; now they are our problems. And, conversely, many of our problems have become theirs. The nature and mission of the Church, the relationship between Church and world, the role of Scripture and tradition, the question of teaching authority (the "magisterium") within the Christian community, the connection between teaching authority and theological exploration, the meaning of doctrine and dogma — the Roman Catholic Church is working through these questions on behalf of the entire Christian community. Of course, there are other Christian communities addressing these questions. Some communities, however, are not capable of that. Much of liberal Protestantism has lost the points of reference, even the vocabulary required for deliberation and debate on such questions. Most of conservative Protestantism, especially fundamentalist Protestantism, is not aware of the questions.[3]

Catholics are suspicious of the Protestant enthusiasm for Catholicism that Neuhaus represented before his ecclesial transition into the Roman Catholic faith. Similarly, they are suspicious of the enthusiasm that I represent. Many Catholics have spent their lives reacting against an authoritarian church. I am often sympathetic with such concerns, but the problem with that perspective is that it creates a false sense of security on the part of many Catholics. The Catholic Church could be criticized in the past because it was assumed that its fundamental structure would remain in place — bishops would continue to be bishops, Rome would still be Rome. In like manner, the "old Catholic moral theology" could be criticized without fundamentally challenging the assumption that the distinction between moral theology and fundamental theology made sense — that is, Catholic moral theology should no longer be "legalistic," but yet it was assumed that the structure of moral theology was still sound. As a consequence of these assumptions, criticism of the Church too often has been a distraction from the real business at hand: namely, helping the Church face the challenge of modernity. Catholics, in the name of reform, work to make the Church look like American democracy, failing to see that this cannot help but result in a church that is no longer capable of challenging the status quo. If I seem, therefore, too uncritical of Roman Catholicism, it is only because I have to live out the presuppositions of the alternative.

On the Very Idea of Ecumenical Ethics; or, Why Natural Law Is a Misleading Idea for Catholics

I have been asked to address the topic of ethics and ecumenism because Catholics find themselves in a quandary raised by the issue of abortion. The question seems to be how Catholics can continue to be good ecumenical citizens while at the same time maintaining the integrity of Catholic moral insights.

My simple answer is that I do not want Catholics to be good ecumenical citizens—I want them to be Catholics. There is nothing more important for the future unity of the Church than for them to be Catholics. For unless Catholics draw on the integrity of their hard-won wisdom about matters such as abortion, they will have failed in their calling to be a church that holds itself in judgment for the Church's disunity. I would argue that inherent in the Roman Catholic commitment to the magisterial office is the willingness to see the divided nature of the Church as a sign of Catholic unfaithfulness; Catholics have failed to help us see why Christians who find themselves separated from Rome should be what Catholics think we should be.[4] In short, Catholics have been so anxious to be like us that they have failed in their ecumenical task of helping us see what it means for any of us to be faithful to the Gospel on which our unity depends.

Of course, there is every reason for Catholics to be confused about these matters. After all, it was the strategy of most ecumenical movements in this century to concentrate on deeds rather than creeds. We assumed that there was little chance of reaching agreement in matters of belief, but at least we could join hands as people of good will to fight for justice, to protest on behalf of the oppressed, to stand for basic moral values. Moreover, such a stance seemed particularly well-suited to Catholicism since Catholic ethics was putatively based on natural law, and thus did not require any peculiar theological justification or ecclesiological practices to be rendered intelligible.[5]

Therefore, unlike Protestant accounts of the moral life that, at least in theory, maintained a much tighter connection between theological conviction and moral behavior, Catholics seemed to have a moral tradition particularly well-suited for ecumenical endeavors. In other words, it mattered not whether

Protestants believed in the authority of the magisterial office or had a correct understanding of nature–grace. All that mattered was that Catholics and Protestants could agree that certain forms of behavior are incumbent on Christians and all other people of good will. We may not have been able to agree about the status or nature of the sacraments, but at least we could agree that all Christians, Protestant and Catholic, ought to be for justice. If natural law meant anything it ought to mean that.

At a theoretical level this seems straightforward and clear. The problem, however, is that this account of natural law ethics failed to acknowledge or notice that it was only intelligible as long as Catholicism presupposed a social order whose practices had been formed by Catholic habits. I remember a story a Protestant observer at Vatican II told me that nicely illustrates the point: A bishop asked his theological advisor, "Now explain to me again why only Catholics seem to believe that contraception is wrong even though our position is based on natural law reasoning common to all people."

In an odd way, when Catholics came to America they learned that their "natural law" ethic was community and tradition specific, but it is not yet a lesson that they have taken to heart. Catholics came to America with a moral theology shaped by the presuppositions of Catholic Constantinianism. Natural law was the name given to the moral practices and principles discovered as essential to Christian living, if not survival, in that barbarian wilderness we now call Western civilization. Catholics could continue to believe in the theoretical validity of a natural law ethic even, or perhaps especially, interpreted through Kantian eyes, as long as they saw their lives centered, sociologically and historically, in Europe. After all, Protestantism, whether in its Lutheran, Calvinist, or Anglican forms, still had to make do with societies that had been formed as Catholic. (This is but a reminder that Protestantism remains both theologically and sociologically a parasitic form of the Christian faith. Without Catholicism, Protestants make no sense—a hard truth for Catholic and Protestant alike to acknowledge.)

That changed when Catholics came to America. By "came" I mean when Catholics took up the project of being Americans, rather than being Catholics who happen to live in America. For when they came to America they had to live in a society that was putatively Christian, and yet a society in which they were not "at home." The Catholic Church knew how to live in cultures that were completely foreign—in India and Japan—but how was she to learn to live in America, a culture that at once looks Christian but might in fact be more foreign than China?

It was a confusing challenge for Catholics. They came here with the habits and practices of a Constantinian ethic, allegedly based on natural law presuppositions, and they discovered that to sustain those habits they had to become a sect. Protestant Constantinianism forced Catholic Constantinians to withdraw into their own enclaves — into their own ghettos — in order to maintain the presumption that they possessed an ethic based on natural law grounds. What a wonderful thing God did to Catholics. Contemplating it can only confirm what an extraordinary sense of humor God must possess.

For example, Catholics came to America thinking that societies had the obligation to educate children about the true and good. Yet when confronted by putative neutral public education that presumed that everyone agreed that church and state ought to be separated, Catholics were forced to build their own school system. Where else would Catholics learn that the life of the mind could not and should not be separated from the life of prayer? I do not wish to be misunderstood. I am aware that there were many reasons for Catholics to live in ghettos, not the least of which was Protestant anti-Catholicism (which is still more virulent than Catholics generally are willing to acknowledge). Nor do I wish to invite Catholics to wallow in romantic nostalgia for the often wonderful and terrible forms of life those ghettos produced. Rather, I simply want to call attention to the sociological form that was needed to sustain the Catholic project of a natural law-based moral theology.

Catholics in the Hands of Tolerant Protestants; or, Being Killed by Kindness

The problem for Catholics is no longer how to survive in a hostile environment dominated by Protestant and Enlightenment presuppositions. Now the great problem is how to survive liberal tolerance. Until recently, Catholics could depend on Protestant prejudice to keep themselves Catholic — that is, it may not have been clear what it meant to be Catholic, but at least Catholics could depend on Protestants to tell them why they were peculiar. However, as Protestants have become increasingly unclear as to what it means for them to be Protestant, it has become equally difficult to know — at least in matters moral — why being Catholic is different. From a Protestant perspective, as long as we are characterized by a general uncertainty about what we are about, it just seems to be a matter of courtesy to invite Catholics to become part of our amorphous search for identity.

This is a particularly dangerous situation for everyone. Catholics desiring to show that they have a positive attitude toward Protestants end up telling Protestants what we already know — for example, that moral matters such as abortion and divorce are extremely complex, so it is very hard to have predetermined moral stances on such issues. But if Catholics, thus, end up telling Protestants what they already know, consider the plight of Protestants! We end up telling secularists what they already know! These are strange results for traditions that are called into the world on the presumption that they have something to say that the world needs to hear.

In short, one of my worries is not that Catholics will fail to be ecumenical, but that when they come to cooperate with Protestants they will have become what we already are—that is, a denomination. In *The Restructuring of American Religion,* Robert Wuthnow documents the decline of mainstream Protestantism in America.[6] He confirms what I think many have sensed: that members of Protestant churches now depend less on belief in the particular theological and ecclesial heritage of their denomination than on how their religious organization provides a means for individuals to express their particular interests. American Protestants are no longer distinguished by whether they are Presbyterians or Methodists, but by whether they are "conservatives" or "liberals" within their denominations. Moreover, the meaning of conservative and liberal is determined primarily in terms of the options available within the context of the American political system rather than by larger theological and moral questions.

This has not happened to American Protestantism by accident, but rather is the result of our success. Conservative and liberal Protestants could disagree about the divinity of Christ, but they were in agreement that there was a pivotal connection between personal faith and the larger society. Wuthnow characterized their reasoning in the following manner:

> The good society depends on individuals acting responsibly to uphold moral and democratic values; but a sense of personal responsibility is best supported by conceptions of individual accountability to the sacred; and this sense of accountability requires acknowledging the higher authority of the divine, guilt and punishment whenever responsibility to the divine is not maintained, and the possibility of divine forgiveness, redemption, and even ennoblement.[7]

In our current context, this sounds remarkably conservative, so it is easy to overlook the assumption that the primary social task of mainstream Protestantism was to create and sustain a society that provided freedom for something called the individual—that is, our task was to make democracy work. Wuthnow suggests, therefore, that the supermarket with its myriad consumer products has become more of a symbol of freedom than the traditional flag-waving Fourth of July parade. "Freedom means the opportunity to choose from a variety of products, to select a full complement of goods that meet our individual needs and desires. It means having the financial resources with which to purchase any gadget of seeming use in our quest for personal development and self-expression"—and, of course, it means freedom to choose our "faith."[8]

In short, Protestantism helped to create, and legitimate, a form of social life that undermined its ability to maintain the kind of disciplined communities needed to sustain the church's social witness. In an essay written over twenty years ago, "The Voluntary Church: A Moral Appraisal," James Gustafson noted that the movement from the "gathered church" to the voluntary church almost irresistibly involves a compromised form of church. The decisive criteria for the voluntary church is no longer holiness of life, but rather

> the will to belong. The theological and experiential marks on which the in-group was defined from the out-group have lost their power. The zest for purity in the churches has given way to an acceptance of the impossibility of its achievement, and consequently to a more or less open membership. Now, instead of being gathered out of the body of strangers into the family of saints, the strangers volunteer to join the community of those like themselves, who find something meaningful in religious life for themselves, their children, or their neighborhood. Men admire the saints among them, and perhaps wish to join their small number. If they fail, however, there is no serious disruption of church life.[9]

What I find so interesting about this process is that it is also happening to Roman Catholics. They are becoming like Protestants, one denomination among others. There is no true church here, but rather one more association of people who, at best, share a common search for meaning. No doubt there is little that Catholics can do about this as they are subject to economic and social forces that make this process almost inevitable. What I find odd, however, is that the kind of moral theology that Catholics are generating in the name of freedom underwrites this process as a good.

Catholic Moral Theology
and the Ecumenical Task

How should Catholic moral theology be done if Catholics are to be full participants in ecumenical dialogue and action? The question of how Catholics should relate to Protestants is of relatively little moment, given the social forces I have described. The more important question is: How can Catholics and Protestants alike, in this American context, maintain communities that are capable of disciplined, and Christian, moral discourse?

It is exactly this challenge that most Catholic moral theologians, whether they be of the left or the right, fail to make central for their work. Catholics on the left want the Church to be a morally disciplined community in order to speak in a determinative fashion about war and economic justice, but to speak less decisively about abortion, contraception, and divorce. Catholics on the right want the Church to speak decisively about abortion, sexual ethics, and divorce, but less decisively about war and economic justice. One would think that this difference would be the result of some fundamental disagreements about methodology of moral theology, but I think this is not the case. Rather, I fear that this kind of dispute already reflects a church that has lost its moorings for ethical reflection.

The issue can be framed in an even starker fashion. I would maintain that the natural law basis of Catholic moral theology was insufficient to prepare Catholics for the challenge of negotiating a society like America's. As a result, disputes between conservative Catholic moral theologians and liberal Catholic moral theologians do little to help Catholics locate the challenge they faced and continue to face in America. Natural law underwrote the assumption that Catholic moral theology could be written for anyone irrespective of his/her relation to faith in Jesus of Nazareth. But "anyone" in America turned out to be the "individual" of the Enlightenment whose very being depended on the refusal to acknowledge or spell out his/her particular history.

Thus, Catholic moral theologians have embraced the American project as part and parcel of what it means to do faithful moral theology. For example, consider some of the titles of recent works by Catholic moralists—Charles Curran, *American Catholic Social Ethics: Twentieth Century Approaches;*[10] John Coleman, *An American Strategic Theology;*[11] David Hollenbach, *Justice, Peace, and Human Rights: American Catholic Social Ethics in a Pluralist Context;*[12] Dennis McCann, *New Experiments in Democracy: The Challenge of American Catholicism;*[13] *American and Catholic: The New Debate;*[14] and George Weigel, *Catholicism and the Renewal of American Democracy.*[15] It would be a mistake, of course, to read too much into titles, but it is at least interesting that Catholic thinkers seem to think that Catholics can and should be modified by the designation "American."

This emphasis on "American" might be interpreted as a purely descriptive account of the unavoidability of the American reality. No doubt at times it does mean no more than this. But it also means more since there is the suggestion, not only among these authors in particular but also among American Catholic moral theologians in general, that "American" is a normative recommendation that should change how moral theology is done. Moreover, it is a recommendation that is in continuity with the deepest wellspring of past Roman Catholic moral theology—namely, that grace completes nature. Thus, moral theology can first be based on the assumption that there is no fundamental tension between the general societal ethos and a specifically Catholic moral conviction.

For example, Dennis McCann argues that the Americanist heresy condemned by *Testem Benevolentiae* was not a heresy at all. Rather, Americanism is not shameful "indulgence" but, as Max Stackhouse has recently pointed out, "a liberation to new duty given by the grace of God, which leads to voluntary community, disciplined personal life, lay intellectuality, and social outreach." Indeed, as Leo XIII feared, this liberation is a liberation from the church; but he failed to grasp the Americanists' hope that such a liberation also occurs for the sake of the church. At stake in the "certain liberty" for which Americanists stand condemned is, in Stackhouse's terms, the revolutionary American principle of "self-governing association" and its extension to all the institutional sectors of society. America thus is an experiment in which the basic, primordial freedom of the church to order its own life is taken as the basis for the organization of political, economic, educational, familial, and other aspects of life.[16]

The difficulty, according to McCann, is that the "certain liberty" valued by Hecher, and later by Murray, has not been fully realized by the Church's "search for self-identity" after Vatican II.[17] Yet he is convinced that the future is with the Americanist as it is the

consistent tendency of Catholics to define their own integrity in terms of this nation's ongoing experiment in "self-governing association." In this sense, the Americanist heresy is rooted in the very foundations of Christianity in this country, a heritage common to the whole spectrum of American Protestant and Catholic communities of faith. It has become, and inevitably must become, the agenda for American Catholicism whenever Catholic people consider fully the logic of their circumstances here—how it is that their habitual patterns of organizing themselves for participation in our common life are religiously significant.[18]

McCann argues that it is the task of future generations not only to make America more American by a fuller institutionalization of that "certain liberty," but to make the Catholic Church itself more American. The Church must become the same kind of voluntary, self-governing institution that already characterizes most of American life.

According to McCann, the primary virtue for a church so constituted, internally and externally, is civility. Appealing to John Courtney Murray, McCann suggests that civility should be understood as "a disposition to conduct politics not as open warfare among conflicting interest groups, but as skilled and self-disciplined public 'conversations.' "[19] As such, civility is not just a political necessity, but a religious virtue:

Its faithful exercise makes each of the communities participating in the American "public church," as well as their respective members, more disposed to regard each other in public as mutually interdependent, as bound to each other, in Martin Marty's terms, "by explicit or tacit agreement, to mutual communication, of whatever is useful and necessary for the harmonious exercise of social life."

"Civility" thus is the ecumenical virtue *par excellence;* for in our pluralistic context, it is an indispensable precondition for building the Kingdom of God in America. Pluralism may exist without "civility," but a pluralistic society cannot, if it lacks the sense of social interdependence which this virtue fosters among diverse communities who, both because of and in spite of their differences, remain pledged to one another for the sake of the common good.[20]

I must admit I thought that after John Murray Cuddihy's *The Ordeal of Civility: Freud, Marx, Levi-Strauss, and the Jewish Struggle with Modernity,*[21] no one would be able to recommend civility without apology again. For as Cuddihy points out, civility is that part of the modernization process that requires the bureaucratization of private affect and public demeanor. It is the great bourgeois project to adapt the individual's inner life to the socially appropriate.

"Niceness" is as good a name as any for the informally yet pervasively institutionalized civility expected — indeed required — of members (and of aspirant members) of that societal community called the civic culture. Intensity, fanaticism, inwardness — too much of anything, in fact — is unseemly and bids fair to destroy the fragile solidarity of the surface we call civility. Civility, as the very medium of Western social interaction, presupposes the differentiated structures of a modernizing "civil society." Civility is not merely regulative of social behavior; it is an order of "appearance" constitutive of that behavior. This medium is itself the message and the message it beamed to the frontrunners of a socially emancipating Jewry came through loud and clear: "Be nice." "The Jews," writes Maurice Samuel looking back on the epoch of Emancipation, "are probably the only people in the world to whom it has ever proposed that their historic destiny is — to be nice."[22]

It may well be unfair to juxtapose Cuddihy's account of civility to that of McCann's. McCann would certainly protest that he is concerned to save particularity in the name of healthy pluralism. But it is not enough to save pluralism. One must be able to show, given the context of the Enlightenment ideology and institutions indicated by Cuddihy, that the forces of modernity that grind all genuine disputes into calm "conversations" can be resisted.

Nor is it enough, as McCann and Hollenbach do, to appeal to "justice as participation," as if the very evocation of that phrase represents a coherent social theory or policy. Hollenbach, for example, notes that the disagreements among Rawls, Nozick, Sandel, and Walzer concerning justice could be seen as a vindication of MacIntyre's and Hauerwas's analysis of the moral anarchy of our society and our allegedly sectarian social strategy. Rather than a confusion about justice, according to Hollenbach, what we have is the beginning of a genuine argument about justice. We do, that is, if we realize that there is not one meaning to justice in some univocal sense. All of the inter-locutors in the current disputation have got their hands on some part of the reality we are in search of. Socrates knew this phenomenon well: dialectic, that is argument, is a process of sorting through a host of opinions to discern what is true in each, in search of that which is most true, most good. The argument about what justice means is as old as Western civilization. The quality of the argument today may well determine whether this civilization has a future, or whether its future will be in any sense civilized. In the face of these high stakes, I think the sectarian retreat of MacIntyre and Hauerwas is ultimately, if unwittingly, a failure of nerve. It fails to appreciate new possibilities present today for expressing love of one's neighbor by engaging in the march of cultural transformation.[23]

"Justice as participation" turns out to be another way of saying that Catholics should be good Americans.

Of course, I do not mean to imply that everyone who calls for an "American Catholic moral theology" agrees with McCann's and Hollenbach's understanding of that project. (Indeed, I assume that there are significant differences between even the two of them.) In particular, I find John Coleman to be especially sensitive to the challenge facing American Catholicism. As he notes,

> What seems abundantly clear is that the American Catholic Church cannot have its cake and eat it too. It cannot hunger after unitary prophetic strategies which presuppose authoritarian patterns within a largely hierarchical church or a restricted lay autonomy and, simultaneously, foster a human relation and voluntary model premised on pluralism and a personal freedom. . . . It [the church] cannot accept the game of pluralism and still expect to impose its unique agenda on the societal outcomes.[24]

Coleman urges the Catholic Church to explore all the creative possibilities of the human relations and voluntary model of the Church in spite of the liability of that church's penchant to become captured by class-based moral consensus. As he puts it, "with the collapse of the immigrant church and the increasing education of American Catholics, the church is fated to that model in America."[25] A sobering prediction indeed.

At stake in these sociological observations is not only the question of the Church's accommodation to this society, but questions of how moral rationality is understood and practiced. In the interest of joining the arguments in our culture about matters such as abortion, the Catholic Church is tempted to underwrite those forms of Enlightenment rationalism that deny their traditioned character. Catholics, more than any other people, must resist the presumption of modernity that those from other traditions are "really just like us" because Catholics speak a putatively universal language that makes their behavior intelligible. What must be admitted is that Catholics and non-Catholics live in different worlds. That is why Christians finally do not seek to convince the other; we seek to convert. These are complex matters involving matters of relativism and truth that cannot be explored here. Suffice it to say, however, that at least one of the ways we know the truth of the Catholic faith is when we recognize its unwillingness to substitute for the reality of the Church the insubstantial universal reasons for knowing and worshiping God rightly.

Abortion and Ecumenical Relations

I am aware that I have not addressed the question of how abortion fits into this account. Indeed, it may seem that I have said little about moral theology, but instead have been addressing the general historical and sociological situation of Catholicism in America. Moral theology more properly deals with concrete issues such as how to reason about abortion, suicide, contraception, and so on. Instead of addressing these issues, I have criticized the Americanism of Catholic social ethics in order to defend my "sectarianism," or, to put the issue summarily, I have suggested that there is nothing wrong with Catholics that could not be made better if they would just quit being nice and let the "nasty" side come out.

This suggestion relates directly to how Catholics should articulate their concern about abortion to the wider society. Michael Schwartz, in "The Restorationist Perspective: Catholic Challenge to Modern Secular America," notes that abortion has become the test case for the honeymoon between "Americanist Catholics—who are usually well-educated and upwardly mobile—and the secular culture to which they have surrendered."[26] These Catholics, Schwartz notes, are subject to the paradoxical attitude that secular culture adopted toward postconciliar Catholicism:

> Catholicism is still despised to the extent that it claims to teach with authority, but that contempt is no longer mixed with fear, only with condescension. The pope is unable to assert his authority effectively over even the clergy, much less the laity. And so we have the new strain of anti-Catholic sentiment expressing itself by praising those Catholics who separate themselves from the beliefs and practices of their church. To the extent that the reality of the church is despised, so individual Catholics who subordinate their Catholicism to some secular ideology are held up as models of intellectual honesty, courage, and all-around decency. The only good Catholic, it would seem, is a bad Catholic.[27]

Schwartz observes, however, that for such Catholics a crisis was occasioned exactly when their "new-found ecumenical friends decided that the next great step in the advance of civilization was to authorize the killing of babies. We were tolerant, and we desperately wanted to be accepted. But we were still Catholics, not barbarians. We drew the line at murdering the young."[28] In opposition to those in power, Catholics knew that this was not another question to be resolved by interest group politics. Catholics knew they had a duty to stand for life, to choose, as Schwartz puts it, Christ over Caesar.

This frames the issue properly. For if the strategy I have recommended in this essay is close to being right, it will remind Catholics that opposition to abortion involves much more than just opposition to abortion. In fact, opposition to abortion does nothing less than to put Catholics at odds with the primary ethos and institution of the liberal culture that has just accepted them. To be against abortion means more than politics as usual. As Schwartz says,

> The unfortunate truth is that most Catholics in America look to something other than the church for their basic direction in life. There are among us today people who call themselves Catholic but who are, above all, something else: feminists, Marxists, Republicans, evolutionists, pacifists, or whatever. Not everything in these ideologies is in conflict with Catholicism, and not everything in them is in harmony with Catholicism. But where these secular ideologies are in conflict with Catholicism, those who have placed their faith elsewhere insist that the church must change to conform itself to the higher truth proclaimed by the ideology of their choice. No secular ideology can save. None of them, ultimately is the truth. Only the Catholic faith answers the hunger of the human heart. Only the Catholic faith is true. Only the Catholic faith can bring us to the wholeness which consists in seeing God as God really is. It is not, I am saying, the church which must change to accommodate to the things of the world, but the world must be transformed, folded under the mantle of the Bride of Christ.[30]

I have resisted the opportunity to critique the methodology of past Roman Catholic moral theology except for a few generalizations about natural law as the presumed starting point for Catholic moral reflection. But if Schwartz is right, as I think he is, it means that moral theology cannot be divorced from those practices and virtues that derive their intelligibility from theological convictions. After all, Catholic convictions about the wrongness of abortion have never been derived from abstract principles about the "right to life," but rather have been rational just to the extent that Catholic people were formed by practices that made them a community capable of welcoming children into the world. What is "natural" about that practice is that is the way we were created—a claim about "nature" that unavoidably requires acknowledgment that there is a Creator.

As a way to make these arguments concrete, let me suggest a different way to test the issue of ecumenical ethics. Rather than thinking about how Catholics can participate in, for example, the California Conference of Churches, Catholics might want to ask whether the bishops ought not to command that all Catholics participate in Operation Rescue. Catholics would then have to associate with the most despised of our society—Bible-believing fundamentalists—in nonviolent action. Indeed, as Charlotte Tow Allen reported in the December 8, 1988, *Wall Street Journal* article entitled "Anti-Abortion Movement's Anti-Establishment Face," there are tensions between Catholics and Protestants in the anti-abortion movement.

> Evangelicals rely exclusively on the Bible for moral authority. "I don't see how someone could believe abortion is murder without believing in the Bible," says Michael Hersch, director of Operation Rescue in Atlanta. This can be disconcerting for those who believe abortion violates natural law as well. Catholics have a long tradition of incorporating natural law principles into their theology, which makes it easier for them to discourse on issues with Jews, atheists, and other non-Catholics.

Yes, far too easy, but what a wonderful opportunity God has given Catholics to discover the richness of being Catholic, and, therefore, to call us all to the unity of God's good kingdom.

Notes

1. This essay is a revised version of the Tenth Paul Wattson Lecture at the University of San Francisco on 27 February 1989. The issue I was asked to address was "Ethics and Ecumenism: Can Christians Divided by Moral Issues Be United?" I was honored to be asked to deliver the Wattson Lecture since I admire the Society of the Atonement's tireless work in service to the prayer, "That all may be one."

2. If you ever wonder where Protestant liberalism has gone to die, you will discover it in the soul of many Roman Catholic theologians.

3. Richard John Neuhaus, *The Catholic Moment: The Paradox of the Church in the Post-Modern World* (San Francisco: Harper and Row, 1987), 66–67. I do not share Neuhaus's sense that this is "the moment in which the Roman Catholic Church in the United States assumes its rightful role in the culture-forming task of constructing a religiously informed public philosophy for the American experiment in ordered liberty" (283). I do not think it is the church's task, Protestant or Catholic, to generate such a "public philosophy," and I am particularly distrustful of what "ordered liberty" means. Nonetheless, I share his strong claim that the essential crisis for our time and the church is unbelief. I read his book as a call for the church to recover its theological integrity— a recovery that surely has, as Neuhaus rightly suggests, extraordinary social implications.

4. For an attempt to affirm the importance of the papacy from a Protestant point of view, see Robert Wilken's and my article, "Protestants and the Pope," *Commonweal* 107, no. 3 (February 1980): 80–85.

5. I do not mean to obscure the different accounts of natural law within Roman Catholic moral theology. Indeed, it is my own view that the position that I have just characterized—that natural law could be divorced from theological claims—has little to do with the kind of natural law position represented by St. Thomas Aquinas. However, this account of natural law ironically was accepted by both "conservative" and "liberal" Catholic moral theologians. For an excellent critique of this turn in natural law theory, see Russell Hittinger, *A Critique of the New Natural Law Theory* (Notre Dame: University of Notre Dame Press, 1987).

6. Robert Wuthnow, *The Restructuring of American Religions* (Princeton: Princeton University Press, 1988).

7. Ibid., 58.

8. Ibid., 279.

9. James Gustafson, *The Church as Moral Decision Maker* (Philadelphia: Pilgrim Press, 1970), 110.

10. Notre Dame: University of Notre Dame Press, 1982.

11. New York: Paulist Press, 1982.

12. New York: Crossroads, 1988.

13. Kansas City: Sheed and Ward, 1987.

14. Edited by Joe Holland and Anne Barsanti (South Orange, N.J.: Pillar Books, 1988).

15. (New York: Paulist Press, 1989). Weigel says:

Catholic incarnational humanism is a more attractive vehicle of evangelization than the various dialectical approaches found in fundamentalist and evangelical Protestant worlds—and far more adequate than the apologetic accommodationism that has characterized the Protestant mainline for over a generation. Catholic liturgical sensibilities are proving attractive to those who find the lecture-as-worship model a bit aesthetically thin after a while. Catholicism's classic natural law approach to moral reasoning could make an enormous contribution to a pluralistic democracy trying to determine the right role of religiously-based values in public policy discourse. The ideal of the "communitarian individual" in American democratic capitalism coheres nicely with Catholicism's central social-ethical principles of personalism, the common good, and subsidiarity.(25)

In the light of such a quotation, I am tempted to simply say, "I rest my case." At the very least, we must ask Weigel to show what form of the "classical natural law" reasoning is so helpful for a "pluralist democracy." Not only do I think that appeals to "pluralism" are empty in the face of the fragmentation of American society, but I also think that Weigel does not appreciate how controverted any questions about practical reasoning are today. It is interesting that in this respect Weigel appeals to "common human experience" as the basis for natural law in thinkers such as Simon, Maritain, and Murray (197), but he seems innocent of the problematics of such an appeal. Even stranger, Weigel fails to understand that the same appeal to "common human experience" is what underwrites the program of liberal Catholic theologians of whom Weigel is so critical. In this respect, Weigel manifests the same difficulties as his great hero,

John Courtney Murray, who wanted to provide historical placing of Leo XIII's *Rerum Novarum,* but still wanted to make the precepts of natural law ahistorical. Like being pregnant, it is difficult to be only partly "historical."

16. McCann, 13.

17. The appeal to John Courtney Murray among those wishing to find a role for Catholicism in America is subject matter for a book in itself. One constantly wishes that the "real John Courtney Murray would stand up." I cannot see how the same person inhabits the pages of McCann, Curran, and Weigel. I think this is partly due to the incoherence of Murray's own position: Murray tried to combine Catholic social thought, which shares much with what is being called "communitarian" today, with liberal social theory. In the last chapter of *We Hold These Truths,* Murray rightly noted that the liberal social theory of Hobbes was ultimately incoherent, and offered Catholic natural law as an alternative. But his "natural law theory" certainly cannot be seen as originating the sustaining ethos behind American constitutional practice. Even if it were, his natural law remains far too rationalistic to sustain the kind of duties characteristic of the early encyclicals.

18. McCann, 27.

19. Ibid., 56.

20. Ibid., 176.

21. Boston: Beacon Press, 1974, 13–14.

22. Ibid., 13.

23. Hollenbach, 78–79.

24. Coleman, 146–47. For an equally powerful, if not more powerful, analysis of this dilemma, see Gustafson, *supra.*

25. Coleman, 147.

26. In *American and Catholic,* edited by Holland and Brisanti, 90.

27. Schwartz, 88–89.

28. Ibid., 90.

29. Ibid., 91.

30. Ibid., 95–96.

13

A Jewish Appreciation of Catholic Social Teaching

Matthew Berke

Is it good for the Jews? Among Israel in exile, this question has perennially been the standard for measuring all issues, great and small, as well as providing the punchline for more than a few jokes. ("Father!" exclaimed the immigrant's son, breathlessly, "Did you hear that Babe Ruth hit three home runs today?!" "Yes," replied the father, "but is it good for the Jews?")

That papal social teaching might be "good for the Jews"—that is, that its success might coincide in significant measure with Jewish ideals and interests—is a thought that would have seemed absurd to most generations of Jews throughout the common era. After all, the papal teaching of contempt was responsible, directly or indirectly, for much of the persecution and forced isolation of Diaspora Jews since the Middle Ages. In the early modern period, when Jews finally began to win a measure of civil and religious equality, every gain was achieved in the teeth of a reactionary opposition that often included the Catholic Church. Even within the memory of people living today, the Catholic magisterium was frequently hostile to toleration, pluralism, and democracy. Not surprisingly, Jews for the past two centuries have tended to favor laws and institutions derived from liberal political theory and the Enlightenment, especially (and contrary to Catholic preference) the idea of a secular public arena, free of religious establishment or bias.

During the past three decades, however, papal teaching has undergone significant change (or as Catholic apologists would say, "development"), forcing

235

us to revise our image of the Catholic Church as an eternal foe of Judaism and the Jewish people. *Nostra Aetatae* (1965), a document produced by the Second Vatican Council, repudiated collective blame of the Jews for the Crucifixion; subsequent Church documents and educational practices have been at pains to denounce anti-Semitism and to present Judaism in a favorable light. The present pope, John Paul II, has shown a special concern for improved relations between the two faith communities, explicitly rejecting the old supersessionist argument that the New Testament cancels God's covenant with the Jews and affirming the continuing religious validity of "living Judaism." In December of 1993, the Vatican finally extended full diplomatic recognition (withheld for the previous forty-five years) to the state of Israel.

The Church's general social teaching has also been of more than passing interest to Jews. Doctrinal developments effected during and after Vatican II have brought about what Catholic ethicist and theologian George Weigel calls "the Catholic human rights revolution." Religious liberty, once regarded as an anathema or as a circumstance to be endured only when there is not a Catholic majority, is now described as the most fundamental of all human rights, a requirement of our freedom and of "the dignity of the human person." Consistent with this view, the Church has renounced all claims for using the state's coercive apparatus. ("The Church," says John Paul II in *Redemptoris Missio,* "imposes nothing, she only proposes.") While not becoming democratic in its own internal governance or accepting the naturalistic anthropology often associated with a liberal worldview, the Church has embraced the whole constellation of institutions commonly regarded as classically liberal: pluralism, democracy, market economics, and, above all, universal respect for human rights. This transformation has not been merely theoretical: by virtue of its active opposition to various dictatorships around the world, the Church has emerged as an unexpected champion of the free society.

These developments are, quite naturally, a source of gratification and relief for the Jewish community—especially the Church's refutation of the deicide charge, its recognition of living Judaism, and its unequivocal endorsements of religious liberty and tolerance. Some of these points might perhaps belong under the category of theological instruction rather than social teaching, but from a Jewish standpoint they are a necessary precondition for any serious interfaith dialogue, on social and moral issues or on anything else. It would perhaps be too much to say that Jews warm to the general idea of Catholic social thought, though. Most probably regard it as something inimical to their interests, which are seen to have security and space only to the extent that liberal, secular principles dominate the public sphere. This attitude reflects in part a lingering suspicion based on long, and unhappy, historical relations—including continued disquiet about the role of the Church during the Holocaust era. (At the signing of the diplomatic pact between Jerusalem and the Vatican, Israel's deputy foreign minister, Yossi Beilin, gave poignant expression to the prominence of history in the Jewish mind: "Behind the agreement," he said, "there are very few years of light and many more years of darkness."[1]) It reflects also a continuing unease about how Church teaching might work its way into law and public policy on a variety of current issues, such as contraception, abortion, divorce, and school prayer.

It is difficult to gainsay a basic common sense that gives priority to the weight of Jewish experience and that recognizes, realistically, that differences between the Jewish community and the Catholic Church can be expected to persist indefinitely into the future. Nevertheless, one may still suggest that Jewish well-being — to say nothing of justice — requires that old stereotypes not blind us to new realities, that we not refight old battles when newer, more dangerous, threats surround us. At the close of the twentieth century, it seems unlikely that Catholicism will pose a threat to Jewish life. Far more dangerous than the reemergence of a triumphalist Catholic Church is the general decline in civilized values, public morality, and intellectual life that has increasingly come to characterize our society over the last few decades. The tendency to anarchy, of course, is a problem for everyone; but it is also probably the case that Jews — a prosperous and culturally prominent minority about whom ancient libels arise whenever society is under stress — are more likely than most to be immediate victims of social breakdown.

It is in this context of cultural stress that a sober Jewish appreciation of papal teaching must take place. For it is one of the curious aspects of the current social situation that liberalism, the public philosophy usually associated with Jewish equality and well-being in times past, seems unable to arrest the barbarism of modern culture; indeed, contemporary liberalism is implicated in many of the most corrosive moral and intellectual trends of our time. The other side of the coin is this: the Catholic Church, our former nemesis, now constitutes a major force opposing social disintegration. If, in the past, it was tardy in recognizing the providence of a liberal democratic order, today Catholic teaching not only embraces that order, it also serves a crucial (in some respects unique) role in fortifying its essential first principles — in particular, the idea that moral truth is not an oxymoron but a necessary element for any kind of civil, tolerant, and reasonable public life, and also the conception of society as a differentiated body whose various agencies must always protect their proper autonomy from the encroachments of the state.

In assessing the social role of Catholic teaching, it is necessary always to remember that the ultimate desire of the pope is for all people to "come to Rome." Yet, at the same time, we can also appreciate the fact that the Church has in recent years taken upon itself the task of reintroducing a kind of baseline morality into Western society; even if it cannot convert everyone to Catholicism, the Church appears determined to halt the progressive paganization of contemporary culture. The key documents of the Church's latest social teachings tend to be addressed (directly or indirectly) "not only to believers but to all people of good will" (see, for instance, *Veritatis Splendor* #3). The Church's success in combating neopaganism, it seems to me, is wholly consistent with the ideals of Judaism and the long-term security of the Jewish community; or to put the matter more bluntly, it is good for the Jews. The remainder of this essay will be devoted to exploring common ground with Catholicism, using as principal points of reference John Paul II's most recent encyclicals: *Centesimus Annus* (One Hundred Years, 1991) and *Veritatis Splendor* (The Splendor of Truth, 1993).[2]

Normative Standards

Judaism has always been concerned, at least in some measure, with the moral condition of the larger human community. Traditionally, distinctions were made between, on the one hand, evil idolators and, on the other, righteous gentiles who have a share in the world-to-come by virtue of observing the so-called Laws of Noah. The Noahide code (implied in Genesis 9:4–7) prohibits idolatry, blasphemy, murder, adultery, robbery, and eating flesh cut from a living animal; it also requires the establishment of law courts. Christianity of course surpassed this bare ethical minimum and developed a moral and religious tradition as complex as that of Judaism. Maimonides, the most revered Jewish teacher of the Middle Ages, saw in Christianity part of God's preparation of the nations to receive the fullness of the law; he also recognized that Christianity clearly worshipped the God of Abraham, Isaac, and Jacob (albeit in an incarnational and trinitarian form not acceptable to Jews). Franz Rosenzweig, probably the preeminent Jewish thinker of the twentieth century, went so far as to speak of Christianity as a kind of partner with Judaism in God's covenant and in the salvation history of the world. Maimonides and Rosenzweig may not represent the typical, everyday view of Christianity among Jews throughout the ages, but neither are they minor currents. The point is well established: the moral state of the nations is not a matter of indifference to Jews, and Christianity, when it is not an implacable enemy, can be accounted a positive influence.[3]

A passage in the Jewish prayerbook, recited when the Torah is returned to the Ark, is perhaps useful in understanding the Jewish ethical ideal in this context: "Behold, I have given you a good doctrine, My Torah: do not forsake it. It is a tree of life to those who hold it fast, and all who cling to it find happiness. Its ways are ways of pleasantness, and all its paths are peace." At least two principles are implied in this passage that might apply not only to Judaism but also to other religio-moral systems, Catholicism in particular: first, that morality involves not just an ultimate ideal or aim but a system of specific rules and prohibitions that help keep life on a straight path to its ultimate good; and second, these rules, taken as a whole over the long run, not only lead to, but themselves constitute, a good life.

Because of an emphasis on love and grace over, even against, a complex of life-regulating rules, some expressions of Christianity can be criticized for a susceptibility to antinomianism. Roman Catholicism, however, clearly avoids the antinomian temptation through its many rituals, spiritual disciplines, and solemnly prescribed ethics; these elements might well be seen, from the Jewish standpoint, as a Christian counterpart to the system of *mitzvot* (commandments). Though the Christian ethic was summarized by Jesus in a pair of precepts taken from the Hebrew Scripture—that is, to love God wholeheartedly and to love your neighbor as yourself—Catholic teaching never assumes that human affairs can be regulated simply by referring all of life's decisions to the ultimate principle of love; there are always specific requirements of right and wrong, which, says John Paul II, "have the capacity to clarify the daily decisions of individuals and entire societies" in such areas as "human sexuality, the family, and social, economic, and political life" (VS #4). Papal teaching recognizes that people cannot live in an ethical wilderness, between God and the Devil, without such rules. The story is recalled of the rich young man who asks, "Teacher, what good must I do to have eternal life?" and is told, "If you wish to enter into life, keep the commandments" (VS #6, with reference to Matthew 19:16–17). Thus, says the pope, "the Church's Magisterium also teaches the faithful specific particular precepts and requires that they consider them in conscience as morally binding" (VS #110).

It should be noted that the commandments are not regarded here as arbitrary, life-denying impositions that are alien to man's real impulses (VS #41), being accepted only in order to receive a payoff from God in the next life. Ethical requirements bind the conscience because they are *true*—true, that is, with respect to "what man is and what he must do" (VS #10) in order to flourish and enjoy the fullness of life in this world as well as the next, as an individual and as a member of the social body. "In fact, human freedom finds its authentic and complete fulfillment precisely in the acceptance of that law" (VS #35).

Throughout *Veritatis Splendor,* the pope repeats the idea that being moral involves living in truth. Because "particular, everyday choices" may be in accordance with or contrary to the truth, they inevitably " 'shape' a person's entire moral life" and "give moral definition to the very person who performs them, determining his *profound spiritual traits*" (VS #65 and #71).

The Plague of Relativism

Of course, the ethical teachings of Catholicism and Judaism differ over many "specific particular precepts." Without minimizing such differences, I believe it is fair to say that there is an underlying similarity between the two religions in the search for and commitment to truth, combined with a will to subordinate one's own immediate impulses and desires to that truth. Even in liberal Judaism—that is, the Conservative and Reform movements—this normative aspect is retained (albeit tenuously in the case of Reform). At this particular point in history, I would argue, specific differences between Catholic and Jewish teaching seem less significant than the abyss that separates both from the moral relativism so influential in the contemporary secular culture. An examination of relativism, with special attention to the critique of it in *Veritatis Splendor* and *Centesimus Annus,* reveals its corrosive effect on the reasoned discourse of a democratic society and on the public morality, as well as pointing to common ground between Catholic and Jewish approaches to ethics.

Though relativism is sometimes an elaborately worked out ideology, it is perhaps more often a sensibility that is held confusedly and inconsistently along with other unrelativistic beliefs. Its main idea is that there are no timeless and universal moral truths, only culturally determined norms and subjective preferences. In the absence of any final standards, the individual is completely free to determine right and wrong for himself or herself, and to live accordingly. Moral sovereignty resides in "conscience," which is understood not in the Jewish or Christian sense of the will to conform action to an objectively true and authoritative standard, but rather as an inner psychic sense or motive of the self that cannot be judged by any external criteria. No duties or restraints are binding upon the individual other than those that have been consented or contracted to—except that the individual must respect the absolute autonomy of other individuals, and refrain from judgments upon the "values" or "choices" of other autonomous selves. At the social level, policy and law are to be guided by the demands (usually described as "needs") of the times rather than by any sort of immutable or objective truth.

In one form or another, relativism has insinuated itself at every cultural level, from the high skepticism of the educated elite classes to the vulgarity of TV talk shows for the masses. At the elite level it is the U.S. Supreme Court, in the 1992 case of *Planned Parenthood v. Casey,* justifying the abortion right (and by implication much more) not on constitutional grounds nor even through reasoning about the rightness or wrongness of the act itself, but rather on the ground that an abortion license is necessary to safeguard the right "to define one's own concept of existence, of meaning, of the universe, and of the mystery of life." Relativism at the middle-brow level is anthropologist Joseph

Campbell's famous dictum to "follow your bliss," and at the popular level it is expressed in any number of familiar nostrums: "Yes, I think it's wrong, but I can't impose my values on anyone else"; "Nobody can tell you what to do, you just have to look into your heart and decide"; "There's only what's right for you." And so on.

Superficially, relativism appears to be a kind of live-and-let-live public philosophy, one that has, in diluted and unconscious ways, commended itself to many Christians and Jews—people of good will who have legitimate fears of an overbearing government that might seek to suppress every vice or enforce every virtue. However, the problem with the false humility and restraint of relativism is that it does not hold freedom accountable to what is true or good; thus it ends up insisting that church as well as state refrain from judging the morality of various acts. Whether held as an unconscious reflex or a conscious ideology, relativism is, from the standpoint of both Judaism and Christianity, an incoherent and, ultimately, very dangerous error. While Christian ethics contains elements that are in tension with Judaism, relativism is the very antithesis of Judaism and Jewish well being. Its influence creates a moral vacuum at the heart of culture, and ultimately this vacuum is filled by an ethic of pure power that reduces politics to a conflict of wills, with little or no role for moral reason.

Papal teaching seems to have a good fix on the specific flaws of relativism, why it is a threat to the common good and even to Jews in particular. It recognizes that democratic politics can function only when people can reason together. But reason can take place only if there are universal truths that are accessible to, and binding on, all. If there is no truth except the subjective truth of the individual, or of the ethnic group or sex, then citizens can at best emote toward one another—a form of communication, to be sure, even (in its place) a valid and necessary one, but hardly an adequate means for the deliberations of a democratic society. Ultimately, without moral truths, there is no way to arbitrate differences or decide upon policies except by recourse to power. Though the success of human community depends upon a variety of devices— including power relations—it is impossible to maintain order or justice if people do not, at least in some measure, know and voluntarily subordinate immediate desires to "the universality of the true good," the "common law" of all rational beings (VS #51). "If one does not acknowledge transcendent truth, then the force of power takes over, and each person tends to make full use of the means at his disposal in order to impose his own interests or his own opinion, with no regard for the rights of others" (VS #99).

Of course, the resort to pure power assertion is supposed to be precluded by the proviso about not oppressing others or abridging their autonomy and freedom. But the proviso turns out to be a complete anomaly within the relativist worldview, having no force, psychologically or logically. It has no force psychologically because once the self has habituated itself to asserting its own impulses and desires, untethered by conscience or law, the requirement of mutual respect and tolerance is reduced to a frail reed that cannot stand amidst the stampede of egoistic urges. "[W]hen man shows little concern for seeking what is true and good . . . conscience gradually becomes almost blind from being accustomed to sin" (VS #63, quoting from *Gaudium et Spes* #16). The proviso has no force logically because freedom and autonomy cannot stand alone in what is essentially a nihilist epistemology. Freedom can be understood as sacred and inviolable only if we know certain truths about human beings as creatures made in the likeness and image of God; but this is a foundational claim that can never be a public truth within a relativist framework. What is frequently overlooked is that once the transcendent dimension is lost, there can be no ground for respecting other people's freedom. To quote the Thomist philosopher Jacques Maritain, whose writings foreshadowed the Catholic human rights revolution: "Whenever we say that a man is a person, we mean that he is more than a mere parcel of matter, more than an individual element in nature, such as is an atom, a blade of grass, a fly, or an elephant. Where is the liberty, where is the dignity, where are the rights of an individual piece of matter?"[4]

Those expecting to see a liberal and humane social order constructed on the basis of relativism seem to assume that the normal, nonpathological disposition of the majority of people is a kind of sentimental benevolence. This is a terrible delusion. But even assuming that most people are reasonable, compassionate, and tolerant most of the time, the fact remains that in the truthless universe of relativism these virtues have no more standing than their opposites. If there is no transcendent truth, we cannot demand or expect people to respect a notion of rights based on human freedom and dignity, unless that respect just happens to coincide with their subjective preferences. Nietzsche, the ultimate relativist political philosopher, recognized this fact when he described humane impulses and human rights talk in terms of a "slave morality" by which the weak use conscience to manipulate the strong. He saw that relativism establishes an amoral universe in which it is as reasonable to be cruel as to be kind. Consistently applied, relativism becomes nihilism. This realization was not lost upon various tyrants and mass murderers in the twentieth century. And it is an ever-present, even inevitable, possibility in our own time when nihilism, under the guise of relativism, tries to show a human face. *Veritatis* (#99), citing from an earlier papal document, is correct in noting that "the root of modern totalitarianism is to be found in the denial of the transcendent dignity of the human person who, as the visible image of the invisible God, is therefore by his very nature the subject of rights which no one may violate—no individual, group, class, nation, or state." Hence the pope's repeated denials of the "claim that agnosticism and skeptical relativism are the philosophy and basic attitude which correspond to democratic forms of political life" (*Centesimus Annus* #46). And this: "Here we recall the Jewish people in particular, whose terrible fate has become a symbol of the aberration of which man is capable when he turns against God" (CA #17).

In sum: human rights and toleration can be grounded only in the affirmation of immutable moral truths rather than in the impossibility of ascertaining such truths.

> [F]reedom attains its full development only by accepting the truth. In a world without truth, freedom loses its foundation and man is exposed to the violence of passion and to manipulation, both open and hidden. . . . Authentic democracy is possible only in a state ruled by law and on the basis of a correct conception of the human person. . . . As history demonstrates, a democracy without values easily turns into open or thinly disguised totalitarianism. (CA #46)

Is our current democratic society, impoverished as it is in "values" and intellectual integrity, actually "turn[ing] into open or thinly disguised totalitarianism"? Not imminently, to be sure. But neither is it alarmist to suggest that our political and cultural life is increasingly characterized by an ethos of unreason and power. Right-wing fringe groups are, for now, only a minor part of this new unreason. The most significant practitioners are influential and institutionally well-placed activists of left or "liberal" persuasion, who have instituted a stifling form of ideological conformity known as Political Correctness, or PC, which now dominates American campuses, and has spread, progressively, throughout much of the rest of public life. Like the Marxian Communists of a previous generation, these activists turn public affairs into cultural and political warfare. Today at elite universities the main preoccupation is no longer to transmit and elaborate Western intellectual traditions—moral, religious, literary, and political—but rather to discredit Western achievements, subjecting them to thoroughgoing deconstruction as so many manifestations of the will to power and domination—against women, homosexuals, nonwhite non-European races, and so on.[5] "Rights" are claimed but usually as self-evident propositions—or simply asserted in threatening tones—with no sense that reason and deliberation might distinguish legitimate from illegitimate claims. Indeed, brave souls seeking to employ disinterested reason in arbitrating such claims are often told that their traditional modes of thought simply do not apply to issues that passionately engage feminists, gays, or racial minorities.

This situation calls to mind the plea of Kant (from his essay "What Is Orientation in Thinking?"): "[C]onsider what you do and where you will end with your attacks on reason." In fact, I believe, we already have a foreshadowing of where these attacks will lead. Contempt for moral truth and moral reasoning has a tendency to lead to broader epistemological skepticism. Can it really be surprising that in this time of deconstructing venerable truths and debunking all authorities that we witness such outrages as Holocaust Revisionism, that is, the claim by charlatan "scholars" that Hitler's mass murder of European Jewry never occurred? Or that certain black radicals openly promote their own mythical history in which Jews figure in world affairs primarily as slave traders, financial manipulators, and perpetrators of genocide? These phenomena may not have been intended by our politically correct intellectual elites, but they are malignancies that grow well in the soil of a deconstructed culture. One suspects that many more varieties of cynical nihilism may be on the way. Historical parallels are always imprecise, but the frequent comparison of contemporary America to Weimar Germany is not without merit; perhaps the missing element in our situation is just a large catastrophe or upheaval that would reveal the moral fault lines in society.

In any case, it is in this context of cultural and intellectual fragmentation that Jews should think about papal social teaching. The heirs of the Enlightenment have largely declared intellectual bankruptcy (often in so many words) with respect to foundational issues of morality and metaphysics. In that, they are very much unlike the liberals of an earlier time, that is, the liberals of the American founding, whose worldview blended Enlightenment rationalism with Reformation Christianity; those liberals could assert, "We hold these truths. . . ." Modern liberals may continue to assert the classic liberal values of tolerance, pluralism, and democracy, but they are unable to provide an intellectual context in which such ideals make sense, or a social environment in which they can thrive. That is why Catholic social teaching is so important today: it reinforces the intellectual foundations that make democracy possible. It is a curious irony of history, but a historical reality nonetheless, that the Catholic Church, which many of the American founders regarded as an institution utterly antithetical to their ideals, should now be so important in defending the order they established. John Adams, one of the premier anti-Catholics among the founders, once asked of Thomas Jefferson (in a letter of 19 May 1821), "Can a free government possibly exist with the Roman Catholic religion?"

Were he alive today, Adams might have to consider favorably the proposal of theologian Richard John Neuhaus that the wider culture can look to Catholic teaching for a compelling reaffirmation of basic truths about the American experiment in ordered liberty. Neuhaus's phrase for describing the Church's educational task in this regard, "the Catholic moment,"[6] might perhaps alarm Jews and other non-Catholics who misunderstand it to mean the Church's seizing an opportunity, during a moment of cultural upheaval and flux, to convert everyone to Catholicism. That of course is not the intended meaning of the phrase; the notion of a Catholic moment shouldn't be any more threatening than the idea that 1776 was the Calvinistic Anglo-Protestant moment, though it in no way forced all citizens to become Anglo-Protestants.

Restoring Personal Morality

Catholic social teaching's affirmation of moral truth against relativism has not been solely on a high cultural and intellectual plane. Indeed, since the beginning of the modern tradition of papal social teaching, a thread running through the encyclicals has been a recognition that political prudence "will be of no avail to secure [society's] well-being" unless there is a solid foundation of personal morality among the great mass of people (cf., Leo XIII's *Rerum Novarum* [1891], #82). While continuing to give close attention to the larger, structuring institutions of the political and economic order, the latest encyclicals display this same concern with necessary, foundational elements of morality — most notably in the area of sexual relations and the family. This aspect of papal social teaching seems to have special poignance in our own time, a period of social breakdown that is not attributable, for the most part, to an unsoundness of basic political and economic institutions, but rather to moral, spiritual, and intellectual corruption.

For instance, the sexual revolution, by eliminating age-old taboos, has created, or at minimum contributed to, a series of social problems that seem to be spinning out of control: for starters, tens of millions of legal abortions since 1973, a phenomenon that coarsens our moral sensibilities and at the same time generates increasingly uncivil and violent confrontations between proabortion and antiabortion factions. The sexual revolution has also been a disaster for family life, contributing to an epidemic of divorce and a proliferation of impoverished, fatherless children. In the black underclass of our cities, illegitimacy rates are now at 80 to 90 percent, a situation that is unsustainable economically (since most receive public assistance) as well as politically: the products of dysfunctional ghetto families become caught in a cycle of social incompetence and dependence, increasing their own sense of alienation and resentment and engendering feelings of fear, and finally anger, in the rest of the citizenry. It is an open question whether the ghetto-centered plague of drugs and crime can be successfully opposed within the limits of the Constitution, or whether we should expect increasing levels of anarchy culminating (one assumes) in some undemocratic form of reaction.

Rather than seeking to counteract these trends, most of our elite institutions have capitulated, in one way or another, to a fashionable moral relativism with respect to sexual ethics. Much of our public school system — certainly that por-tion in which parents have lost control to education professionals—now acts as an agency of cultural disintegration that distributes condoms, preaches "safe" sex, announces the moral parity between homosexuality and heterosexuality, and, in collaboration with the courts, obstructs any effort to impart to children a religiously grounded morality (sexual or otherwise). Entertainment and the arts have been largely degraded, celebrating lewdness and license, and, perhaps even worse, presenting a kind of casual acceptance of irresponsible and immoral behavior. During the 1992 presidential campaign, a major controversy arose over the television show "Murphy Brown" when the program's leading character, a single woman, decided to have a child out of wedlock. A brief word of criticism by then-vice president Dan Quayle, made in passing during a speech about the nation's mores and standards, provoked a storm of indignant reaction. From coast to coast, entertainment, artistic, and intellectual elites denounced the Quayle remark as a harbinger of censorship, religious repression, and so forth. The whole incident—far from being a tempest in a teapot—was really a perfect symbol of the moral collapse and confusion of our era.

Given the difficulty that public personages have in speaking the simplest moral truths in our current cultural climate, the pope is certainly on target in seeing confusion about human sexuality and the family as being at the very center of "a genuine crisis" (VS #5) in morals and understanding. Contemporary secular culture has not only liberated sexual energies from their procreative function, but also separated them from the sanctifying context of marriage. This separation has had disastrous consequences, as described above. The response to these consequences by our social elites has been, for the most part, to ignore or deny their origin in the collapse of genuine sexual ethics, and to conceal this denial by redefining the idea of family—so that it can include almost any child-rearing or domestic arrangement—and by invoking the rubric of the welfare state to shame the public into paying higher taxes to support single parents and, if possible, federalized day care.

In contrast, Catholic teaching emerges in today's culture as a badly needed voice of sanity and common sense, which can be endorsed—in most of its main features, if not in every aspect—by Jews and other non-Catholics. *Centesimus Annus* (#39) denounces the ideology of sexual license in which

> people are discouraged from creating the proper conditions for human reproduction and are led to consider themselves and their lives as a series of sensations to be experienced rather than as a work to be accomplished. The result is a lack of freedom, which causes a person to reject a commitment to enter into a stable relationship with another person and to bring children into the world or which leads people to consider children as one of the many "things" which an individual can have or not have, according to taste, and which compete with other possibilities.

Moreover, the family, traditionally understood, is presented as a positive model (a "sanctuary of life") that forms part of a larger "human ecology" every bit as much in need of careful maintenance as any other habitat in nature (CA #38 and #39).

> The first and fundamental structure for "human ecology" is the family, in which man receives his first formative ideas about truth and goodness, and learns what it means to love and to be loved, and thus what it actually means to be a person. Here we mean the family founded on marriage, in which the mutual gift of self by husband and wife creates an environment in which children can be born and develop their potentialities, become aware of their dignity and prepare to face their unique and individual destiny (CA #39).

In response to the devastation of family life, through divorce and illegitimacy, the pope (in CA #47) has asserted a series of rights for children, including "the right to live in a united family and in a moral environment conducive to the growth of the child's personality." Such a proposal is perhaps not practicable—how does one guarantee children their "right" to "a united family" and "a moral environment"?—but in the boldness of its formulation and in its emphasis on the needs of children over those of adults, it presents us with a wholesome way to rethink some of our social problems.

These views are, in the main, consistent with Jewish ideals and interests. Judaism has always regarded the sexual impulse as natural and healthy, if expressed within the context of marriage. Unlike Catholicism, rabbinic Judaism has always rejected celibacy as a counsel of perfection for the pious; and rarely has it been tempted to sexual morbidity and pessimism. Even insofar as the sexual drive is seen as a manifestation of the evil impulse, it has merited rabbinic endorsement on the ground that without it "no man would build a house, marry a wife, and beget children" (Genesis Rabbah 9:7). Nevertheless, Judaism, like Catholicism, has always seen the danger of sexual license and, traditionally, regarded with horror such offenses as sodomy, pederasty, adultery, and incest (cf., Leviticus 20:13; 15–16; 10; 11); cross dressing, too, is seen as a dangerous perversion (Deuteronomy 22:5) and a signal of the breakdown of restraint and self-control. Judaism has always held abstention from licentiousness as a high ideal (Leviticus 19:2 and commentaries), both for the sake of a righteous life for the individual and to protect the integrity of the family, which has always been the unquestioned center of Jewish life. Judaism has far less in common with the image of the family as it is understood in the (ever-changing) definitions of modern liberalism than with the pope's vision of the family as "the first and fundamental structure," wherein one learns the "first formative ideas about truth and goodness, and [about] what it means to love and be loved, and thus what it actually means to be a person" (CA #39).

In this ideal regarding sexual relations and family life, it is possible to see areas of congruence between Catholic and Jewish teaching. There are, of course, major points of difference, too: for example, birth control, divorce, abortion. Despite its various statements condemning artificial means of contraception, from *Humanae Vitae* (1968) through *Veritatis Splendor,* Catholic teaching on this topic is unlikely to convince a majority of Jews (or Christians, for that matter, perhaps including Catholics) that the Church has it right on this matter. Most Jews would regard as intolerable any laws restricting the free use of contraception. Though Orthodox Judaism still prohibits certain forms of contraception, even here exceptions are allowed: for example, to protect a married woman of fragile health who might be endangered by pregnancy. (One of the main differences between Catholic and Jewish ethics is the fact that in Jewish teaching there are exceptions to almost every rule, whereas in Catholic teaching, there are many rules that admit no exceptions under any conditions — birth control being one such case.) It is not possible in the context of this essay to debate the fine points of the issue. However, those who look with favor on much of papal teaching can only hope that the firmness and prominence of the Church's prohibition against contraception does not detract from the attention that is clearly merited for other aspects of its teaching that, from a non-Catholic standpoint, are surer and more important. The same principle would seem to apply to the issue of divorce. The trivialization of marriage and the consequent dissolution of family life is certainly an issue that engages both the principles of Judaism and the survival of the Jewish community. Divorce, while permitted by Judaism, has always been considered a tragedy and a defeat, not only for the divorcing couple but for the family and Jewish community as well. The sense of divorce's cosmic significance can be gauged in the old saying about the angels weeping in heaven whenever a divorce occurs. Nevertheless, divorce is considered by Judaism as sometimes being the lesser of evils, and an option that should not be foreclosed by civil or religious law. From an outsider's perspective, it seems that Catholicism perhaps recognizes this reality in an indirect way by its granting of annulments.

The question of abortion is also a stumbling block for a Jewish appreciation of papal social teaching. According to Catholic teaching, the fetus is, from the moment of conception, a human being in the fullest sense, with all the rights of personhood; therefore no abortion may be performed in any circumstances because it would be to take an innocent life. While traditional Judaism does not allow elective abortions — permitting the practice only in rare cases of grave medical emergency for the mother — the majority of non-Orthodox Jews today do favor the current abortion license (in effect, for any reason at any time) established by the U.S. Supreme Court in the 1973 case of *Roe v. Wade.* Reflecting this view, the Conservative and Reform movements have widened the narrow range of abortions allowed by traditional Jewish law.

I make this observation with a certain sadness, and with the hope that the basic humanitarian impulse of liberal Jews, derived from their religion and displayed in abundance in many other fields, might ultimately be applied to the protection of unborn life. Moreover, I would also hope that Orthodox Jews, who permit abortion only in certain limited situations, might overcome their reluctance to enter the broader public discussion on the issue. This reluctance stems from the fact that despite its restrictions on abortion, traditional Judiasm does not recognize the fetus as fully human in the sense of possessing full human and legal rights. Many Orthodox Jews doubtless fear that prolife legislation (as proposed, for instance, in the Republican party platform of 1992) would ultimately forbid all abortions, even those exceptional cases where the life of the mother is at stake.

Some of these differences between papal and Jewish teachings are significant, to be sure. But on balance, it seems to me, Catholic social teaching must still be regarded as beneficial, or at minimum potentially beneficial, to the Jewish community. In contrast to the Church's ambiguous role as part of the counter-Enlightenment, its counterrevolutionary actions against the sexual revolution clearly represent a positive influence on society overall, and indirectly to the Jewish community, which is no more immune than other religious communities to the allures and corruptions of a "liberated" culture. The Jewish divorce rate, once extremely low, is now comparable to that of the general population, with all the unhappy consequences that flow from it: for the divorced man and woman, for their children, and for the stability of a Jewish community that is already edging closer to complete assimilation. Moreover, Jews can never feel entirely safe in a decadent culture, one whose sexual and family life, and whose entertainments and amusements, increasingly resemble the sort of pagan environment condemned by the Torah and the prophets as an abomination and a mortal danger for those who strive to live according to God's law. If the proper analogy for contemporary society is not Sodom and Gomorrah but Weimar Germany, that is no comfort, since we all remember what followed Weimar.

Immediate Practical Issues

The importance of papal social teaching is partly that it can affirm forthrightly and unabashedly the essential truths that ground the free society. But it is significant, too, that the Catholic Church has a massive institutional means for dis-

seminating these truths: its system of parochial schools. Free from the ideological and economic interests of powerful national teachers' unions, as well
as from the many legal obstacles to the enforcement of order and discipline,
Catholic schools have had enormous academic success among poor minority
students in inner-city neighborhoods, where social disintegration is most
advanced.

But the most salient fact about the parochial schools, in terms of reestab-
lishing moral truth among the youth, is that they can appeal to conscience in
ways that are unthinkable for public schools. Anyone contemplating a recovery of morals and values must recognize that public schools, which are essentially state institutions, are by their nature prohibited from entering the inner
sanctum of conscience where moral character is formed. Nor can they present
the larger context of life's meaning in which ethics must make sense. Religion,
not the state, is the proper agency for forming moral consciousness; ethics, after all, is not something purely external to the inner life that can be taught and
learned in a compartmentalized fashion, like mathematics, but rather something that is integral to the whole of life and, as the pope puts it, "touches man
at the very depths of his being" (VS #21). Conscience, he rightly observes, has
binding force because it involves "*the witness of God himself,* whose voice and
judgment penetrate the depths of man's soul, calling him *fortiter et suaviter* to
obedience" (VS #58).

Clearly, a public school, even when it refrains from distributing condoms or
teaching the moral equivalence of homosexual unions, still cannot and should
not be a major conscience-forming agency; to attempt this task would violate
the separation of church and state in the truest sense, for it would wrongly involve the state in the business of "touch[ing] man at the very depths of his being." The Catholic promotion of parochial schools—in particular, the attempt
to win public approval for a system of vouchers, by which tax money would
follow students to whatever school their parents choose for them—represents
not simply a way of bringing more business into diocesan schools, but also of
ensuring the transmission of moral values in society. Education is hardly a matter of "choice" for its own sake, or for the sake of efficiency—though these
purposes might be served as well—but rather of limiting the comprehensive
influence now possessed by a purely secular agency, that is, the public (or state)
school.

"Subsidiarity" is the name of the general principle by which Catholic
thought seeks, among other things, to vest primary responsibility for education
in the family and Church. Subsidiarity stipulates that society should not be a
unitary entity whose various agencies and associations are basically instru-
mentalities of the state; rather, the plurality of subsidiary agencies, associations, and smaller communities within the larger society must be understood

as having a large measure of autonomy to perform their proper functions without being subsumed or dictated to by society at large, especially the state. Thus a large degree of freedom, within its own proper sphere of action, must be given to family, religion, labor union, business enterprise, voluntary association, and so on. The aim of the state should not be to take over their functions in a kind of totalitarian manner, but to enact such laws and policies that enable the subsidiary communities to perform their jobs properly. The virtual monopoly on education held by the state school system is, if not totalitarian, at minimum in violation of the subsidiarity principle, because it gives to the state a function that properly belongs to the family, assisted by the Church—the formation of conscience and character. Having an educational monopoly run by a government bureaucracy also violates the spirit of pluralism since it tends to exclude the teachings and perspectives of distinctive religious traditions.

The movement for school choice may have been a predominantly Catholic concern at one time. But today it is a matter that should actively engage American Jews as well. It cannot be denied that at one point in our history, the public school system served a useful function by integrating newly arrived Jewish immigrants into the mainstream culture. But now that Jews are successful, prominent, and generally at ease in American society, we find that the institution of the public school doesn't so much bring Jewish children into the mainstream as help lead them out of Judaism and toward assimilation. For the children of non-Orthodox Jewish families, the study of Hebrew and of Torah, performed reluctantly a couple of times a week at the local synagogue, is a kind of marginal activity that can rarely keep up, let alone compete, with the "real" work of public school, or, for that matter, with soccer practice, music lessons, social life, etc. Not only do public schools have children for most of the day—with a claim on much of their time even after school, through extracurricular activities and homework—they also propose to teach "values." (And as we know, these are most unlikely to be Jewish values, or even broadly Judeo-Christian-Islamic values either.)

The critical issue for the diaspora community today is a dangerous decline in the sense of Jewish identity and religious interest. There is no single action that can adequately respond to the problem, which at this point has reached near-crisis proportions. Surely, though, a strong Jewish day-school movement will help fix Jewish identity more firmly for children who attend such schools, and may even become the core agency of a larger revival of Jewish life, culture, and learning. While most Orthodox children, and a fair number of Conservatives, already attend Jewish day schools, it is imperative that this institution be exploited more fully, by liberal as well as traditional Jews. Day schools may not be right for all Jewish children, but their very presence and success—should it come to that—will undoubtedly help in the creation of a more healthy, secure, and authentic Jewish environment generally. One should not be surprised if what comes out of such a robust Jewish environment—intellectually, culturally, even religiously—is of more interest and value to the larger community than the contributions of a secularized and assimilated Judaism.

A vital day-school movement will require, first and foremost, a recognition on the part of Jews that such an institution is needed. It will also require political and legal changes on behalf of educational choice—a school voucher plan, for instance. Without that sort of political reform, the Jewish day school, like any other religious and private school, will remain financially unattainable for the majority, even when the desire is present. If such reform does come to pass, it will succeed in large measure through the efforts of the Catholic Church— in part because of the Church's institutional and political strength, but also because of its social teachings, which have over the years argued consistently and cogently for the justice of pluralism and choice in education. Insofar as Jews think about the future of the diaspora community, they must at least consider seriously the role of day schools, as well as the political change necessary to make them a major force. In the process of such consideration, papal teaching concerning subsidiarity will merit close attention. On the education issue, we may discover a common interest with the Catholic Church based on reason and equity.

Conclusion

Of course, the thesis of this essay—that Jews can, as never before, view Catholic social teaching as a benevolent or at least nonhostile force—depends upon the permanence of the Catholic human rights revolution and its complete internalization by the Church. Some Jews, and others, may argue that such a development is unlikely or impossible. The Church, they may say, is an undemocratic hierarchy, highly secretive in its deliberations, insufficiently self-critical, and highly defensive about the institutional sins it acknowledges only when confronted with overwhelming external pressure. Moreover, Roman Catholicism prescribes, with awesome detail and rigor, standards for the whole of society, not just Catholics (unlike Judaism, which reserves its most demanding requirements for Jews, allowing for greater pluralism and flexibility in the ethics of the larger society). The Church, this argument might conclude, cannot restrain its will to domination; if it is not exercised directly through public officials and magistrates, then it will be done indirectly through Catholic majorities, where they exist.

It is not possible to say with certainty whether the Catholic human rights revolution will finally be consolidated and developed—or reversed. I think it is fair to say, however, that for the present and the foreseeable future the Church, through its social teachings, has committed itself and its credibility to the democratic consensus of the modern world. In past times, when the Church straightforwardly rejected tolerance and liberals accepted the basic moral truths of Scripture, Jews may have been correct in identifying their security and well-being with a secular public realm. In our time, however, when our secular intellectual culture has largely jettisoned the idea of moral truth, the Church helps to rebuild the foundations of liberal democracy that are being eroded by moral relativism. If there are problems with the idea of the Catholic Church as a bulwark of liberal democracy, there are greater problems without it; the survival and flourishing of disapora Jewry is no longer well served by a public philosophy that is wholly secular and liberal. A public realm without God or transcendental truth is ultimately dangerous for society as a whole and especially ominous for vulnerable Jewish minorities. Surely it is better for Jews to live among the sons and daughters of Noah than among the children of Edom.

Notes

1. Quoted in *New York Times,* 31 December 1993, A1.

2. *Centesimus Annus.* In *Origins* (CNS Documentary Service, 16 May 1991, vol. 21). *Veritatis Splendor* (St. Paul Books and Media: Boston, Mass., 1993). [All further references in the body of the text are to these editions.]

3. Maimonides's teachings on Christianity were influenced by the earlier writings of Judah Ha-Levi; his inchoate notion of Christianity's positive role was extended and amplified by later commentators such as Rabbi Menahem Meiri in the fourteenth century. For a fuller account, cf. David Novak, *Jewish-Christian Dialogue: A Jewish Justification* (New York: Oxford University Press, 1989).

4. Jacques Maritain, *The Rights of Man and Natural Law* (New York: Scribner's, 1943), 2.

5. While all intellectually responsible people would acknowledge the West's "crimes, follies, and misfortunes," the distinguishing mark of today's cultural elite is insistence that these calumnies *define* Western civilization. Of course, this is also a cultural elite that retains ties, albeit perversely, to the humane ideals and truths that emerged out of the religious traditions of the West, and continues to trade on a sense of conscience cultivated only within Western civilization.

6. Richard John Neuhaus, *The Catholic Moment: The Paradox of the Church in the Post-Modern World* (San Francisco Harper and Row, 1987).

14

Catholicism, Liberalism and Communitarianism: Concluding Reflections

George Weigel

Father John Courtney Murray, whose name has been invoked more than once in this volume, had a Lincolnian view of the United States that was quite unabashed in its American exceptionalism. Unlike those great nation-states of Europe that had been formed out of distinctive ethnic cultures, the United States was, in Murray's view, a "proposition country"—a democratic experiment originating in certain moral claims about the human person and rightly ordered human communities. That singular foundation meant that the United States (for all its economic and military power) was a considerably more fragile country than the nation-states of Europe. For while France could survive foreign occupation and Poland political dismemberment, even as England had survived the transformative traumas of industrial revolution and democratization, America—or at least an America in moral and cultural continuity with its founding—could not survive the erosion, among its people, of those foundational ideas on which the American experiment rested. Like Lincoln, Murray asked whether, and how, a nation so conceived and so dedicated could long endure.

Murray once compressed into a single, elegant sentence the worst-case scenario to which his Lincolnian concerns gave rise, when he warned that "the noble, many-storied mansion of democracy [could] be dismantled, levelled to the dimensions of a flat majoritarianism, which is no mansion but a barn, perhaps even a tool shed in which the weapons of tyranny may be forged." That would happen if the moral "consensus" that had formed the American people and sustained the American democratic experiment should collapse in the general public, and among the institutions (including mainline Protestantism and the American academy) within which the consensus had been nurtured and by which it had been transmitted to new generations. But even if that "evil day" were to come, Murray believed that there was an American community capable of leading a revival of the experiment: a revival based on a restoration of the experiment's moral foundations. That was the Catholic community, which, Murray believed,

> would still be speaking in the ethical and political idiom familiar to them as it was to their fathers, both the Fathers of the Church and the Fathers of the American Republic. The guardianship of the original American consensus, based on the Western heritage, would have passed to the Catholic community. . . . And it would be for others, not Catholics, to ask themselves whether they still shared the consensus which first fashioned the American people into a body politic and determined the structure of its fundamental law.[1]

A lot has happened since Murray sketched that possible "Catholic moment" in the unfolding drama of American history. And while the generation of Catholic intellectuals immediately following Murray was less than enthusiastic about securing the moral foundations of an American democratic experiment that many of them found riddled with racism, militarism, imperialism, and, latterly, sexism, a successor generation to the successor generation has now arisen. As this book makes plain, it has energetically taken up the task that Murray envisioned.

The conversational partners in that enterprise are, happily, far more ecumenical and interreligious than they tended to be in Murray's day (thanks to colleagues like Matthew Berke and Jean Bethke Elshtain); there are still able representatives of Murray's own generation (like Francis Canavan) on hand to provide sage counsel; there are dissidents and intellectual provocateurs to be engaged (as the contributions of Kenneth Craycraft and Stanley Hauerwas — both of which would have brought a gleam of satisfaction to the eyes of Joseph Clifford Fenton and Francis Connell, Murray's great antagonists — nicely illustrate). But that there are younger American scholars articulating an intellectually powerful, politically distinctive, and assertively Catholic "take" on the contemporary American situation is, I think, established beyond reasonable dispute by the essays you have just read by Gerard Bradley, Robert George, Kenneth Grasso, Robert Hunt, Mary Keys, and Christopher Wolfe.

More than the cast of characters has changed since Murray's time, of course.

As Father Neuhaus indicates in his foreword, the American academy has largely abandoned the democratic culture-forming task that Murray envisioned for it, and although Father Neuhaus does not say so here, I doubt that he would disagree with me that the Protestant mainline establishment has also downed tools on the work of securing the moral foundations of the American experiment. Evangelical Protestantism has, however, emerged as a major moral-cultural and political force in American public life, in ways that were simply unimaginable when Murray was writing the essays that became *We Hold These Truths;* and, perhaps even more astonishingly, significant leaders in that evangelical community are looking to the Church of Rome, and (imagine!) to the Bishop of Rome, for public leadership on fundamental questions of personal and social morality at the end of the twentieth century.

But, and here we return to the debit side of the historical ledger, both the federal judiciary and the national Democratic party have become committed to a construal of American liberties that Murray would have found offensive, even odious: the notion of liberty as the freedom of the unencumbered, autonomous, imperial self to autoconstruct his or her own universe of meaning, value, and action, so long as no one (or no one in whom the courts declare a "compelling interest") gets hurt. If Murray would have found it hard to imagine a United States in which Roman Catholics and evangelical Protestants made common cause on deeply contested issues of public life and informed their new public alliance with the teaching of papal encyclicals, I dare say Murray would have found it just as hard to imagine an America in which political correctness and ideological multiculturalism terrorized the campuses, abortion-on-demand was the law of the land, lethal violence ruled the streets of too many urban areas, and the out-of-wedlock birth rate was approaching 30 percent of all births across the socioeconomic spectrum. But, then, perhaps I give Murray too little credit: for the toolshed in which those weapons of tyranny he warned about might be forged is, by some lights, precisely what is being constructed by a Supreme Court that teaches the American people that "the heart of liberty is the right to define one's own concept of existence, of meaning, of the universe, and of the mystery of human life."[2]

In these new circumstances—which, arguably, constitute the gravest moral crisis in American public life since the Civil War—the imperative is to extend and develop, rather than simply exegete, the kind of distinctively Catholic thinking on American democracy that Murray represented. Happily, for those who would make that effort, there are ample resources at hand in the social magisterium of Pope John Paul II: another development that Murray would have welcomed, but which he could not have possibly foreseen.

Much of modern Catholic social doctrine has, until John Paul II, had something of a reactive quality about it. Beginning with Pope Leo XIII in 1891, the great truths of the tradition of Catholic social and political thought were deployed in response to the economic, social, cultural, and political developments (and derangements) of the modern world. On occasion, there was a considerable substantive step forward, as when Pope Pius XI's *Quadragesimo Anno* (1931) enunciated the principle of subsidiarity as a centerpiece of Catholic social doctrine. And to be reactive, it must be emphasized, is not to be reactionary (as John XXIII's *Pacem in Terris* forcefully demonstrated in 1963). But the general pattern from Leo XIII through Paul VI was for the magisterium of the Church to respond to certain phenomena (the industrial revolution, the rise of fascism, the post-war divisions of East/West and North/South) that history had put onto the human agenda.

With the social magisterium of John Paul II, and particularly with the encyclical *Centesimus Annus,* something rather different is afoot. For John Paul's vision of the threefold "free society"—a law-governed democratic polity, an entrepreneurially creative free or market economy, and a vibrant moral culture (in which free men and women freely seek and adhere to the truths about the human person that have been created in them by the Lord of history)—is a bold proposal significantly ahead of the curve of debate in both developed and developing countries, most especially including the United States. Indeed, measured against the depth and visionary reach of John Paul's social doctrine, most of what passes for social and political analysis in the American academy and in the press today is, to put it gently, thin gruel indeed. It is as if the pope, urgently aware of the impending conclusion of two thousand years of Christian history and eager to strengthen his brethren (Luke 22.32) for their entry into the Third Millennium, has deliberately decided to seize an intellectual position in front of the contemporary argument over the right-ordering of society, in order that the Church's social doctrine might act as a magnet drawing that debate into more fruitful channels of inquiry and reflection.

Be that as it may, the social doctrine of John Paul II picks up and develops, in intriguing ways, themes that Murray brought into play two generations ago. Murray's defense of the American notion of "limited government" (i.e., a government that acknowledged that much was beyond its competence, and that its primary task was to secure the rights of persons) was not in conflict with classic Catholic social and political thought; indeed, Murray argued that the American Founding was, for all its Lockean and Calvinist antecedents, in essential continuity with the Christian civilization of the West, unlike the French eruption of 1789. But Murray's notion of "limited government" lived in relative tension with the generally high or expansive view of the state that had characterized modern Catholic social teaching (and that had, until Vatican II, colored the Church's position on the question of church–state relations). With John Paul II, we begin to see hints and traces of a development of social doctrine in which the Church more assertively proposes the limits of the legitimate scope of state authority and the reach of state social policy.

This is in part, one suspects, a reflection on the Church's (and John Paul's) experience of totalitarianism in both its nazi and communist forms. To be sure, these are the extreme cases; and yet the modern bureaucratic state, even in established democracies, does seem driven by certain internal dynamics toward a constant expansion of the scope of its power. (These forces were first identified and analyzed by Max Weber; their influence has been amplified by the rise of that "new class" of politicized intellectuals that has arisen in all developed postindustrial countries.) John Paul II is surely aware of these developments. But his sharp critique of the humanly demeaning effects of the social welfare state (what the pope terms, in *Centesimus Annus,* the "Social Assistance State"[3]) is not, to repeat, reactive. Rather, it is more deeply rooted in a constructive analysis of the acting human person and of what John Paul dubs the "subjectivity of society."[4]

This papal neologism, which is perhaps the most creative innovation in *Centesimus Annus,* has interesting points of tangency with both Murray's thought and the recent experience of the human rights resistance in east central Europe. For what Murray called the *res sacra in temporalibus* (which Robert Hunt describes in his contribution to this volume as "the spiritual truths of personal, family, and communal life") are what a generation of dissidents in central and eastern Europe experienced in the relationships and the free associations they came to call "civil society." And, with those dissidents, John Paul II understands that the "subjectivity of society" is both the most secure line of defense against the totalitarian temptation and the essential foundation of any democracy that truly promotes human flourishing. Those relationships and associations that nurtured in individuals a commitment to "living in the truth," as Václav Havel put it, were the key to the moral revolution that made the nonviolent political overthrow of communism possible; and, as Murray insisted decades earlier, it is precisely those relationships and commitments that make the democratic experiment possible.[5]

This notion of the "subjectivity of society" (which, in John Paul's thinking, is more than the mere aggregate of the "subjectivities" of the acting persons who compose a society) casts new light upon another deeply controverted issue in modern democracies: the question of "individualism." There is much criticism—much of it warranted—about the radical individualism of postmodern Western societies. And yet those same societies are beset by ever-encroaching state power, reaching ever deeper and farther into the nooks and crevices of personal and social life. A society that is, in its high culture, radically individualistic is, in much of its social and political practice, increasingly authoritarian: the "nanny state," as some Americans have aptly dubbed it.

In these peculiar circumstances, John Paul's "subjectivity of society" challenges both the philosophical proponents of radical individualism and the bureaucratic overseers of the nanny state to a different view of human relationships in society: one in which individual rights are ordered to the fulfillment of personal responsibilities and the pursuit of the common good; one in which the state has a limited sphere of authority, but a range of voluntary associations ("mediating structures," or what Mary Ann Glendon has called "communities of common memory and mutual aid") shape far more of the texture of public life. Murray understood that "public" was broader than, and thus not synonymous with, and thus not reducible to, "political." The social doctrine of *Centesimus Annus* teaches a similar wisdom.

The collapse of European communism in the revolution of 1989 led in short order to some fevered speculations about the "end of history" in the uncontested triumph of democracy and the market. Those fantasies were quickly shattered in the killing fields of Bosnia, and by the difficulties in consolidating democratic polities and market-oriented economies that virtually all postcommunist societies experienced. The multiple crises of the new democracies were a powerful reminder that democrats are made, not born: which means that democracy requires, in the citizenry, a critical mass of certain distinctive virtues if the grand experiment of self-governance is not to self-destruct. But that lesson (which seems to be an iron law of history, this side of the coming of that Kingdom that truly is the "end of history") is not for new democracies only: it must be relearned, at the end of the twentieth century, by the established democracies of the West.

All of which suggests that the crucial questions for the future of democratic capitalist societies are cultural, rather than narrowly political or economic. In one respect, the "end of history" enthusiasts of the early 1990s were correct: for at least the foreseeable future, the great arguments of public life will not pit capitalists vs. socialists or democrats vs. authoritarians and totalitarians. Rather, the great arguments will be about the moral–cultural ligaments of democratic capitalist societies. And, at the most basic level, the argument will be about whether any such connective and community-forming tissues are necessary.

Put yet another way, and to bring the issue home to the United States, the great argument will be whether American democracy is to be understood as a republic of procedures, or as a substantive moral experiment in a people's capacity for self-governance. In the procedural republic, the only actors of consequence are the autonomous individual and the state; in the substantive experiment, the acting person comes to know his or her duties, and thus his or her rights, in the many prior communities of civil society—family, religious institution, voluntary association. In the procedural republic, rights and laws are the stuff of the public discourse; in the substantive experiment, rights and laws are ordered toward the ends of human flourishing by prior understandings of rights and wrongs. In the procedural republic, there is no transcendent moral horizon against which the justice of the laws is determined; in the substantive experiment, the very possibility of democracy and the democratic equality of all citizens is established by the mutual acknowledgment of a moral law before which all are held accountable.

The model of the procedural republic is defended, these days, by the all-stars of the secular American political-philosophical establishment; the case for the substantive experiment was adumbrated historically and philosophically by John Courtney Murray, and has now been given a richer phenomenological and theological texture by the social magisterium of Pope John Paul II. We may not know, for sure, whether the case for the substantive experiment will win out, as the twentieth century flows into the twenty-first. We may know, with as much certainty as is permitted in these matters, that if it does not, the American future will have very little to do with the promises inherent in the American Founding.

That the case for a more ample American democracy, a democracy recommitted to the moral truths about the human person on which the Founders rested their case, will be further developed in the years to come by the successors to Murray's immediate successors among American Catholic intellectuals is the very good news contained in this book.

Notes

1. John Courtney Murray, *We Hold These Truths: Catholic Reflections on the American Proposition* (New York: Doubleday Image Books, 1964), 53.
2. Justices Anthony Kennedy, Sandra Day O'Connor, and David Souter, in *Casey v. Planned Parenthood of Southeastern Pennsylvania,* 112, S.Ct. 2791, at 2807.
3. *Centesimus Annus,* 48.
4. Ibid., 46.
5. On "civil society" as the antidote to the communist toxin, see my study *The Final Revolution: The Resistance Church and the Collapse of Communism* (New York: Oxford University Press, 1992), and "The Revolution of 1989 and the Restoration of History" in my *Idealism Without Illusion: U.S. Foreign Policy in the 1990s* (Grand Rapids, Mich.: Eerdmans, 1994). The analysis in both these volumes draws extensively on the east central European dissident literature of the 1980s, particularly the writings of the Czechs Václav Havel and Václav Benda. Key themes in that literature, refracted through the prism of his own extensive experience of anticommunist resistance, helped shape John Paul's analysis of "1989" in *Centesimus Annus.*

Index

263

About the Contributors

Matthew Berke is Managing Editor of *First Things,* a monthly journal published in New York City by the Institute on Religion and Public Life. He has a Ph.D. in political science from Yale University. His articles and reviews have appeared in a variety of magazines, newspapers, and anthologies.

Gerard V. Bradley is Professor of Law at the Notre Dame Law School. He has published extensively in the areas of constitutional law, religion, and public life. His books include *Church-State Relationships in America* (1982).

Francis Canavan, S. J., is Professor Emeritus of Political Science at Fordham University. He has published widely in the area of political theory. His books include *Freedom of Expression: Purpose as Limit* (1986), *The Political Economy of Edmund Burke* (1995), and *The Pluralist Game* (Rowman & Littlefield, forthcoming).

Kenneth R. Craycraft Jr. is Assistant Professor of Theology at St. Mary's University. His articles and reviews have appeared in *First Things, Crisis, Theology Today,* and other journals.

Jean Bethke Elshtain is currently Laura Spelman Rockefeller Professor of Social and Political Ethics at the University of Chicago. A widely published scholar in the area of political theory, her books include *Public Man, Private Woman* (1981) and *Democracy on Trial* (1994).

Robert P. George is Associate Professor of Politics at Princeton University and a member of the United States Civil Rights Commission. Among his many publications in the fields of moral and legal philosophy is *Making Men Moral: Civil Liberties and Public Morality* (1993).

Kennth L. Grasso is Associate Professor of Political Science at Southwest Texas State University. He is the coeditor of *John Courtney Murray and the American Civil Conversation,* and his essays and reviews have appeared in *Interpretation, Responsible Community, First Things, Review of Politics,* and other journals.

Stanley Hauerwas is Professor of Theological Ethics at Duke University Divinity School. A widely published scholar in the field of Christian social ethics, his books include *A Community of Character* (1982), *Christian Experience Today* (1988), *and Dispatches from the Front: Theological Engagements with the Secular* (1994).

Robert P. Hunt is Associate Professor of Political Science at Kean College of New Jersey. He has written on American constitutional theory and the political thought of Reinhold Niebuhr and is coeditor of *John Courtney Murray and the American Civil Conversation* (1992).

Mary M. Keys is Visiting Professor at the Department of Government at the University of Notre Dame. She is a Ph.D. candidate in political philosophy at the University of Toronto.

Ralph M. McInerny holds the Michael P. Grace Chair of Philosophy and is Director of the Jacques Maritain Center at the University of Notre Dame. The author of many books, he has been chosen to deliver the Gifford Lectures for 1999.

Richard John Neuhaus is Director of the Institute on Religion and Public Life and Editor in Chief of *First Things.* He is the author of numerous books and essays, including the widely acclaimed *The Naked Public Square* (1984). His most recent books include *America Against Itself* (1993) and *Doing Well and Doing Good: The Challenge to the Christian Capitalist* (1992).

Michelle Watkins graduated in 1994 from the University of Notre Dame with a degree in philosophy.

George Weigel is President of the Ethics and Public Policy Center, Washington, D.C. He is the author or editor of numerous books and essays on religion and public life. His most recent books include *Freedom and Its Discontents*

(1991), *The Final Revolution: The Resistance Church and the Collapse of Communism* (1992), and *Idealism Without Illusions: U.S. Foreign Policy in the 1990s* (1994).

Christopher Wolfe is Professor of Political Science at Marquette University and President of the American Public Philosophy Institute. He is the author of *The Rise of Modern Judicial Review* (Rowman & Littlefield, 1986 and 1994), *Judicial Activism* (1990), and *Essays on Fair and Liberal Democracy* (1987) and coeditor of *Liberalism at the Crossroads* (Rowman & Littlefield, 1994).